LIVING IS GIVING

PLAYRIGHT PUBLISHING

I was part of the Volunteer Experience 2000

NAME:

VOLUNTEER ROLE:

VOLUNTEER NO:

VOLUNTEERS PARADE THROUGH SYDNEY. PIC RENEE NOWYTARGER

LIVING IS GIVING

THE VOLUNTEER EXPERIENCE

Laurie Smith

Playright Publishing Pty Ltd

First Published in 2001 by Playright Publishing Pty. Ltd.
PO Box 548, Caringbah. 2229.
Sydney. NSW. Australia.
(02) 9525 5943. Fax: (02) 9524 7485.
www.playrightpublishing.com

National Library of Australia
Cataloguing-in-publication data

Living is giving: the volunteer experience

ISBN 0 949853 77 1

1. Sydney Organising Committee for the Olympic Games. 2. Olympic Games (27th: 2000: Sydney, NSW). 3. Volunteer workers in recreation – New South Wales – Sydney. 4. Voluntarism – New South Wales – Sydney. I. Smith, Laurie, 1947 -.

769.069309944

Publisher: Gary Lester

Production Assistant: Jennie Fairs

Designed by Rhys Butler

Printed by Tien Wah Press, Singapore

CONTENTS

VOLUNTEERS PARADE THROUGH SYDNEY. CORNER OF GEORGE AND HUNTER STREET. PIC TIM HUELIN

Forewords

IOC OLYMPIC MUSEUM COLLECTIONS
PHOTO: JEAN–JACQUES STRAHM

Juan Antonio Samaranch
Marqués de Samaranch
President of the International Olympic Committee

The year 2001 has been proclaimed by the United Nations General Assembly as the 'International Year of Volunteers', and the Olympic Movement, the largest volunteer movement spread out in every country of the world, has been mobilised to consolidate the culture of volunteerism.

Millions of volunteers, of all races, cultures and religions, are the foundation of the Olympic pyramid. The development of sport and Olympic education would not be possible without the participation and commitment of sport-loving volunteers; nor, indeed, would it be possible to stage the Olympic Games. We all have pleasant memories of the 47,000 volunteers who ensured the success of the Games of the XXVII Olympiad in Sydney in 2000. Among them was Laurie Smith, the author of this book entitled *Living is Giving – The Volunteer Experience 2000*.

If we had to pay all the Olympic Movement's volunteers according to the workload and their responsibilities, and taking into account the personal expenses they have to bear, we would reach a staggering figure which a government, or an organising committee, would be unable to come to terms with. These facts are described in detail in this book by Laurie Smith which you are holding in your hands, who himself has attended nine Olympic Games and his wife Barbara five.

Volunteerism in the sports world is also unique, in that it deals with several subjects at the same time. The Olympic volunteer is therefore a multifaceted person, who can handle any workload. Often far from their family during weekends and holidays, Olympic volunteers make sacrifices that should not be forgotten.

But volunteerism also derives from the notion of solidarity which exists in all cultures in various forms. In other words, Olympic solidarity, in the widest sense of the term, incorporates this human generosity of being helpful. This notion best describes the Smith family and all the Olympic volunteers whose personal experience and commitment are recorded in this book. It is therefore the duty of society as a whole, and national governments in particular, to pay tribute and salute all the volunteers of the world.

My congratulations and sincere thanks to Laurie Smith for his dedicated contribution to Olympic volunteerism and for writing this book which will enrich the Olympic cultural legacy.

Dr Robert D. Steadward, O.C.
President, International Paralympic Committee

Sport, and most assuredly sport for athletes with a disability, simply would not be, without volunteers. Uncountable organisations, teams and clubs would firstly not exist, secondly not succeed and lastly not endure. When volunteers come forth, as a cohesive unit of committed helpers in sport, even if they have never been acquainted before, they inevitably become as closely related as family members. Many go on to enjoy lifetime friendships built upon the solid foundation of common interests and loyalty, common goals, hard work and long hours. Many volunteers have related to me over the years that the aspect of working within a deadline provides excitement and stimulation. During the Paralympic Summer and Winter Games, for example, despite whatever time has been spent in training and preparation, all volunteers ultimately operate within a time frame of approximately 17 days. This adrenalin rush invariably helps to maintain the enthusiasm and energy necessary for the high-intensity focus and work involved.

Since the first athlete with a disability ever entered competition, volunteers have been the strength, indeed the soul of the Paralympic movement. From Sir Ludwig Guttmann's concept in 1944 of rehabilitating the wounded youth of World War II by organising fundamental sporting events, to the XI Paralympic Summer Games Sydney 2000, our organisation has been constructed within the frame of volunteerism. For the Sydney Games, the number of volunteers exceeded 17,000.

Former athletes and disability sport experts go on to become volunteer members of Commissions established by both the IOC and IPC, from whence they are able to interact with other volunteers of similar backgrounds and interests, and from which position they can address pertinent issues. Others will dedicate their retirement from sport to act as volunteer ambassadors and mentors to aspiring and developing athletes. Within all these groups are committed people who will stay with the Paralympic movement to the end of their days.

The Paralympic Games, along with world and regional championships, enjoy the volunteer services of medical doctors, teachers, nurses, classifiers, coaches, technical officials, office personnel, security, bus drivers, concession and catering staff, protocol assistants, lawyers, information technologists, administrators, accountants, facility and venue workers and managers, from every walk of life and every continent. Many in our movement are veteran volunteers who began as family members of an athlete, then carried on to contribute, for years after the athlete had retired.

The impact of volunteers on our movement has been staggering, having extended far beyond the parameters of any measuring device, likewise, the importance of their contribution. Volunteerism is for those who believe that they can make a difference in the lives of others through the application of their special talents and efforts. For Paralympic athletes and the competitions in which they participate, volunteers undeniably make that essential difference.

I like to compare the impact of our volunteers with that of snowflakes: 'Snowflakes are nature's most fragile elements, but just look at what they can accomplish when they stick together.'

The Paralympic movement will forever be indebted, and is honoured to pay homage to its legion of volunteers, in the past, present and future. It is to these individuals that this book is aptly and gratefully dedicated.

Mr Sandy Hollway
Chief Executive,
Sydney Organising Committee Olympic Games

Laurie Smith has done a wonderful thing in producing this account of the volunteers who contributed so much to making the Sydney 2000 Olympic and Paralympic Games the best ever. It is wonderful because it has been a labour of love, because it is a story which needed telling, and because it can help inspire the great cause of volunteerism generally in our community.

The book was Laurie's initiative, done on his own time and indeed at his own expense. He did it because he is a true believer in the Games and in volunteering. For him the phrase 'Living is Giving' is not a piece of empty rhetoric, a platitude or a mere sentiment. It is a philosophy of life. The President of the International Olympic Committee, Juan Antonio Samaranch, said in one of the IOC meetings during the Sydney Games that this title said so much. The book exists because Laurie, and Barbara who has always given him tremendous support and partnership, believes in giving – and the book is a homage to others who share the same conviction.

The story needed telling because the volunteer effort, in the end, was vital not just to the conduct of the Games but to the quality of the Games. The army of volunteers provided the backbone for the Games workforce. Operationally and financially the Games could not have been delivered without them. But beyond that they provided much of the sparkle, humour, courtesy and helpfulness which was so remarked upon by our own spectators and visitors from overseas.

To a significant extent they were the face of the Games. As such, they did Australia proud. I will long remember a comment again made in an IOC meeting by the chief IOC official, Mr François Carrard, that the work being done by the volunteers at Central Station in directing the crowds efficiently and with good humour was 'the greatest thing I have seen'.

But the book is relevant to the future, and is not only a record of the past. This is because the health of volunteering in Australia will depend in significant part upon recognition – recognition by people in the community generally that volunteering is a personally rewarding as well as socially beneficial activity, and recognition by all of us of the debt of gratitude which we owe to volunteers. In this sense the volunteers for the Games were simply the most visible example of the depth of the volunteering culture in Australia, and how important a national asset this is. It is an asset which should be nurtured and Laurie's book will help to do so.

At one level the story of the volunteers in the 2000 Games is the story of how one of the largest and most complex human resource exercises in Australia was planned and run so excellently by our managers and staff. At another level it is the story of what the people in the program, the volunteers themselves, did so brilliantly. And at another level again, it is simply a human story about ideals, values, ups and downs, times of stress, and times of fun and humour. In other words, a microcosm of life.

The volunteers were people I was privileged to know and to learn from. I am sure Laurie's book will help you to know them better.

Lois Appleby
Chief Executive,
Sydney Paralympic Organising Committee

The XI Paralympic Summer Games were held in Sydney from 18 to 29 October 2000, two weeks after the Olympic Games. Four thousand athletes came from 122 countries to contest 18 sports; a time, an event, a place for the athletes to put to the test their years of hard training and to strive to do their personal best performance in their chosen sports.

Supporting the Games were more than 14,500 volunteers. A team of men and women, from all corners of Australia who, without any doubt whatsoever, achieved their best performance ever.

The volunteers covered all areas of the Games – they were the face of the Games. They were the folk that answered questions, directed people to venues, supported the international visitors as drivers and assistants to the teams, drove buses, worked in the village, at the airport, in the warehouses: everywhere!

Many volunteers gave thousands of hours to work on the Games. I would particularly like to acknowledge the Pioneer Volunteers who provided enormous support to the Paralympics over four years. They worked in 'The Hive', helped in the schools program and with functions and supported us with an excellent transport service!

Many volunteers were away from their own homes for months – especially those who worked on both the Olympics and Paralympics whose home was outside Sydney. Their commitment was outstanding.

During the Paralympics, the spectator numbers increased beyond our expectations. The Australian public performed 'a personal best' in their support of the Games. However, the larger crowds put increased pressure on the venues and the volunteers at Sydney Olympic Park. Despite this pressure the volunteers maintained their enthusiasm and friendliness. They kept the crowds of people moving and excited them in the venues. I saw volunteers leading the spectators in song, in dance, in cheers – making the experience of being at the Paralympics such a happy one for everyone.

The volunteers' good humour, their time, their friendliness, their spirit of doing for others made the Paralympic Games an outstanding success. As Dr Robert Steadward, President of the International Paralympic Committee, said at the Closing Ceremony these were 'the best Games ever'.

There was some magic at the Paralympic Games. It's hard to know just how it came to be. But there is no doubt that the spirit of the volunteers played a huge part in making the Games the success they were.

Thank you for all coming on this journey with us.

Acknowledgements

When taking on a project of the magnitude of this book with no previous experience, it requires good planning, an open mind to ideas and support, passion, dedication, discipline, money and/or stupidity. All these requirements are held together by one precious ingredient – support.

The most devoted person in this area was my life partner, friend and lover, my lovely wife Barbara. She has been my sounding board for ideas, my financier, my computer expert, my shoulder to cry on, my accountant, and most of all walked side by side with me making sure my heart did not over rule my head as I lunged with passion into this exciting project.

I may still be looking for a publisher if it wasn't for the friendship and guidance of Olympic Champion Kevin Berry. I do owe a lot to Gary Lester and Jennie Fairs at Playright Publishing for the support, guidance and faith. Gary and his team had to shake convention in some areas to produce the image being sought, and in this department designer Rhys Butler has done us proud.

In the latter part of the year 2000, I was being overwhelmed with correspondence, and the help provided by Mavis Booth, Brenda Dabelstein, Jill Pioch and Bev Brown was invaluable. There were many SOCOG staff who in the ten months leading up to September 2000, gave me help, support and advice, and a special thank you must go to Sandy Hollway. The cost of this project has been scary, and I must thank my dear father Allan Smith and his wife Alice, for their support, love and encouragement throughout the project.

Marie Fox of Volunteering NSW, please don't underestimate the importance of your advice and support. There have been volunteers like Rob and Pam Callaghan and Garry and Anne Lee who have encouraged and motivated us throughout, but to everyone of you who have contributed to this book – thank you!

Introduction

Why write a book on volunteers, and in particular Olympic/Paralympic volunteers? Well why not? Volunteers are the backbone of society. Many books have been produced on Olympism and Olympic athletes, but there has not been anything dedicated to the volunteer contribution to such events.

These pages are not meant in any way to place as less significant the contribution of the tens of thousands of dedicated volunteers who every day contribute to our Australian community and communities around the world. Rather, I hope this book is a legacy for volunteering generally. Nor is it meant to give greater credit to the volunteer contribution than that of the total team effort which made the Games of 2000 so successful in their planning, execution and cultural significance.

Those who were volunteers, I hope, will treasure this book as a permanent reminder of their involvement. Those who were not, may never appreciate what we as volunteers and members of Workforce 2000 shared. However, if this book helped you understand why friends or relatives developed a special affinity with colleagues who shared this once in a lifetime experience, then maybe we have helped you as well.

We have never pretended that there were not some challenges to overcome. I use the example that the volunteer workforce was of the size of a large country town, bringing with it all the characteristics of that number of people. There were births, deaths, friendships formed, friendships lost, those who registered for their own selfish reasons and those who fell ill. However, the overwhelming attitude of giving, passion, pride, love and dedication made it all so worthwhile.

As you venture through these pages, I hope you laugh, cry and have a better appreciation of the dedication and commitment of the unpaid Olympic/Paralympic workforce, sharing some of the same emotions that I experienced as a volunteer – and as a servant of the volunteers in compiling these memories.

Laurie Smith

(L to R) Steven Grigor, Laurie Smith, Pat Gray and Sandy Hollaway receive the National Australia Day Council Award (opposite page) on behalf of all volunteers from Prime Minister John Howard.

australia day

NATIONAL AUSTRALIA DAY COUNCIL

achievement award

26 January

In recognition of all Australian Volunteers who contributed to the Sydney 2000 Olympic and Paralympic Games

presented to **Pat Gray Steven Grigor**
Laurie Smith Sandy Hollway
Representing all the volunteers

by NATIONAL AUSTRALIA DAY COUNCIL

signed *Lisa Curry-Kenny*

Lisa Curry Kenny MBE OAM

position CHAIRMAN
NATIONAL AUSTRALIA DAY COUNCIL

date 25.1.01

PRE – GAMES VOLUNTEERS

In the 12 months prior to the successful bid announcement, enthusiastic people like Kerry Bray, Vera Rothwell, Richard Rasker, Peter Konnecke, Dora Rothwell, Robyn Brettell, Gill Gorrick, Yanni Athanasopoulos and Suzy Greirson were meeting with Eddie Moore at Sports House, Wentworth Park, to assist the bid in any way possible.

The volunteer program between winning the bid in 1993 and 1996 was co-ordinated out of the SOCOG community relations department with **Louise Walsh** and **Genevieve Tutaan** as the key organisers. In May 1996, **David Brettell** was appointed head of the volunteer program. David and his wife Robyn had already been part of the volunteer program, and were passionate Olympic followers, having just returned from their fourth Olympics in Barcelona.

Soon after the Atlanta Olympic Games, David was joined by **Richard Rasker** and **Cherie Mylordis** as the team to begin the process of developing a plan for the recruitment, training and management of an estimated 50,000 volunteers. Richard had been recruited from the volunteers' ranks, and actually contributed to the early planning meetings by coming in after work and on weekends (high on enthusiasm and passion) before he actually took up full-time duty with SOCOG.

Pioneer Volunteers

At one of the planning meetings, discussions were taking place regarding the growth, recruitment, training and requirements for the first group of volunteers from which David and Richard had come. Richard recalls: 'We felt we would require about 500 volunteers to meet the needs of SOCOG prior to the actual recruitment of the 50,000 Games-time volunteers. We wanted to call this group something meaningful. Atlanta had called them "Internal Volunteers". We couldn't call them "the first group of volunteers" or "early volunteers" … then suddenly out of my brain and my mouth it came "PIONEER VOLUNTEER". It stuck, and thus began the journey for 500 wonderful people to become Pioneer Volunteers and be part of the organisation of the Olympic and Paralympic Games.'

(L TO R) VERA ROTHWELL, PETER KONNECKE AND KERRY BRAY

(L TO R) ROBYN BRETTELL AND GILL GORRICK

The Pioneer Volunteers were never meant to be, and have never been, considered more important or more skilled than any future volunteers. They came together through referrals, written applications and recruitment from selected community groups. But they share a special affinity in the establishment of the successful Volunteers 2000 Program.

Let us indulge in the thoughts of **Richard Rasker**, who by Games-time had been a paid SOCOG staff member for over four years, but came through the volunteer ranks and so will explain why volunteering is such a rich experience: 'Great memories, fun, friendships and the honour of contributing in some way to staging the Olympic and Paralympic Games. No matter how small the contribution, every one of the volunteers will have done something to help stage the best Games ever. Only a handful of athletes can say they are Olympians, even less can say they are Olympic Champions – but through the volunteer program, like the athletes, the volunteers can say they participated in an Olympic Games, were part of the greatest positive experience on earth, and through their dedication they can even proudly say they are champions. Serving athletes to help them perform at their best, showing off our great country to the world's people – all of these experiences make the Games great and help build the pride and passion that drives the volunteers, makes them give more of themselves and in the end, what the volunteers are doing – like the Freemans, Thorpes and O'Neills – is representing Australia at an Olympic Games. And by their smiles, friendliness, enthusiasm, passion and commitment, volunteers not only contribute to staging the Games; they are in fact the very essence and soul of the Games.'

Pioneer Volunteer Teams

One of the best innovations put into place for the Pioneer Volunteers was the formation of teams by district within the Sydney basin and the Central Coast. These teams were named after former host cities of the Olympic and Paralympic Games, and the innovation was put in place by SOCOG co-ordinator of the Pioneer Volunteers, **Kathryn Bendall**, and her assistant **Sally Mulligan**.

As volunteer numbers grew, the team program provided many benefits to both the volunteers and SOCOG. Volunteers would not have far to go in order to meet as a group, and could car-pool when asked to volunteer as a group. Many genuine friendships have developed out of this program.

SOCOG ran a Team Leaders' meeting every month as a means of two-way communication. Each team elected a team leader on a six-month rotation, and these team leaders brought information to SOCOG and returned to update their colleagues at the next team meeting.

Many teams took on other projects within their communities which were either Olympic or Paralympic related. There were fundraising dinners, fashion parades, two-year and one-year-to-go parties and Paralympic school programs.

The Hive

Pioneer Volunteers took over the role of providing support at SOCOG Headquarters in place of the early volunteers who had put up their hands back at Bid time (most of whom actually became Pioneer Volunteers). The volunteers were provided with the Los Angeles conference room to use as their base and co-ordinated workroom to which all project areas of SOCOG would bring tasks to be handled by volunteers. This room was affectionately named The Hive, to where all the workers gathered for 'Queen Bee' Kathryn Bendall.

Many Pioneer Volunteers contributed to setting up The Hive, and while much pride was taken in its initial decoration, there were times that the volumes of material for processing made it look more like a warehouse. While many volunteers actually committed to working specific days of the week out in needy program areas, most SOCOG and SPOC staff and the volunteers don't know how the volume of work could have been processed had it not been for the efficient running of The Hive. The list below is the best record we have of those who contributed in The Hive; for any omissions we sincerely apologise:

Rizk Abdel-Malak, Isobel Armour, Leah (Princess) Armstrong, Wendi Balbi, Jane Betts, Maureen Boyle, Ray Brown, Ron Browne, Margaret Byron, Zita Caldwell, Pam Callaghan, Joyce Chambers, Tony Chatfield, Margaret Childs, Sharron Church, Laurie Coleman, Lyn Comber, Christine Cunliffe, Margaret Davey, Nicole Dawe, Barrie Dawson, Denis Dean, Esther Dean, Evelyn Ferry, Brenda Gardiner, Heinz Gerstl, Doris Graves, Dianne Greenway, Maxine Hall, Susan Hart, Debbie Henry, Norma Holt, Pam Horam, Peter Horam, Stephen Horvarth, Pamela Kirkham, Anneke Kunz, Julia (Julie) Larsen, David Leathley, Barbara Lee, Garry Lee, Anne Lee, Lyn McHale, Frank McHale, John McKearnan, Belinda McLeod, June McMannus, Marguerite McNeal, Peter Melhuish, Hannah Mills, Joyce Moody, Jenny Moscrop, Dora Mulvey, Alwyn Murray, Ken Murray, George Nolan, Kim Owens, Rosemary Owens, Julie Pegrum, Shannon Penny, John Purdy, Glad Pye, Fran Rogers, Marie Rumsey, Frank Sanney, Bill Shelley, Ari Shukla, Pat Sleeman, Lyn Stephenson, Margaret Stewart, Ralph Stilgoe, Joan Stilgoe, Di Stuart, Noel Taylor, Dorothy Williams, Norm Williams, Shirley Williams, Ann Windibank

THE HIVE – LEVEL 5 – SOCOG HEADQUARTERS, JONES STREET, ULTIMO

FRANK MCHALE (SEATED), RIZK ABDEL-MALAK AND JULIE LARSEN, PREPARING MANUALS IN THE HIVE

(L TO R) HANNAH MILLS AND JOYCE CHAMBERS STUDYING CHILDREN'S ARTWORK

PIONEER VOLUNTEER GERARD LANDON

RESULTS / TIMING VOLUNTEERS AT THE OLYMPIC SWIMMING SELECTION TRIALS

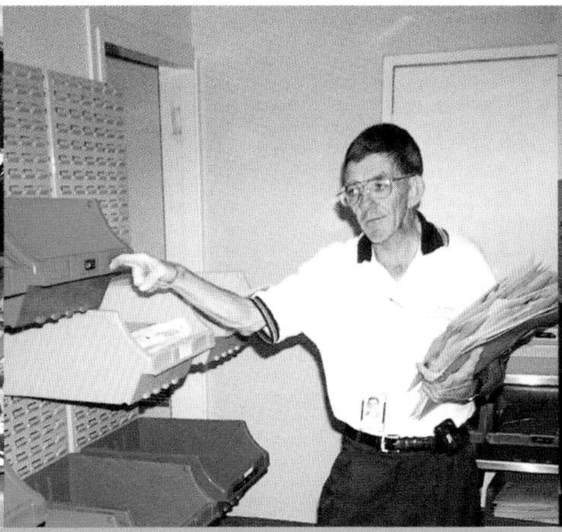

Eighteen thousand articles were submitted by Primary School students in response to the Art Program, and for three years **Joyce Chambers** and **Hannah Mills** sorted and catalogued the students' contributions. Thousands of selected pieces took pride of place in decorating the athletes' rooms in the Village, and then became treasured souvenirs which the athletes took home as a reminder of the contribution of Australian children to making their Olympic experience even more special.

The mail must be delivered

While many have contributed to collecting, processing and delivering mail throughout SOCOG Headquarters, a dedicated trio of Pioneer Volunteers have become the most familiar faces. They are **Gerard Landon, Doug Baker and Len Rayner**. Between them they have contributed thousands of hours of volunteer time, and not just 'doing the mail run', but at test events at nearly every venue.

Many SOCOG staff have stories of commendation about the trio. A member of the Paralympic Games staff – **Mary Clarke** – says: 'Gerry has been a body always there at the beginning and always staying to the very end to clean-up. He identifies with the ethic of rolling up the sleeves without counting the cost, and establishes a great rapport with those with whom he is associated.'

Both **Ken and Nancy Laycock** have had their fair share of health problems in recent years, but during January 2000 at the Tennis test event, Ken recalls: 'A young man wanted to get closer to get a photo of Pat Rafter, explaining to me that his sister-in-law was going into hospital the following day for her first treatment for cancer, and had come especially to see Pat play. Not knowing how I would achieve it, I asked if she would like to meet him.

'I contacted a supervisor, explaining the situation, and before long it was arranged for when he came off court. We escorted her to the players' exit, and as Pat came off court the supervisor spoke to him. Pat came forward and greeted her and chatted for a while. He then put his arm around her for a photograph.

Ken and Nancy Laycock ready for the closing ceremony

Kim Jeung and brother-in-law Anthony

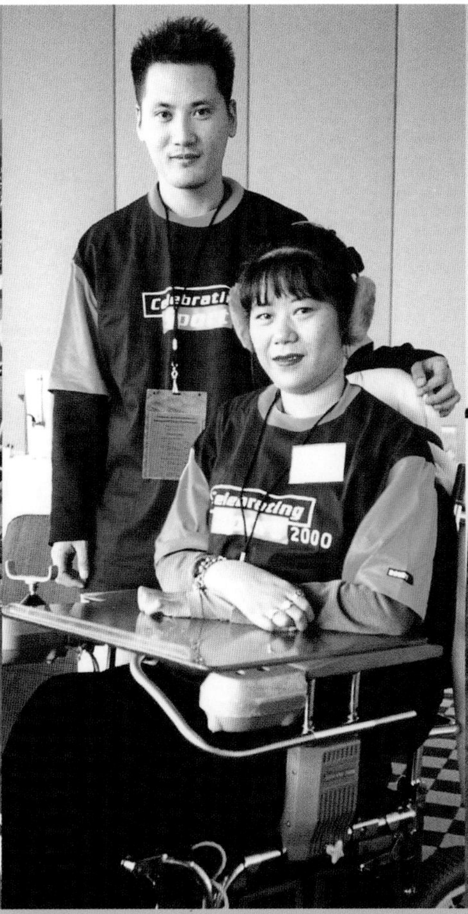

Olympian Jenny Murray (nee Steinbeck) volunteering at the Olympic swimming selection trials

'This to me was a very special encounter, made perfect by Pat's generosity. Pat Rafter we salute and thank you for making a young lady's burden lighter.'

Lindsay Mitchell sustained considerable head injuries in a motor vehicle accident in 1986, after which he spent two years in hospital. Lindsay became involved in volunteering in the community in order to meet new people, which resulted in him working at test events for Sailing, Tennis, Diving, Gymnastics and Synchronised Swimming in the lead-up to the Games.

Sue Cole volunteered in test events for Baseball, Athletics, Shooting, Swimming and Basketball, providing pre-Games experiences which had her singing the praises of fellow volunteers and organisers. 'I've gained some wonderful friends and all of the money in the world could never give me the pride and satisfaction of being a volunteer for the Sydney 2000 Olympic Games.'

Kim Jeung was born in Cambodia, but came to Australia in 1991 because of the civil war in her homeland. One year later Kim was in a car accident that made her a quadriplegic.

Kim decided that she would like to assist people in communicating, she herself being fluent in five languages. Due to her restrictions in her motorised chair, her brother-in-law, Anthony, accompanied her to her first test event at Weightlifting in March 2000. Kim recalls: 'I was nervous when I arrived, but my supervisor explained carefully my duties, which really helped my confidence. I would like to thank the organisers, teammates and supervisors for helping me fulfil one very important event in my life – to be part of the Olympic and Paralympic Games.'

Philippe Le Scoul came to Sydney from Altona (Melbourne) to be a Liaison Officer for the French Gymnastics Team during the test event. There were the not so good aspects, such as the 11-hour bus trip each way, and the blisters from long hours at the venue, but as Philippe says, 'These challenges were nothing compared to the wonderful experience with the athletes and fellow volunteers, and I couldn't wait to get back in September for the Big One.'

'I had the most incredible time at the Baseball Intercontinental Cup as a volunteer in Spectator Services. It was great to feel wanted and appreciated, and I am sure I was running on adrenalin for the whole two weeks.

'My son was a bat/ball boy and was befriended by the Japanese Team. Although only 15 years of age, he stands 6ft 2ins and has a very large frame – they nicknamed him "Jumbo". After the final game, one of the players gave him a bat which had been shattered during the game, plus a brand new ball – and said, "Thank you Jumbo." This story my son will tell to his children I'm sure.' ... **Tricia Squibb**

In January 2000, **Laurie West** drove over seven hours from Normanton to Cairns in North Queensland, bought a return airline ticket to Sydney, and came down to be accredited as a volunteer working at the Diving test event for one week. All this so as he could do it all again in September as a Spectator Services Host at the Olympic Stadium. Laurie says, 'It was just an unbelievable experience, and I have so many stories to tell the folks back home in Normanton.'

Laurie West in the staff break area – aquatic centre

(L to R) Graeme Turnbull, Pam Cameron, Hanny Sterki, Pat Moro and Wendy Munton (doping control volunteers at synchronised swimming test event – April 2000)

Staff and volunteers at the diving test event

Double Trouble – Double Games

Twin sisters **Margaret Stewart and Shirley Williams** created havoc around SOCOG Headquarters and test events as most people could not tell them apart. It wasn't till Margaret and Shirley were seen together that many SOCOG staff and Pioneer Volunteers weren't amazed that 'this lady' seemed to have more than 24 hours in a day.

Shirley and Margaret have the distinction of being involved in both the 1956 Melbourne and 2000 Sydney Olympic Games. In Melbourne they were employed as catering staff in the Olympic Village, in Sydney – well! As Pioneer Volunteers they have been everywhere, and despite accident and illness, their passion to 'help their country' has never faltered since the morning they walked south over the Sydney Harbour Bridge from Shirley's house at Milsons Point to hear the announcement as to which country's bid had been successful for the staging of the 2000 Olympic and Paralympic Games.

Norm and Dorothy Williams have established a unique double – Norm carried the Olympic Torch in 1956 and Dorothy has carried it in 2000. It is not known if any other married couple has achieved the unique distinction of carrying the Olympic Torch for different Olympics but in the same country.

'I began manning Olympic stands creating awareness before we won the right to host the Olympic Games, and after that magical announcement I continued in similar roles even after SOCOG was formed. I then had the privilege of becoming part of the Pioneer Volunteer Program. In 1998 I was involved in a motor vehicle accident and spent nine weeks in hospital with the threat of having my leg amputated.

'That was the low point – my leg was then saved, I got back to working in SOCOG Headquarters and eventually moved into the area of Doping Control, which became my greatest pleasure as a Games-time role. I was also accepted as a Torch Bearer for the Olympic Torch Relay, another highlight which contributed to making 2000 an unbelievably special year.' ... **Pam Cameron**

BASKET CARRIERS AT THE OLYMPIC SWIMMING SELECTION TRIALS

TWIN SISTERS MARGARET STEWART AND SHIRLEY WILLIAMS WORKING IN THE HIVE

(L TO R) SUE BATTEN AND JUNE MCMANUS (ACCREDITATION – GYMNASTICS TEST EVENT FEBRUARY 2000)

(L TO R) JOE AYOUB, ROGER COX, LOUIS VASQUEZ, JULIA STENTON, KEVIN LUCAS AND KERRY BRAY IN FRONT. COURSE VOLUNTEERS FOR THE HOST CITY MARATHON IN APRIL 2000

VOLUNTEERS UNDER THE GUIDANCE OF ANNE GREEN (DARK SHIRT), PREPARE TO ASSIST DISABLED ATHLETES AT THE OLYMPIC SWIMMING SELECTION TRIALS

Kathy Munro became a Pioneer Volunteer, and spent most of her pre-Games volunteer time working with SPOC on the Link Elite Athlete Program (LEAP), something she became very emotional about. 'The wonderful team of Debra Pinkerton and Heather McDonald made us feel so much part of the organisation. I participated in as many test events as possible before taking up my Games-time role as Spectator Services Team Leader at the Aquatic Centre. This was a magnificent venue to be involved with, but I also had a wonderful time during the Paralympics in the Superdome, as so many of our LEAP school students came through the venue, and it was so special to see the results of our efforts.'

My time with Olympic Legend John Akwhari

'Having been born in Tanzania, I was keen to make contact with the Tanzanian Team while working in the Athletes Village. I was especially privileged to meet John Akwhari, who had become famous as the man who had embodied the Olympic Spirit in Mexico City in 1968. After finishing last in the marathon more than one and a half hours after the winner he said, 'My country didn't send me to start the race. They sent me here to finish.'

'John asked me if I knew Bruce Ronaldson who had been his school teacher and first coach years ago. John had an old letter from Bruce written from Oxford in England. After many phone calls to International Directories, I found Bruce Ronaldson. Armed with a Telstra phone card I took John to the public phone in the Village and we called Bruce. It was a great reunion for them both who hadn't seen each other for I guess at least 30 years. A very special Olympic moment!' ... **Graeme MacLean (Pioneer Volunteer)**

It says it all!

WHO WANTS
TO
VOLUNTEER?

Pioneer volunteer Margaret Davey

Pioneer volunteer Ken Willoughby MBE, making distribution boards for broadcasters

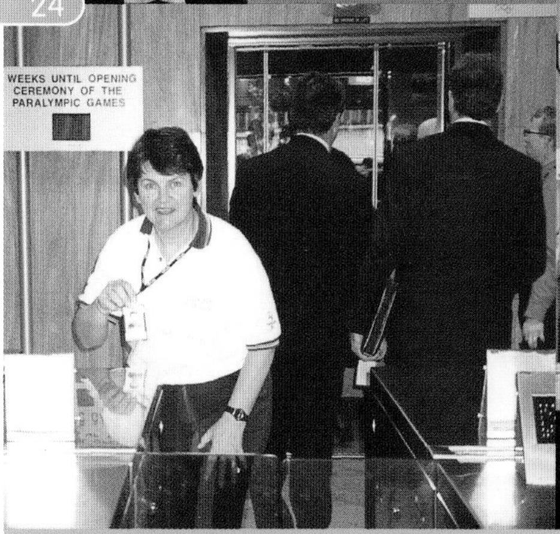
WEEKS UNTIL OPENING
CEREMONY OF THE
PARALYMPIC GAMES

Pioneer volunteer Joyce Moody about to scan her pass at SOCOG headquarters. A taxi driver was once heard to say, 'They must be a dedicated lot, always bowing to the Olympic rings as they enter the building!'

Barrie Dawson 'models' the new volunteer uniform to fellow pioneer volunteers in the Hive

Who says volunteering doesn't pay?

Pioneer Volunteer, **Rizk Abdel-Malak** was working at the Sailing test event when he found two-thirds of an old grey $100 note stuck to the wharf. He was going to keep it as a souvenir, but decided to take it to the bank where it was inspected, and because one digit of the number on the reverse side was visible, Rizk was given a new $100 note.

Pioneer Volunteer **Albert Simonian** moved to Australia from Jordan in 1992 after finishing his PhD in Budapest, and being fluent in English, Arabic and Hungarian. Albert says: 'Because I enjoyed the friendships and opportunities being part of the volunteer program, my wife Maysoun has now become a language specialist with SOCOG. We are proud of this country, and when people asked why we do it for no payment, we say it is our commitment to our new country.'

Pioneer Volunteer **Margaret Davey** at age 73 was 'in everything', and she had to have amassed over 3000 hours of volunteer time prior to Games-time. People half her age would love to keep up her pace, and while making this volunteer commitment, she went off and won nine Gold Medals in swimming at the Australian Masters Games. Well done Margaret.

The Rothwell Family has made preparing for the Olympic and Paralympic Games a real family commitment. Three generations were volunteers, Vera and her mother Dora became involved before Sydney even won the bid. Once the Pioneer Volunteer Program was established, her son Deryck became involved. All three contributed enormously to SOCOG's build-up before their Games-time roles. Both Deryck and Vera were Olympic Torch Bearers, and Deryck went on to be a volunteer in the Olympic Youth Camp. Vera has also contributed a regular 'Volunteer' column in *The Park Record*, in Park City, Utah, as a lead-up to the 2002 Winter Olympics. Passing on the Baton!

'It all began with a "meet and greet" at the Nikko Hotel for the World Junior Athletics Championships in August 1996, the year I retired. It concluded with a party after the conclusion of the Paralympics, for those of us fortunate enough to have worked in the Athletes Village. What happened in between was the most amazing four years, and all I can say is I was born in the right place at the right time!' ... **Joyce Moody**

Frank and Lyn McHale spent many hours working in The Hive, and alternated every Tuesday going to help out with the auction of the Objet d'art whenever it was being conducted in the Pitt Street Mall. On 29 June 2000, Lyn came away the proud owner of piece Number 444. She took it home under cover of darkness and produced it on Frank's birthday, 9 July 2000 – What a surprise!!!

Elaine Briers carried the euphoria from Melbourne in 1956 to Sydney in 2000. Elaine in her younger years was fortunate enough to be a secretary in the media, which gave her accreditation to both ceremonies and many other events, an experience which motivated her to become involved with the Pioneer Volunteer Program with SOCOG. She became a familiar face in her role at the staff shop on the seventh floor, and it was obvious that associating with staff and volunteers working on the success of the Sydney Games helped her relive her Melbourne experiences, but at the same time inspired her for her role in Protocol with the Federation States of Micronesia.

No excuses

John Purdy and Barbara Lee were volunteers at the World Junior Athletics Championships in 1996, but deteriorating health, and a subsequent liver transplant for John in August 1997, prevented them from continuing their roles till March 1998. John says: 'Once I got my new lease on life there was no holding us back, as we both enjoyed the friendships and working relationships with our Barcelona Pioneer Volunteer team members, and colleagues in The Hive and other areas of SOCOG. We had a great journey to our ultimate fulfilling Games-time roles in Medical for Barbara and Doping Control for me. Thanks for the experience.'

Ken Willoughby's passion for working on 'Big Aussie Projects' began with the Snowy Mountains Scheme, so he certainly wasn't going to let the Olympics and Paralympics pass him by! However, the date 11 April threw Ken some 'curved balls'. On that date in 1996, Ken had a stroke – a setback he put behind him. Then on 11 April 2000, Ken was diagnosed with lung cancer. An operation in May left Ken struggling, but with his usual determination, Ken recovered sufficiently to carry the Olympic Torch on Day 98 of the Torch Relay, and to successfully complete his Games-time volunteering. Well done Ken, we are proud of you!

PIONEER VOLUNTEERS NOEL DUNN AND CAROLE BARTLE ASSISTING AT THE OLYMPIC JOURNEY PARADE – MARTIN PLACE, 1997

PIONEER VOLUNTEERS (ON THE ARENA OF AN INCOMPLETE OLYMPIC STADIUM) AT THE ANNOUNCEMENT THAT THE OLYMPIC TORCH RELAY WOULD COMMENCE ITS AUSTRALIAN JOURNEY AT ULURU

PIONEER VOLUNTEERS ENJOY THE HOSPITALITY AT PRESIDENT, MICHAEL KNIGHT'S, OLYMPIC STADIUM SUITE

One year to go ...

And the winner is ... Sydney!!! Who can forget the night?
When Mr Samaranch rose to speak and the words came out just right.

That was almost six years ago, it's strange how time can fly,
Now we've got just one to go – I feel like I could cry.
So much has happened in this time, so many things we've done
We've grown and learned along the way, it isn't always fun.

2000 seemed so far away, on that fateful night
This time next year we'll know for sure, if we've done it right.
Our hearts will swell with pride and tears will surely flow
But for now we'll keep on working hard, because there's still one year to go.

It's tempting to imagine where we'll be one year today
But there's still so much to do, let's not wish the time away
And if you really wish it were now, just think how much we'll miss.

Of course we'll have our memories, time will never erase those
And albums crammed with photos, of the highs and lows
But what I hope will stay with us, through all the years to come
Are all the friendships that we've made, and pride in what we've done.

So let's not wish for the time to go too fast
Let's spin out every minute, and try and make it last.
The good news is, we've longer than you know –
Because 2000's a leap year, there's 366 days still to go!!! ... **Vera Rothwell**

PIONEER VOLUNTEERS AT THE ROYAL EASTER SHOW 1998

A SMALL CONTINGENT OF THE TOKYO PIONEER VOLUNTEER TEAM

'We were overjoyed at being invited to be part of the Pioneer Volunteer Program, which led to – directing traffic in pouring rain, directing cyclists in the RTA Cycle Sydney Race, Marching in the Olympic Journey Parades in Newcastle, Canberra and Tamworth, helping at the Wheelchair Basketball Gold Cup and Wheelchair Tennis. These were just some of our pre-Games commitments.

'Come Games-time, we would stand on Wyong Station at 4.30 am talking to strangers in the same beautiful uniform and we all shared the same goal. Only another volunteer can understand the feeling of accomplishment and camaraderie that exists with us today.' ... **Denis and Esther Dean**

Passion from Pioneers

'I was accompanying Paralympian Stewart Pike at the Aquatic Centre, and asked how I could help him. He said, "You can swim the 100 Fly for me." He obviously didn't know how well I CAN'T swim butterfly!' **Barrie Dawson**

'When the Great Stadium Walk was offered to the public on 21 February 1999, my husband Frank and I went. We were hooked, and the next month I went with my friend Margaret Childs for an interview, and later Frank became an ORTA Driver. It has been so rewarding.' ... **Leah Armstrong**

'I'd truly describe the most exciting day during this period as the day we got the news that I'd be carrying the Olympic Torch.' ... **Julie Pegrum**

'I retired as Principal of Parramatta High School at the end of 1996, and my life has been special ever since. My daughter Christine, son John and his wife Yvonne have all joined me in becoming Pioneer Volunteers.' ... **Ken Murray**

'I had been doing a presentation as part of the Speakers Group to people at a nursing home. When I finished, I overheard two ladies in the front; one said to the other, "What's he been talking about Mavis?" The other said, "I don't know, but he hasn't called out one of my bingo numbers!!!!" ... **Barclay Wade (Olympian Tokyo 1964)**

'When we worked at the Pan Pac Swimming in 1999, a young Canadian swimmer began chatting with me, and during the course of our conversation we discovered that my brother, who lives in Canada, not only taught him, but had also taught with his mother. We were now friends for life! Unfortunately injury prevented him from competing at the Olympic Games.' ... Toni Walsh

'The Opening Ceremony was very exciting. We helped everyone get ready in their special uniforms, and tried to prepare them for the huge number of people who would be watching them. When Madagascar came out into the Stadium, I cheered from my place way up in the stands. Everyone around me turned and asked me "Madagascar?" "That's my team," I said.' ... Glenn Fisher (NPC Assistant – Madagascar)

'I was born with a form of dwarfism, and will never compete in the Olympic Games, but I have always loved sport and the Olympics. I could have asked for no greater honour than to share the work with all the wonderful volunteers who made The Hive their domain over the past two years. To cap it all off, carrying the Olympic Torch was just unbelievable.' ... Belinda McLeod (Pioneer Volunteer)

'The past four years have been the most unbelievable of our lives, and have given us the impetus to take on other adventures to enhance our future in a continuing positive manner. When we were offered the opportunity to become involved with the Pioneer Volunteer Program with other enthusiasts on the Central Coast we were like two excited kids! The adventure in no way disappointed us, and in fact far exceeded our wildest expectations.

'The act of doing things like meeting Olympians, speaking to groups of excited school children, working at SOCOG Headquarters, seeing Olympic events at close quarters, and carrying the Olympic Torch were all situations we will cherish forever, but the friendships developed are the greatest legacy for our future.' ... Garry and Anne Lee

Denise Tugwell and her two daughters Holly and Heidi, embraced the Olympics back in 1997 by becoming part of the Pioneer Volunteer Program. Heidi then went off to Japan to study, and came back to the experience of a lifetime as a volunteer at the Olympic Youth Camp. Meanwhile, Denise and Holly became active in test events and finally Doping Control, which became their ultimate Games-time roles with an exhilarating face-to-face contact with the world's elite athletes.

Rob and Pam Callaghan couldn't get enough of the Olympic/Paralympic experience – to the point that their children were banning the use of the 'O' word around the house! They did have one 'fault' though – they did not know when to say No! It got to the point where whenever Rob took a phone call from Pam his response was 'What have you committed us to now?' Their roles in Protocol at both the Olympics and Paralympics were fulfilling, and made good use of their people skills. They, like many volunteers, look at the friendships developed as the major legacy of the experience, and their children are proud of Rob and Pam's involvement.

The constant activity for Reception at SOCOG Headquarters meant that full-time receptionist, Susan McElhone, was supported by a core group of volunteers, and others who would assist as required. Those who became familiar faces, and experienced the buzz of excitement in the build-up were: Faye Dunn, Vera Rothwell, Lee Steel, Anne Windybank, Pam Kirkham, Kayleen Howe and Gai Hamer.

Pioneer Farewell

Well this is finally it, my fellow Pioneers
Next year we'll just be part of 50,000 volunteers
Our last night as a group has come around so fast
So let's now share together a few memories of the past.

Between us all we've worked at wide and varied places
Helping run events with cheerful, smiling faces
We've met royalty, officials, athletes, fans and more
We've carried their bags, driven their cars, and opened up their doors.

Who can forget ASOIF, or the air of the airport at dawn
And reaching for the coffee cups at 4.30 in the morn
Or sailing regattas spent overseeing the car park
Or long days at athletics, and driving home in the dark.

We experienced all kinds of sports at Sydney's Greater West Games
Some even presented medals in a glorious burst of fame!
We've had roller skating, badminton, volleyball and yet
There hasn't been a single thing that I ever want to forget.

Right along beside us on this Pioneer Journey of ours
Volunteer Services Staff were also clocking up the hours
Our thanks go out to all, but three I'd like to name –
Kathryn, Sally and Debs – without you it just wouldn't have been the same.

It's hard to think just what it is that we'll miss the most,
Will it be Pioneer Journeys, or perhaps the Pioneer Post?
But never mind, you know things could be worse –
At least now you'll be free of all this Pioneer verse!

I wish that this experience could go on and never end
Because I know what I'll miss most are all my Pioneer friends
Thank you all for everything that you've so willingly done
And when you look back and remember, hasn't it been fun?

However, my friends, our special time draws to a close
Look around and just be proud that you were one they chose
Ignore the negative, no matter what is said
Be sure the best Games ever are only nine months ahead.

A thousand hours or five hundred, fifty, or even ten
No matter what time you've given, you'll always remember when
You were part of something special, a memory you'll hold dear
And proudly tell your grandchildren, yes, I was a Pioneer Volunteer! ... Vera Rothwell

Susan McElhone and Lee Steel

Pam Kirkham

Gai Harmer

Olympians volunteering at the Olympic swimming trials – (L to R) Georgina Parkes, Shane Lewis and Karen Stephenson (nee Moras)

Amsterdam pioneer volunteer team debrief – back (L to R) Joye Walsh, Jim Breen, Janis Gardner, Marijke Newnham, David Magnusson, Judy Lucas, Kym Scollay, Robyn Stutchbury (partly obscured) and Seated (L to R) Marie Rumsey, Deborah Gardner, Julie Pegrum, Geoff Rowell, Angela Turek, Noel Tait

Pioneer volunteers Ralph and Joan Stilgoe, who made a total commitment to their Olympic volunteering, as they have done in their lives of community volunteering

Volunteers Parade...

ain't
nothing
yet!

THE
GALLERIES
VICTORIA

TORCH RELAY VOLUNTEERS

In this segment there are so many diverse groups of people to recognise. Those community people and volunteers who were honoured to carry the Torch in either the Olympic of Paralympic Torch Relay, were given great acknowledgement, and rightly so. However, there were escort runners, State Emergency Service volunteers, Rural Fire Service volunteers and countless community groups and individuals who gave of their time over months and even years, to make the two Torch Relays the outstanding success they were.

Every cauldron-lighting ceremony involved a community volunteer task force supporting Local Council and SOCOG staff. Most of these volunteers received very little recognition, and contributed their time and effort in a way that they often do for other community events – just because they want to! Every Council District through which the Torch Relays passed was given the opportunity to have their volunteers recognised in this souvenir memento – some chose to, others did not! It has been a passion of the author to give due recognition, and those of you who's names or organisations are not mentioned in these pages – you know you are appreciated, and there is a wide-held belief that you are the backbone of society.

'Knowing how many people had carried the flame before me, and how many were yet to, made it an unforgettable honour. Having positions available to the public encouraged Australians, it showed that the Games were for the people. Having rain and an uphill run did not deter me, as I was encouraged by friends and family running beside me.

'Even though it was a terrific experience, the aspect of the Games I enjoyed most was the way Australia pulled together and welcomed the world. Being a volunteer in Spectator Services at the Equestrian and Athlete Escort in the Paralympic Ceremonies, I got to mingle with a myriad of nationalities, and am even writing to a PNG Paralympian.' ... **Naomi Walton**

Very few rural communities had the distinction of hosting both the Olympic and Paralympic Torch Relays, however, one such community was the Southern Highlands of NSW, centred on Mittagong, Bowral and Moss Vale. In 1992, before Sydney had won the bid, and long before this community knew they would have even one, let alone two Torch Relays passing through their district, a group of passionate and dedicated volunteers became pro-active in promoting their region. This resulted in some very successful fundraising, and the opportunity to host several Olympic and Paralympic Teams for pre-games training.

Naomi Walton being congratulated by her friend Natalie

Torch relay community volunteer Margaret Hawkes shares the moment with spectator services hosts

(L to R) Chris Sturtridge, Jack Hutchinson, Shaun Sayers and Alan Shaw – community volunteers at Deepwater (north of Glen Innes in the New England district of NSW)

To the best of their records, the following are the volunteers who contributed over eight years, culminating in very successful Torch Relay Celebrations:

Robyn Abbott, Lorraine Acton, Gillian Adamson, Margaret Alcock, Emma Alcorn, Jill Anderson, Elizabeth Armstrong, Anne Aughey, Sally Bailey, Lucia Bainat, Gail Barr, Lloyd Barwell, Graham Bell, Jan Bell, Jenny Bennett, Judy Berg, Vivian Berney, Jennifer Birnie, Gordon Blinman, Raewyn Bolte, Shirley Brereton, Olga Broekhuizen, Bernard Brown, Ruth Brunsdon, Max Bulluss, Belinda Butler, Meryl Caldwell-Smith, Flavia Cancian, Richard Cant, Laurel Cheetham, Benita Chittenden, Judy Clark, Lizzie Clarke, Barbara Clayton, Rosemary Cork, Susan Covey, Graham Covey, Geoff Cowgill, Bessie Cowgill, Terri Crichton, Rosalie Daw, Pat Denning, Judith Dey, Annette Dirickx-Jones, Freda Doy, Annette Dubokovich, Jill Dyson, Renee Eccleston, Robyn Ferguson, Janice Fletcher, Anna Fletcher, Christine Florance, Gay Free, Bill Free, Elaine Gardner, Arthur Gardner, June Gardner-Brown, Barbara Ginnane, Joan Glendenning, Sheila Hall, Francis Halpin, Patricia Hammond, Peter Harris, Brian Harrison, Patricia Harrison, Norma Hart, Gillian Hawkey, Sue Henderson, Eunice Hicks, Jewel Hillier, Marie Hodgson, Vince Holloway, Margaret Holmes, Marika Holmik, Denise Horvath, Penny Hoskins, Kath Howard, Glenys Howarth, Jackie Hussey, Jen Huxley, Lynette Jacobsen, Caroline Jefford, Joy Jefford, Mary Johnson, Ian Jones, Alan Kahn, Pat Keight, John Keight, Pamela King, Richard Knapman, Richard Knight, Paul Leape, Lydia Lee, Clive Lee, Bette Lewis, Miles Lochhead and Waterpolo Club members, Jenny Lockyer, Pam McDevitt, Margaret McDonald, Hazel McGregor, Denis McIntosh, Alan McKern, Jean McKern, Jenny MacLennan, Alistair MacLennan, Gwen MacPherson, Philipa Mainwaring, Reg Marsh, Todd Martin, Susan Maude, Bruce Mayo, Mavis Mayo, Leila Merson, Jim Merson, Shan Moore, Doug Morrison, Lois Morrison, Kim Morse-Evans, Susan Morton, Ron Mulveney, Lorna Mulveney, Jan Murray, Karen Murray, Steve Muston, Jean Napper, John Napper, David Neumann, Laurie O'Neill, Pam O'Neill, Cynthia Parker, Val Penna, Helen Peters, Dianne Randall, Bryce Randall, Elaine Russell, Cliff Russell, Ellie Russell, Petronella Ryan, Ray Ryan, Ann Sandars, Anne Sayer, Richard Seymour, Sandra Sharpe, Jane Shirlow, Ray Smee, Robin Solomon, Judy Spakman, Peter St Clare-Groth, Debbie Stanley, John Stanton, Elizabeth Symonds, Pam Tallents, Rhona Todd, Peter Tomlinson, Jane Turnnidge, Emma Turnnidge, Maureen Varnavsky, Josie Vittiglio, Cosimo Vittiglio, Judy Walker, Muriel Walton, Margaret Warby, Jean Warne, Alan Watkinson, Margaret Waudby, Annie Wentworth, Pat Wheatley, Ann Williams, Thelma Wilmot, Anna Wisken, Barry Wood, Pam Wood, Patricia Yeomans, Jenny Zantis and Anna Zaranski.

Like most volunteer co-ordinators, **Cindy de Warren**, the Brisbane Olympic Torch Relay co-ordinator, had a considerable task in bringing together and training sufficient volunteers for the expected large crowds in the Brisbane CBD. She did have some great support, but recognition of her efforts has been expressed by **Lea Sruhan, Sandra Beattie, John de Warren, Margaret Dickerson** and **Mary-Lou Collins** who continued on to be a Spectator Services volunteer in Sydney for the Olympic and Paralympic Games.

'I am an ordinary working girl, but being a volunteer assisting the Maryborough City Council on 18 June 2000, as a Torch Relay volunteer made this year one of the best and exciting years of my life. Something I will cherish forever.' … **Judy Turner**

The Torch Relay Crew consisted of basically paid staff who remained throughout the 100 days, plus volunteers who joined the convoy for approximately one month at a time. However, there were a small number of volunteers who did remain for the full period, and within this select group were five young ladies from Melbourne, who became known as 'The Melbourne Storm'. They were, **Anna Reinstein, Julia Van de Linden, Brooke Bond, Rebecca Griffiths and Lisa Meehan**. They did not know one

SES volunteers help assemble the stage for torch relay celebration at Taree

Community volunteers with school children preparing to perform in torch relay celebrations at Glen Innes

Torch relay co-ordinating committee at Nowra on the South Coast of NSW

Emma Alcorn has a disability (Down syndrome), but that did not prevent her from being an active member of the Southern Highlands volunteer group assisting with the torch relay, nor did it prevent her from being a very proud torch bearer.

Noleen Cregan (volunteer hostess) assists "Joyous" torch bearer Kristy-Lee Trajcevski

(L to R) Kath McCabe and Helen Smith – community volunteers at Grafton on the North Coast of NSW, join in the fun of 'painting the town purple!'

THE FIVE MELBOURNE GIRLS AFFECTIONATELY KNOWN AS THE MELBOURNE STORM, ENHANCED THE EXPERIENCE OF LOCALS WHEREVER THEY WENT. (L TO R) ANNA REINSTEIN, JULIA VAN DE LINDEN, BROOKE BOND, REBECCA GRIFFITHS AND LISA MEEHAN

TORCH BEARER ROBERT HEATHWOOD AND COMMUNITY VOLUNTEER RUSSELL COX

ARMIDALE/DUMARESQ SES VOLUNTEERS WHO ASSISTED WITH TRAFFIC DUTY. (BACK ROW – L TO R) JASON BABINGTON, TIM YEOMANS, MARK BABINGTON, ANDREW GAIN, STEVE BISHOP, ROBERT BABINGTON, FRANK HUTTON, DAVID MCKAY AND BOB NORMAN (MIDDLE ROW) DAVID ARCHER, DAN KENNEDY, KIRSTY SHAKESHAFT, DAVID PIDDINGTON, DEAN BABINGTON, NICK JONGERDEN, ROSEMARY MCKAY AND PAUL BABINGTON (FRONT ROW) EDDY WHEATLEY, CHRIS SMITH, NOEL (NORM) HATCH, DAN ALTER AND IVY RANKIN

PARTICIPANTS AND ORGANISERS OF THE NGUIU COMMUNITY (BATHURST ISLAND) OLYMPIC TORCH RELAY CELEBRATIONS: (BACK ROW – L TO R) BERNIE MCCARTHY, JULIE MCDONALD (OLYMPIAN), GARY OTTEN, AUGUST STEVENS AND BILL WINDRED (FRONT ROW) NICKY TIPILOURA, ANGELA KING AND WENDY BOCK

another before this adventure, but each one knew at least one of the other four (too complicated to explain the relationships). They were each hosts on one of the nine shuttle buses, where, with the driver, they welcomed Torch Bearers and Escort Runners, introducing them to one another, and making them feel comfortable for the experience ahead.

Rebecca comments: 'The Torch Relay was just an altogether amazing experience that created a bond between all involved. A connection that no one else can fully comprehend or understand. After all we did not just work with our colleagues – we lived with them for three months. The experience of "living out of a bag" and going from town to town is one that one can only truly get if you were there.

'I think that as members of the core (100-day) crew it was often too easy to forget that whilst we got to live and experience the power of the flame 24 hours a day, others saw it for three minutes or even less. It would have been easy to become complacent and almost cynical toward the event were it not for the amazement on peoples faces the first time they saw or held a torch.

'It became (subconsciously) important that we treated each new lot of Torch Bearers as if they were our first. After all how could we possibly downplay their special moment just because we were so fortunate to witness many many moments. I think that actually they (the Torch Bearers and general public) were what made the event special for us.'

Thank you to the following Bundaberg community volunteers:

Jane McRae, Jody Walters, Coral Sweeney, Mark Evans, Deirdre Choveaux, Catherine Rodgers, Barbara Hancock, Steve Hancock, Noel Muller, Maurice Wilson, Peter Cambourne, Dorothy Hooper, Olive Pollock, Melissa Bauer, John Heiner, Roy Thorn, Darren Gilby, Michael Verdel, Matthew Badger, Betty Reddacliff, Nicholas Trembath, Ellen Trembath, Sylvia McNamara, Arthur Algar, Carolyn Kennedy, Vickie Germain, Bernie Wray and Teddy Gyngell.

Community volunteers wishing to contribute to the success of the Torch Relays come from varied backgrounds and nationalities. One such volunteer in Perth is Hana Byambadash from Ulaanbaatar, Mongolia, who is here in Australia with her husband Battulga and son Mark, as a postgraduate student at Curtin University. Hana has become involved in other volunteer projects, but says, 'I am proud of my contribution to the celebrations of the Sydney 2000 Torch Relay. My involvement in this event made it a truly memorable occasion for my family and friends.'

Murray Bridge, South Australia, had a dedicated group of volunteers assisting with Torch Relay celebrations, they were:

Graham Peake, Shane Snell, Craig Hattam, Travis Deed, Bevan Laube, Tony Samblich, Ron Liebelt, Trevor Mundy, Mark Jeansch, Fred Toogood, Peter Hoffman, Ray Symes, Bill Wilson, Peter Rischbeith, Gary Page, Michael Frith, Robert Butcher, Don Watt, John Clarke, Dennis Roberts, Russell Norman, Paul Mumford, Rob Bridge, Helen Peake, Sarah Peake, Rebecca Toogood, Alicia Ninnis, Trudie Hansen, Elizabeth Twomey, Shirley Liebelt, Gloria Mundy, Benita Jeansch and Barb Toogood. Thank you for a job well done.

Atherton Shire Council in Far North Queensland, would like to thank the following community volunteers for their effort in Torch Relay preparations:

Jim Liston, Robert Van Riet, Don Brandon, Rod Chaffey, James Crompton, Grace McLaren, James McMurdo, Arthur Leinster, Trevor McLeod, Brian McLaren, Frank Matthew, Jeni Matthew, Geoff Redington, Domenico Isabella, Barry Wadsworth, Denis Guilfoyle, Peter Bunyan, Maurie Spencer, Kevin Ramke, Robert Cross, John Fleming, Cheryl Piccone, Bruce Magill, Terry Clark, Lyn Clark, Colleen McIvor, Don Scheffler, Carol Sanderson, Janet Leinster and June Spencer.

Cairns Community Volunteers:

Ross Britton, Kylie Britton, David Buckham, Gillian Buckham, Ken Clark, Ron Crew, Mena Crew, Antoine David, Kate Dhosi, Terry Gibbs, Karen Gibbs, Karen Hales, Julie Hughes, Trevor Keeling, Rob Kelly, Andrew Kerrison, Stuart Lovell, Brenda Lovell, Anthony Lovell, Kev Maher, Jon Mamonski, Alan McDonald, Sandy McEachan, Mary-Ann McEachan, Richard McIntosh, Janet McKay, Paul McLean-Williams, Peter Merlin, Brian Mills, Maggie Moffat, John Muller, Stuart Munro, Dick Opie, Alex Popov, Graeme Reardon, Peter Richardson, Eddie Robertson, Peter Rothary, Don Sanderson, Isobel Sanderson, Mick Schramm, Steven Scott, Jim Spencer, Ken Stone, Mike Woods, Doug Wyeth and Janette Wyeth.

Noosa Enterprise Group were very proud of the community volunteers and Surf Life Saving Club members who made their Torch Relay celebrations such a success. They were:

Denise Alenaddaf, Mrs D. Ballard, Brian Bannsett, Derek Bartels, Kaye Bartholomaeus, Cheryl Bean, Phil Beard, Philip Beard, Jen Beattie, Nadia Bellerby, Robyn Benaud, Peter Best, Rex Betts, Tony Blacksell, Noel Bloxsome, Geoff Bowden, Fran Boyd, Scott Braby, Glenda Brown, Gloria Bruzzone, Nick Carter, Margaret Chinn, Andrew Clarke, June Colley, Colin Crisp, John Crossley, Durn Dart, Steve Dawson, Greg Dinsey, Greg Duff, Ida Duncan, Glen Elmes, Joyce Farlow, Joyce and Richard Faunce, Bill Fielder, Vicki Fleming, Neil Fraser, Tony Frost, Greg Furner, Michelle Gameiro, Janet and Jock Gemmell, Murray Gleadhill, Jenny Hales, Ray Ham, Terry Hanly, Jane Hanson, Ross Hickey, David Hodgkinson, Milosa Jackson, Darren Johnson, Gerard Johnson, Jan Johnston, Belinda Keene, Ray Kelly, Margaret King, Julie Kinloch, Geoff Lander, Ron Lane, Helen Leyden, Gina Linch, Edward Linton, Anne Linton, Rosemary Loader, Trevor Luff, Winifred Lupton, Bill Magin, Hugh McCredie, Alec McIntosh, Janet McKenna, Terry Nash, Brian Nicholas, John Nissen, Mick O'Donohue, Jan Officer, Dale Officer, Chas Olsen, Paul O'Neil, Cr Frank Pardon, Bernard Paul, Sue Pearce, James Penman, Rick Phillips, Cameron Porter, Kathy Profke, S. Reckenberg, Peter Riley, Lynn Robertson, Richard Rowe, Tony Rowe, Stan Ryan, Ann Scanlon, Fran

John and Carol Symington, community volunteers Noosa, Queensland, who organised a cocktail competition between the bar tenders of Noosa – the prize – the Noosa flame cocktail trophy!

Selwood, David and Louise Shepherd, Bronte Shields, Jullian Smith, Julie Spencer, Robyn Stewart, Barry Stewart, David Stewart, Mary Stewart, Chris Strid, John and Carol Symington, Patricia Tidswell, Chris Treweek, Ian Treweek, Bianca Treweek, Peter Uldrich, Mark Upson, Jill Van Dorsselaer, Ben Van Dorsselaer, Ian Van Dorsselaer, Terry Waldock, Margie Wallace, Marlene Wells, Fran Wing and Joy Woodley.

Sunshine Beach SLSC: Karla Blair, Margaret Blair, Rochelle Blair, Jill Cleveland, Kiani Cleveland, Sierra Cleveland, Amanda Frost, Dustin Frost, Kay Frost, Tony Frost, Matt Green, Russell Green, Linda Harney, Rob Harney, Sarah Harney, Bonnie Molloy, Kate Molloy, Ivan Molloy, Kady Moore, Quincy Moore, Shayla Moore, Warick Redwood, Molly Redwood, Taylor Redwood, Johanna Redwood, Anne Ryan, Phil Ryan, Rebecca Ryan, Alan Skuse, Hannah Skuse, Pam Skuse, Gary Steed, Jason Steed, Susan Steed, Elle Spring, Merran Spring, Bethany Stevenson, Jenny Stevenson, Lauren Stevenson, Phil Stevenson, Ben Vincent and Rebecca Vincent.

Peregian SLSC: Mick O'Donohue, Lyn Bollen, Russell Porter, Chris Cameron, Nic Jorna, Wendy Jorna, Evelyn Jorna, Harry Light, Chris Brown, Tony Quinlan, Peter Brooker, Barry Higgins, Louise Dodd, Graeme Duckworth, Wendy Robson, Paul Jones, Alan Collins, Leon Sharpe, Roy Wood, Jenny Wood, Alan Tinker, Olwyn Hanna, Rod MacRae, John Flowers, Willy Van Bakel, Peter Van Bakel, Lex Moses, Steve Coolican, Scott Cash, Ken Sell and Ben Stockwin.

Noosa Heads SLSC: Brian Clancy, James McArthy, Marius Van Gemeren, Natalie McArthy, Rowan Simpson, Gemma Gannon, Blaire Charleswood, Drew Charleswood, Lauren Penny, Ryan Trama, Joshua Ellis, Sean Clancy, Tarryn Penny, Sam Johnston, Adam Trama, Mitchell Collins, Mia Powter, Chantelle Ellis, Lucy Ricketts, Ngaire Paszer, Nathan Burgess, Jake Bartholomaeus, Kya Bartholomaeus, Jackson Winter, Kelly Winter, Matthew Hayes, Lochie Hayes, Kate Maggs, Tim Maggs, Zana Affleck, Chloe Newcombe, Jacqueline Newcombe, Henry Callaghan, Fraser Biden, Harrison Biden, Kyle Gannon, Morgan Hill, Brodie Hill, Luke Sanders, Rory Sanders, Brooke Bowden and Ellie Bowden.

Torch Relay crew and town officials were very appreciative of the catering provided by the **Tourism and Hospitality Students and Staff at Grafton** on the NSW north coast. They were:

Sharon Anderson, Roslyn Butterworth, Clinton Corbett, Katrina Cleaver, Megan Debreceny, Stephanie Flay, Lorraine Graham, Kim Kelly, David Lavallee, Brian Martin, Lisa Powick, Josephine Stedman, Brett Williamson, Sarah Dawson, Catriona Gillies, Stephanie Pate, Leanne Dickson, Rachael Dawson, Kristy Lee Dundon, Luke Hanson, Kimberley Hulbert, Catherine Moloney, Ben Perry, Dean Schweikert, Justin Spurway, Roseanne Wensec, Vicki York, Carmen McAuley, Shelly Alderman, Kathleen Hinton, Lyndel Bailey, Mart Meulenbroeks, Marc Ratnam, Sue Goodman, Caroline Spriggs, Sarah Brophy, Cheryl McGurren and Debie Brown. Thank you for your contribution.

The Maddern Family (Jenny, Tony, Rowan and William) from Katherine in the Northern Territory were community volunteers as the Torch Relay passed through their community. Jenny recalls: 'As I stood "controlling the crowd" watching the torch and runners coming down the section of laneway I could feel the excitement of the crowd.

'Two of my sons and my husband also volunteered and I hoped that they were close by and able to see. This special moment in time brings a country and its people together, makes us appreciate our freedom and to be part of an event that may never come our way again. The torch passed, we heard the boom of an FA18 flying very low over our heads just as the cauldron was lit. The plane rose very steeply above us and the afterburn could be seen distinctively making the hair on your arms stand up both with the fear of war and the sound of peace. We as a family were very pleased and proud to have had the chance to be there and involved.'

Citizens Radio Emergency Service Teams (CREST), has a main role of monitoring the CBRS emergency channels, but also provides safety communications for bike rides, fun runs, road closures for street fairs/functions, etc. Newcastle City Council approached CREST to perform traffic control duties for the Newcastle Leg of the Olympic Torch Relay on 27 August 2000. CREST was also approached by Lake Macquarie City Council to provide communications and members for crowd control duties for the celebrations at Speers Point the following day.

Following is a list of CREST members who helped out on both those days:

Newcastle CREST: Evan Longworth, Brian Durrant, Stan Pedersen, Chris Davis, Allan Batty, Scott Longworth, Helen Longworth, Kevin Longworth, Nathan Bryant, Kristy O'Connor, Terry Sneddon, Geoff Bridge, Sharon Townsend, Peter Townsend, Jean Henderson, Ron Stevenson, Mark Polosak, Stewart Elphick, Diane Elphick and Jennifer Elphick. Prospect CREST: Graham Rees and Robin Hunt. Sydney CREST: Des Cottle. Muswellbrook CREST: Jack Wood.

Although it had rained in the lead-up to the event, it didn't dampen the spirits for celebrations on Day 50 at Maryborough, Victoria. The Central Goldfields Shire Council was appreciative of the support of the following volunteers:

Don Bruce, Ian Zimmer, Peter McRae, Jim Field, Brian Thomas, Peter Haywood, Peter Walsh, Bryce Rawlings, Noel Jennings, Tyson Ohlsen, Robert Osborn, Peter Brown, Trevor Potter, Grant Kennedy, John Caufield, C. Phelan, Anthony

TOURISM AND HOSPITALITY STUDENTS AND STAFF – GRAFTON

Torch Relay volunteer crewmember Rosemary Owens with torch bearer Jack Lockett (109 years young)

Community volunteers Sophie and Judy Shaw with a local escort runner at Moe, Victoria

Ohlsen, C. Wallace, David Boyes, Peter Treble, Charles Bovalino, Shane Dellavedova, Charles Knight, Bernie Waizel, Geoff James, David Brown, Graham Costono, John Selmon, John Bryant, David Tynan, Robert Rowe, Charles Townsing, Gerald Harris, Rodney Brown, Eric Tunks, Daryl McLeish, Kerri Long, Steve Phillis, John Bond, Lynne Cougues, Neil Shankar, Jenny Stewart, Barry Rinaldi, Christian Harriott, Peter Bigmore, Brian Lennen, Chris Egan, Anne Canterbury, Martin Mark, Wayne Belcher, V. Hanson, Gary Hutchinson, Trevor Stevens, Eddie Meagher, Alf Scott, Mavrice McRath, Ron Hurford, Keith Varker, Eric Symons, Bob Earl, Frank Upson and Norm Rasmussen.

The organisers of Torch Relay celebrations in Newcastle would like to acknowledge the efforts of the following community volunteers:

William Alexander, Stacey Archer, Reg Askew, Suzie Attwell, Linda Aurelius, Ron Aurelius, Leanne Baxter, Toni Bright, Heather Brown, Ken Brown, Peter Burgess, Brad Cox, Nicole Crawford, Kevin Cruikshank, Kate Desmond, Melissa Dial, Sue Dunne, Lindsay Evans, Kevin Fernandez, Craig Foot, Kerry Freeland, Kim Gill, Helen Harvey, Karen Hayes, David Heggs, Denise Hogarth, Vicki Howard, Roy Judd, Karen Lawler, James Mackay, Mick Marshall, Graeme Matthews, Brigette Miller, Tony Milligan, Annette Morrissey, Richard Morrissey, Rachel O'Leary, Bob Owen, Mick Parish, Matthew Pearce, Darrell Peattie, Bruce Pemberton, Martin Potter, Peter Ray, Michelle Seymour, John Smith, Robert Smith, W. Smith, Trish Stallard, Deidre Street, David Thompson, Scott Thompson, Janice Walsh, Andrew Way, Brad West, Doug Evans, Craig Evans, Allanah Everingham, Edward Bycroft, Allan Campbell, Michael Ison, Dylan Holmes, Brett Chapman, Mathew McGuire, Selena Rossington, Robert Hunt, Grant Hunt, Steve Pinder, Kate Hall, Patric Kerr, Matthew Rouse, Shane Plant, Alexander Clancy, Luke Bartley, Richard Coles, Alex Miklovic and Pam Morrison.

'Three years ago I joined the Torch Relay staff as a volunteer, and along with **Sue Cameron, Kathy White, Noleen Cregan, Margaret Gaydon, Paul McGuire and Jane Betts,** we were involved in all aspects of getting the show on the road. We travelled everywhere, talking to businesses, sponsors and schools, as minders of the prototype Torch. This led to me becoming a crewmember with the Torch Relay, and I had the honour of joining the crew in Albany, Western Australia.

'The emotion, excitement and experiences of this adventure were too numerous to mention, but two very special occasions will remain dear to me. First, I had the honour of being nominated as a community Torch Bearer, and carried the flame in Mandurah, Western Australia. Secondly, sitting in the Olympic Stadium during the Opening Ceremony with tears of emotion as the cauldron was lit, knowing the journey had been such a success.' … **Rosemary Owens (Pioneer Volunteer)**

The Central Gippsland Older Adults Recreation Network took pride in contributing to the volunteer involvement in the Torch Relay celebrations in Moe and Morwell, Victoria, under the enthusiastic guidance of Janiene Ayre from the La Trobe City Council. The team of **Merle, Mariae, Joan, Lil, Lois, Bryan, Betty, Judy, Jenny, Brenda, Sophie, Violet** and many others performed duties from preparation of IDs and posting out invitations, to traffic control, blowing up balloons, stage assembly, and making sandwiches, cakes, etc. to feed the crews and other officials. An effort that was much appreciated, and which was repeated at celebration sights all around Australia.

The Meander Valley Region of Tasmania acknowledges the following volunteers and committee members for the successful Torch Relay celebrations in the district:

Stuart Bower, John Cole, Ian Cook, Gary Dalco, Angela Enright, John (Max) Gillies, Mark Gillies, Craig Groom, Max Heyward, Brian Roles, Phillip Saltmarsh, Andy Sherriff, John Tracey, Gary Wadley, Frank Walker, Bryan Watson, David Pyke, Greg Hall, Glenn Christie, Denis Lyne, Peter McKenzie, John Blyth, Paul Taylor, John Kearns, Ian Knight, Colin Elmer and Dennis Hampton.

TORCH RELAY PARTICIPANTS FROM EMMANUEL COLLEGE, WARRNAMBOOL, VICTORIA

MEMBERS OF THE QUOTA INTERNATIONAL CLUB OF ALSTONVILLE-WOLLONGBAR WHO WERE PART OF THE COMMUNITY VOLUNTEERS AT BALLINA – (L TO R) JULIA ADLINGTON, CORAL SCHWERTNER, SHIRLEY ARMSTRONG, ANNETTE FERGUSON AND GAIL BURLEY

The City of Rockingham, Western Australia, Torch Relay working committee:

Cr B. Sammels, Sgt S. Hackwell, Mr D. Dorotich, Mr D. Plummer, Mr S. Hewitt, Mr A. Miles, Mr M. Wadley, John Davis, Mr K. Gaisford, Bill Thompson, Mr G. Kennedy, Mr J. Simmons, Mr S. Blackman, Mr K. Needham, Mr R. Chalmers, Ms Liz Polini, Miss Jodie Payne, Mr S. Hubbard, Mr Ned Fimmano, Geoff Flak and Mr T. Willoughby.

Gold Coast Volunteers – Olympic Torch Relay

Graham Dillon, Mary Ann Boehme, David Treacher, Peter Lockhart, Wayne Hickson, Yasmahne Fryer, Philip Uren, Louise Collins, Alan McFadyen, Marie Bruggy, Alby White, Michael Koryzma, Kate Gore, Michael Taylor, Kathryn Finlayson, John McMahon, David Fitzhenry, Warren Clarke, Tony Patmore, Col Saunders, Tony Pirone, Sara Zaknic, Mark Gough, Moira Lockhart, Cameron Foster, Jill Gideona, Denis Nicol, Karen Fitzhenry, Cheryl Te Amo, Roger Ham, Martin Pavlovic, Donna Buikstra, Wayne Wright, Leo Foster and Angus Lockhart.

Murrindindi Shire (Victoria) – Community Volunteers

Sharon Hedger, Annita Rennie, Graeme and Rosemary Witt, Irene Bates, Dick Marston, Frank and June Buckman, Kay Menzies, Cally Sinclair, Michael Sherriff, Nora Spitzer, Kath Hedger, Cathy Hill, George Vasey, Helen Wardle, Mick and Barbara Cummins, Wal Ackerman, Dot Waite, Bev Parkinson, Jan Fallon, Penny Paxman, Andrew Embling, George Lopez, Gerda Lopez, David Fitzroy, Margo Lawrence, Valerie Nash, Vicki Costello, Lorraine Daniels, Ray Steyger, Barbara Skerritt and Claire McDonald.

Baulkham Hills Shire – Community Volunteers

Rosemary Derwin, Rod Sayers, Wendy Priestly, Lawrence Hookkee, Jan Hookkee, Robert Barker, Bruce McCarthy, Rosemary McLellan, Narelle Murray, Jo-anne Aboud, Karen Shalavin, Westher Coleiro, Patricia Bright, Denise Dawes, Judith Shipway, Martin Brannan, Judy Hawes, Patricia Hunt, Elaine Cater, Phil Pettit, Noela Campbell, Danielle Wilson, Michael Viset, Helen Strickland, Judy Neich, Elaine Neich, Lesleigh Perkins, Amy Devlin, Margaret Hawkes, Sue Nicholson and Douglas Nicholson.

City of Albury – Community Volunteers

Graeme Hicks, Andrew Chuck, Greg McLay, Anne Darmody, Cathy Nash, Scott Burns, Roger Butson, Steve Stainsby, Leisa Radford, Brian Hillas, Martin Kick, Michelle Harvey, Tony Scammell, Christie Burns, Brad McNeil, Howlong Lions Club, Don McTaggett, Vass Mortimer, Roy Baird, Gay Harvey, David Milne, Rob McDonald, Kevin Jones, Christine Hammond, Nicole Leskie, Peter White and Ron Newell.

Cessnock City – Community Volunteers

Colleen Zambrowski, Pamela Snaddon, Margaret Sheedy, Toni Osborne, Jennifer Leprince, George Davis, Jodie Kenny, Stephen Hedger, Paul Gason, Mr and Mrs Berrell, Mark Peters, Barbara Muirhead, Warren Bracefield, Roger Lewis, Mr and Mrs McCarthy and Mr and Mrs Griffiths.

District of Grant – South Australia – Working Party

Russell Peate, Jim McPherson, Cr Ian Giles, Cr Shirley Little, Sandy Muller and Leah Opie.

City of Mount Gambier – South Australia – Community Volunteers

Eric Arthur, Cyril Blackmore, Donna Bowden, Carol Burge, Ross Clark, Jim Galpin, Russell Hall, Viviene Hutchinson, Ralph Jacob, Olive Lane, Jeanne Lattin, Bruce Messenger, Basil Mewitt, Neil Richardson, June Rogers, Duncan Seebohm, John Scotland, George Stewart, Heather Von Stanke and Barrie Whennan.

Samuel Terry Primary School Torch Relay Dancers

Kaitlin Adcock, Rebecca Amson, Brittney Anderson, Jessika Anderson, Elizabeth Ash, Reece Austin, Talisha Austin, Chelsea Barnett, Gail Bennett, Gemma Brooks, Michelle Christie, Erin Coates, Courtney Coghlan, Becky Collins, Jessica Critchley, Sara Cutler, Jackson Donnelly, Ellen Doyle, Teagan Edwards, James Egan, Belinda Fenton, Joanne Fonti, Amanda Foster, Sarah Fox, Tennille Fuller-Sale, Cassie Gallagher, Melissa Gallagher, Sophie Gatt, Emily Gittoes, Carley Guernier, Haylee Hardimon, Alicia Hearn, Khloe Hearn, Julia Hiatt, Kaila Jamieson, Ailsa Kemp, Jean Kirby, Kaitlyn Lang, Natalie Layt, Caitlin Lofthouse, Megan Lofthouse, Kristie Macdonald, Emma Maestri, Natalie McAnally, Olivia McIntosh, Erin McSweeney, Jamie Miller, Samantha Miller, Shari Moffatt, Emily Mondy, Liana Mullineaux, Rebecca Nicholson, Nicole Ormerod, Laura Palmer, Mitchell Park, Jemima Paterson, Michael Paton, Alannah Pautschnig, Jessica Pennings, Danielle Picot, Jade Pool, Catherine Rogan, Jessica Rook, Danielle Sammut, Melissa Shoults, Alicia Small, Courtney Talbot, Samantha Thomas, Ashlee Towers, Shane Waddell, Amie Walsh, Annette Wilson, Nicole Wilson, Alex Woodley, Alison Woods, Hayley Woods, Rachel Woods, Emma Wren and Samantha Young.

'When I first received my letter about being an Escort Runner, my heart nearly stopped. I was so excited to be actually a part of the Torch Relay. Then the uniform arrived and I became even more excited.

'Then 21 June 2000 came and I was so nervous, but first I had to go to school. The 3 pm bell rang and I was off to Emerald to run in the greatest event of my life. I felt so special, and I was so proud to be an Australian.' ... **Shaun Johnson (Springsure State School)**. Shaun's colleagues **Brayden Copping** and **Matthew Marshall** expressed similar emotion when relating the experience.

Domremy College not only had involvement in the Torch Relay, but Groundsman, **Tony Fenech**, also participated as a volunteer for Olympic Football at the Sydney Football Stadium.

BEAUDESERT FITNESS AND DANCE GROUP, WHICH PERFORMED AT TORCH RELAY CELEBRATIONS IN SOUTHERN QUEENSLAND

SAMUEL TERRY PRIMARY SCHOOL DANCERS (REPRESENTING MOSCOW 1980) AT THE PENRITH TORCH RELAY CELEBRATIONS – (L TO R) HAYLEY WOODS, JESSICA ROOK, ERIN COATES, EMMA WREN AND HAYLEE HARDIMON

ARMIDALE STUDENTS DANCED IN THE COLOURS OF THE OLYMPIC RINGS AT THEIR TORCH RELAY CELEBRATIONS

'I couldn't believe it when I read my name on the sheet. I had been chosen by my school, Northholm Grammar, and SOCOG as an Escort Runner in the Olympic Torch Relay. It wasn't until I arrived at the service station, my collection point for the shuttle bus, that what was about to happen, really sunk in. I couldn't believe the support the crowd gave. I couldn't stop smiling, laughing and screaming with my Torch Bearers, we seemed to be feeling the same emotions for this once-in-a-lifetime experience. The thoughts will forever bring tears to my eyes whenever I recall my run.' ... **Sarah Lumsden**

Siena College in Findon, South Australia, was well represented in the Olympic Torch Relay with two Escort Runners, **Gabrielle Candlish and Karyn Ford, plus Torch Bearer Kate Mandalovic.**

Gabrielle recalls: 'It was great getting to know all the other Escort Runners and Torch Bearers and sharing a special moment with so many strangers. One thing that I enjoyed most was that there weren't any sad faces.'

Karyn recalls: 'I felt a celebrity that day, but most of all I felt proud to be part of the Sydney Olympic Games, and also proud of the Adelaide people who were all so filled with the Olympic spirit on that day.'

Kate recalls: 'To hold my torch up high with the flame burning brightly for everyone to see was one of the greatest moments of my life. It truly made me feel Australian.'

Elizabeth Moloney recalls: 'All of a sudden I heard cheers and singing in the distance and people screaming at me even louder than before. My Torch Bearer, sensing that they were my friends, kindly handed me the torch as we ran past them. I saw people I had never seen in my life, people were out to see the flame and support everyone involved. It was a unique event.'

Emily Currer recalls: 'It was unbelievable for such a small town, but it was good to see just how important it was to all the people who spurred on John Woodrup, the Torch Bearer who lit the cauldron. He was a 90-year-old man who was a well-loved lifesaver and hometown hero, and as he lit the cauldron the response was incredible.'

Sian Bennett recalls: 'Even though my run was over, I felt special for the rest of the day. I made my way to McDonald's for breakfast, and there I met one of my Torch Bearers who was just as hungry as me. Instead of eating breakfast, people just wanted to take photos, and people who were not from Sydney, but travelled a fair distance to see the Torch wanted us to express how we felt about our entire experience on camera so that the people back home could feel part of the Olympic spirit.'

'The biggest thrill had arrived, running down the pathway and onto the stage. I had lots of mixed emotions. I was happy, excited and very proud. The day turned out to be much more than I had expected. Only 2500 school kids got to experience this, and it is something I will probably never have the opportunity to do again.' ... Escort Runner Brenden Honey

'I was always told that there was spirit in Australia and that Aussies were proud to be part of this nation, but I did not really believe this until I took part in the Olympic Torch Relay as an Escort Runner. In my short life of 14 years, this experience would have to be the most memorable and cherished event I have ever been part of. But, the biggest highlight for me was being able to actually hold the torch for a short time while I ran.' ... Lauren Frazer

A mother's pride

'My son Jonathan had an accident a year ago which left him with horrific head and arm injuries. Jonathan was on life support for two weeks in intensive care as he also had both lungs punctured and a brain injury.

'On release from hospital, a doctor suggested he take a year off school. Jonathan was aghast. He actually went back to school a month later, determined to keep up with his studies. He rightly figured that if he didn't use his damaged brain and exercise it, it wouldn't improve.

Escort runner Anthony McLachlan

Hayley Lonnon, escort runner from Domremy College

Community volunteers – Katherine, Northern Territory

Escort runner Jonathan Rofe

Escort runner Michael Schroeder from Mosman High School gets his chance!

Escort runner Louise Maraun from Mosman High School escorts the torch at Taronga Park Zoo

'The closing date for nominations for Escort Runners for the Olympic Torch Relay was two weeks after his release from hospital. It took him two weeks to write a few sentences. He was so weak he would fall asleep in the middle of a sentence, or his mind would go blank due to the brain damage.

'The New Year 2000 came, and we were amazed and elated that Jonathan had been chosen. Jonathan was very frail, and suddenly being chosen was an added incentive to build himself up physically and mentally so he could be fit enough to participate. There were complications, but little by little he managed.

'By the time 12 June 2000 dawned he was awake and ready, as nervous as a racehorse at the gates. He was anxious and excited. As well as this being a day of great honour, it was a personal achievement. As Jonathan ran, he had a grin from ear to ear on his damaged, though beautiful face. On that day, Jonathan most certainly "won". He truly is an example of someone who has tried so hard and broken through and triumphed.

'An extraordinary coincidence has arisen through all this. At the time of Jonathan's birth in 1983, his grandfather (my father) was rushed to hospital with an aggressive brain tumour; he knew he did not have long to live. He sent me the following telegram: *"I have just heard of the arrival of Jonathan, thank you for the wonderful gift of a grandson, you have handed over the Olympic Flame perfectly, and I am very proud of you, today my life is very full indeed, keep up the good work ...Dad."* How did he know to use that example of passing on the spirit?' ... **Janet Rofe**

'It was a great honour to be nominated by my school (Forest High) to be an Escort Runner and a recipient of a Pierre de Coubertin Award. On 15 September 2000, the last day of the Torch Relay, one of the Torch Bearers did not turn up, so the names of the three Escort Runners (**Matt Able, James Ryburn** and mine) were put in a hat, and Matt's was drawn out to be a Torch Bearer. This then meant that James and I had to escort two extra runners each, six instead of four. This prospect was quite exciting.

'After I finished the relay I went to Manly Beach, where I was part of the Surfboat rowing display put on by the Life Saving Clubs for the enormous crowd waiting for the torch to come along from Queenscliff to Manly. The whole experience was overwhelming. It was through the tireless work of the volunteers that made our Sydney Games the most successful and memorable. I am glad I had the opportunity to be part of such an incredible experience.' ... **Shaun Thompson**

'My name is Louise Nixon, and I go to Warners Bay High School. I carried the Torch on Day 92 of the Olympic Torch Relay in Canberra. My Mum, Jenny Nixon, was the Torch Bearer who passed the flame to me. My Nan and Pop came to watch us carry the Torch. My Pop, Dennis Dick, carried the Olympic Torch for the 1956 Melbourne Olympic Games. Three generations of my family have now carried the Olympic Torch.' ... **Louise Nixon**

'I was lucky enough to have had the privilege of escorting the Torch through my home town Forster-Tuncurry, on its journey to the Sydney Olympic Games. It was amazing to see so many people excited like me. I remember holding the Torch with flashes going off everywhere around me, while people were cheering, and I was trying to hold back tears because the feeling was so overwhelming.' ... **Hannah Clark**

'On 7 August 2000, I escorted the Olympic Torch and four Torch Bearers. I was really inspired by quadriplegic wheelchair basketballer, Shaun Groenewegen. I helped push his wheelchair, and this kind man let me carry the Torch several times, which was the greatest feeling. I will never forget Shaun for doing this for me and for sharing this great experience that is a chance in a lifetime.' ... **Leischa Hitches from Berwick Secondary College, Victoria**

'Escorting the Olympic Torch through Kingaroy, Queensland, to me was the opportunity of a lifetime. It was an event that only a selected number of people were lucky enough to experience, and I am very grateful that I was one of those selected few. Being chosen by my school, Nanango State High, was a great surprise, though being chosen by the Olympic Organisers was even greater.' ... **Michael Pickering**

'I was amazed at how many people there were enjoying the experience in Katherine. Most of the people I ran with let me hold the Torch for those once-in-a- lifetime photos. To top off this year, I was

ESCORT RUNNER JADE KRUEGER ACKNOWLEDGES THE CROWD IN TOWNSVILLE, QUEENSLAND

ESCORT RUNNERS (L TO R) ANDREA LYNCH AND KATHERINE JESS, WHO, WITH RICHARD CLAVARINO, WERE NOMINATED BY THEIR SCHOOL – YARRAM SECONDARY COLLEGE, VICTORIA

ESCORT RUNNER MICHELLE KAHN WITH FRIENDS AND TEACHERS FROM MOUNT SCOPUS MEMORIAL COLLEGE, VICTORIA

Escort runner Shaun Thompson and torch bearer Robyn Rainey who had two hip replacements in the previous two years

Jenny Rollo felt humble carrying the Olympic torch on behalf of children with Cornelia de Lange Syndrome

Torch bearer Olive Webb shares the moment with family

also a Paralympic Torch Bearer in Darwin. I bought the torch, and now have it proudly displayed in our house.' ... **Aiden Lewin (Escort Runner)**

Miles State High School provided three Escort Runners for the Toowoomba/Gatton area, they were – **Daniel Haslop, Danny Scotney and Anna Mulholland**. Their comments were:

'We started to run, I was passed the Torch and with great pleasure I held it high and proud for everyone to see. Having run at night and in the rain made it even more special for me with all the lights and camera flashes reflecting off the puddles on the road.' ... **Daniel**

'The changeover of the torch was breathtaking. I started running in the rain with my eyes fixed on the Torch. I couldn't feel the road under me as I felt like I was floating. I tried to find my family in the crowd, but all I could see were the faces of excitement on the four-deep crowds.' ... **Danny**

'As soon as the relay approached the town the rain began to fall and the weather changed to cold and miserable. This had no effect on the overall blast and adrenalin rush that I felt as I supported the Torch Bearers and held the Torch proudly on its journey for a short time.' ... **Anna**

'The fun really started when we were all on the bus. One of the organisers showed us a video to get us motivated, but two ladies on the back seat already had a song they were singing – "Come On Baby Light My Fire", which sounded relevant and pretty amusing. The excitement really hit me as we ran into York Park with such a big crowd cheering and taking photos, I felt so small but so important.' ... **Neil Oliver (Escort Runner)**

'The morning of 15 September 2000 finally arrived. The very last day of the Torch Relay, in which I would be escorting Alderman Frank Sartor, the Lord Mayor of Sydney, Greg Norman, Louise Sauvage and Dr Tony Kidman across the Sydney Harbour Bridge. This was my greatest honour ever and personally I felt very proud.

'There are no words, however, to describe the way I felt when I ran across the bridge, but I suppose I could only say an absolute buzz! I would like to thank my school, Wenona, and especially Mrs Hadley the Principal and our coach Mr Cassarchis for giving me this opportunity of a lifetime.' ... **Lucy Polkinghorne**

'I tried to wave to every single person in the crowd! I didn't want it to end, ever! From the crowd I could hear Mum shout, "Flick". I turned and there were my friends and family. At that moment the Torch was thrust into my hand, I held it high; the full honour of the event hit me, and an indescribable feeling of inspiration overwhelmed me.' ... **Felicity Whitten (Padua College, Victoria)**

Lachlan Smith and Lance Devlin were Escort Runners representing Tamborine Mountain College in south east Queensland. They recall:

'The magnitude of it all didn't really hit me until I ran over the bridge and up the hill into the Main Street of Canungra. It was raining, the mist was coming down and there in front of me was an ocean of Australian flags and people. Prior to that I was nervous, anxious and fascinated by the huge support crew, media attention and hype. However, when I saw all those flags I realised what a privilege and honour it was for me to be part of it. I wasn't nervous any more, I just enjoyed myself as never before and soaked up the atmosphere.' ... **Lachlan**

'Running down the streets of Beaudesert, crowds of people cheering and waving flags, all enjoying the taste of the Olympic festival – the feeling was indescribable! It seemed as though the fun was just beginning when suddenly, it was all over, yet the experience will be remembered forever.' ... **Lance**

'I ran in the Olympic Torch Relay on 4 September 2000 at the age of 12, just two years after having steel rods put in my back to overcome curvature of the spine. The experience was so incredible and a most precious moment of my life.' ... **Crystal Pillar (Torch Bearer)**

BUSLOAD OF 'HAPPY CAMPERS' IN ARMIDALE, NSW

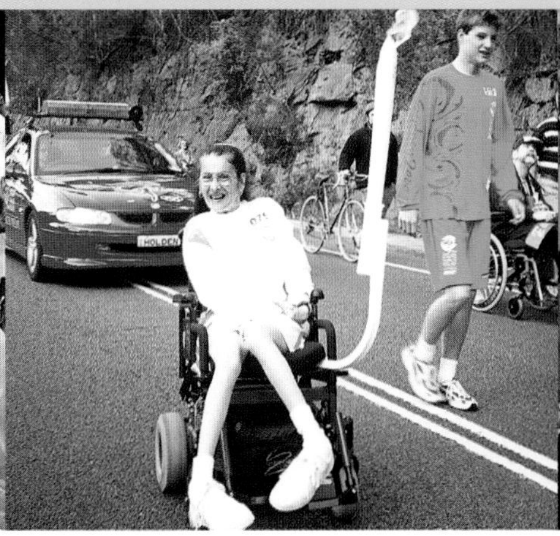

TORCH BEARER JUDITH GEPPERT AND ESCORT RUNNER CHRIS GORDON

ESCORT RUNNER LUCY POLKINGHORNE ESCORTING LOUISE SAUVAGE ON THE SYDNEY HARBOUR BRIDGE (SOMEBODY HAD TO DO IT!)

Assefa Bekele torch bearer and volunteer interpreter

Escort runner Martin Mattner from Coomandook Area School, South Australia

Escort runner Harry Taylor from Geraldton Grammar, Western Australia

'The day I ran with the Torch was a very good experience. I was very proud and excited and felt like a celebrity for a day.' ... **Nathan Manning**, Armadale Senior High School, Western Australia

'I was to be an Escort Runner for the Olympic Torch Relay, and I didn't really worry about anything else, as I was a part of the Olympic Spirit. About five minutes after our briefing, one of the organisers asked me if I would like to be an Olympic Torch Bearer! Before she could get out all the words I said yes, I would love to run with the Torch. The experience has changed my life because I can now say that I took part in helping the Olympic Flame to the Sydney 2000 Olympic Games.' ... **Matthew Woods**, Laidley State High School, Queensland

'My volunteer effort for Sydney 2000 was as an interpreter for Amharic (Ethiopian dialect) and Greek, plus assisting with SPOC security.

'The volunteer program helped me reinforce to myself my belief that if people in a multicultural country such as Australia are able to set their differences aside and work together for progress and to celebrate humanity so can the world. My dream lives on.' ... **Assefa Bekele**

The Katherine Town Council, Northern Territory, acknowledges the contribution of the following Community Volunteers associated with the Olympic Torch Relay celebrations:

Zena Wallace, Derek Cole, Peter Thomas, Chris Keed, Jade Dundon, Chris Stanger, Cheryl-Anne Courtney, Laurel Mason, Brian Headford, Rodney Gregg, Karen Scott, Alison Capps, Eddie Sequitin, Henry Wallace, Ross Roberts, Dian Roberts, Claire Wightwick, Jennifer Maddern, Tony Maddern, Tim Burgess, David Nakken, Dennis Haines, Stephen Clark, Andy Martin, Marco Brugnatti, Joshua Myers, Gary Smith, Noel Orams, Steve Sheahan, Bob Piper, Elizabeth Williamson, Phil Martin and William Maddern.

'I was one of the very lucky people from my school, Gloucester High, to run with the Olympic Torch on 26 August 2000. It was quite emotional, and when the cauldron at the Olympic Stadium was lit, I felt proud to be one of the people who helped get it there.' ... **Anita Landers (Escort Runner)**

Winners are grinners

The results were waited anxiously by everyone concerned
While everybody looked so cool each one of them still yearned
To hear their name called out and know that they would be the one
To carry Sydney's Olympic Flame on our Torch Relay Run.

No lottery result had ever meant so much
Who'd miss out and who would get to touch
The magic torch and hear the cheering crowd –
Oh how they hoped to hear their name out loud.

Then the list was read and all knew who had won
It wasn't hard to tell 'cause they had the most fun
And while the losers tried to smile and say it was all right
The winners celebrated their good luck and partied hard that night.

A strange salute has sprung to life among that lucky bunch
With right arms raised they greet their peers, morning, night and lunch
While lesser mortals roll their eyes and think what could have been
If only they'd got lucky and made the Relay Team.

So those of you who carry the Torch, carry it with pride
While the rest of us are cheering we'll be jealous deep inside
Make sure you hold the flame up high so everyone can see
And if someone trips you up and takes your place, it'll probably be me!!! ... Vera Rothwell

Escort runner Jade Child, with the torch bearers he escorted in Launceston, Tasmania

Darryl Coleman is an adult voluntary worker at Maitland Area School, South Australia, who has given many years service to the staff, students and the community

Escort runner Irene Serebryanikova from Mc Kinnon Secondary College, Victoria. 'My message to other people, should this type of experience ever be offered again – get involved.'

A cold morning on the Mornington Peninsula with Olympic champion Debbie Flintoff-King

Escort runner Joel Ide with his great-grandfather, 86-year-old Fred Chiswick

Escort runner Sam Clayton from Central Coast Adventist School

Escort runner Jeralyn Pickering from Central Coast Adventist School

Paralympic torch bearer Hans Kumpel, who was also a resident centre volunteer in the Olympic and Paralympic villages

Husband and wife pioneer volunteers – Garry and Anne Lee – had the unique experience of both being selected to carry the Olympic torch

Geelong High School librarian Labrini Soldatos, with escort runners (L to R) Jessica Pye, Jared Cobb and Sally Fraser

Torch bearer Geoffrey Thomas and escort runner Leah Wilkinson, from Mary MacKillop College

Escort runners Carley Holland and Mark Gocher, with choreographer of 'Tin Symphony' in the opening ceremony, Karen Johnson Mortimer – all from Aquinas College, Menai, NSW

Escort runner Jason Brown from Hillcrest Christian College, Gold Coast, Queensland. Jason fulfilled the dream of his grandfather Peter Brown, who in 1956, after having been selected as a torch bearer, had to withdraw due to RAAF commitments.

Martin Davis (holding torch) – one of several local constituents nominated by Federal Opposition Leader Kim Beazley to escort him

Torch bearer Paul Kelly and escort runner Damon Petrie from International Grammar School, Ultimo photo by D. Petrie

'I was honoured to be nominated as an Escort Runner by my school, St Patrick's College, Sutherland, but I had no idea what "share the spirit" really meant until I met other Escort Runners and Torch Bearers at the assembly point at Sutherland. Truly it was a wonderfully exciting day that I will never forget, and it made me look forward to the Olympic Games and my work as a volunteer photo assistant at the Main Press Centre, Sydney Olympic Park – another great experience.' …
James Banister

Swan Hill in Victoria made a considerable contribution to the Sydney Olympic Games – Drivers **Vince Foott, Ray Curnow, Paul Pellegrino, Jan Butcher, Lyn Merrett, Craig Davies, Bill Northey, Val Hedwards and Col Hedwards**, all took on the challenge of Sydney's roads.

Swan Hill College contributed the following Escort Runners and Torch Bearers: **Emma Balwinson, Leah Merrett, Alex Watson, Deanne Frame, Tim Medlin, Alan Medlin, Bill Kemp, Kacey Williams, Marcus Luckel and Alex Minney.**

ANZAC Hill High School in Alice Springs created so much enthusiasm for the Olympic Torch Relay that six participants represented the school. They were Escort Runners **Frances Sharp, Tim Blacker and Ali Morton,** plus Torch Bearers **Brendan Kelleher, Ken Swanson and Colin Hodges.**

HEY! WE'VE GOT A TORCH RELAY TO RUN HERE! BILL KYTE PASSES ON THE 'OLYMPIC SPIRIT' AT RUTHERGLEN, VICTORIA

PARALYMPIC TORCH BEARER NAGISA HIRAOKA REPRESENTED THE JAPAN CLUB OF SYDNEY AT NARARA ON THE CENTRAL COAST

(L TO R) ESCORT RUNNERS LEAH MCMAHON AND ELIZABETH HUMPHRIES REPRESENTING SANTA MARIA COLLEGE, NORTHCOTE, VICTORIA

TORCH BEARER BRENDAN KELLEHER

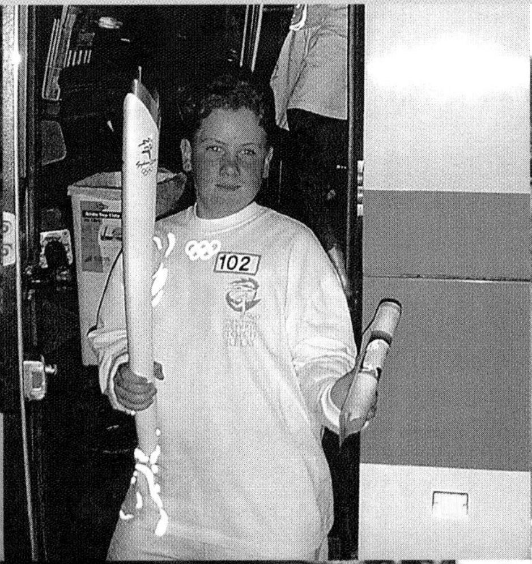

COMMUNITY VOLUNTEERS CHERYL-ANNE COURTNEY AND CHRIS STANGER – KATHERINE, NORTHERN TERRITORY

'I KNEW IT WOULD BE GREAT TO CARRY THE TORCH – BUT NOTHING COULD HAVE PREPARED ME FOR HOW GREAT IT WAS.' ... STEVEN ALCOCK NORTHCOTE, VICTORIA

TORCH BEARERS VERN EZZY AND STEWART JEPPESEN WITH ESCORT RUNNER JOSH ABELL FROM CAPRICORNIA SCHOOL OF DISTANCE EDUCATION

TORCH BEARER KIM PERRY FROM ENDEAVOUR SPORTS HIGH

ESCORT RUNNER SHAUN THOMPSON AND TORCH BEARER MATT ABLE

ESCORT RUNNER SHANNON WYLIE FROM ELANORA STATE HIGH SCHOOL, QUEENSLAND – 'I WAS TO RUN THE MOST UNFORGETTABLE TWO KILOMETRES OF MY LIFE.'

(L TO R) ESCORT RUNNERS CAMERON UNICOMB, GAVIN ELLIS AND JOANNE MAIN FROM NEWCASTLE GRAMMAR SCHOOL

COMMUNITY TORCH RELAY VOLUNTEER MIKE VERDEL WITH TORCH BEARER AND WIFE PATRICIA. TOGETHER MIKE AND PATRICIA FORMED CAMP QUALITY CENTRAL QUEENSLAND

COMMUNITY VOLUNTEER PRASAD SUBBA,
MOE, VICTORIA

ESCORT RUNNER BROOKE FETTERPLACE SHARING THE EXPERIENCE

Volunteers Parade...

TEAM
THANK YOU

ALGERIA

CEREMONIES

Foreword

by Ric Birch Director of Ceremonies

I wish there was another word for volunteer. It doesn't do justice to people who give their time, their skill and their knowledge, always unselfishly and often without acknowledgment. So I'm delighted that Laurie Smith has undertaken to document the role of the volunteers at Sydney in 2000. But it's only part of a big picture. There are so many fields of human endeavour in which the volunteer has made a contribution, or a breakthrough, or a sacrifice. Volunteering has always been part of our society, part of our lives. Volunteers with the SES, helping cover up Sydney's roofs after the huge hailstorm, volunteer firemen losing their lives in the bush, volunteers in wars and conflicts, volunteers helping the homeless and the lost, volunteer lifesavers and the volunteers who have made possible the Olympic Games.

It has become almost obligatory to thank the Olympic volunteers, 'without whom the Games could not have been held', but there is a danger that the speeches of appreciation can totally overlook the passion and emotional involvement that volunteers bring to their work – certainly where Ceremonies are concerned. There is no possible explanation for the hours of work, the dedication and commitment that volunteers give to a project apart from passion. It's impossible to be a volunteer unless you care very deeply.

The Sydney Olympic Opening Ceremony alone engaged the passion of more than 17,000 volunteers! The most visible were the 12,700 performers, but everything that was worn or carried by the performers was only possible because some of our other 4500 volunteers had helped to make it. Backstage there were stage managers, assistant stage managers, stagehands and assistant stagehands – and they were almost all volunteers. Lights that needed to be lifted, boxes that had to be moved, cables that were dragged, costumes that were carried, props that had to be stacked, audience kits placed on seats – all this was done with volunteers. Transport of tens of thousands of people for all the rehearsals was organised and co-ordinated with the help of volunteers. The workshop in Redfern where the amazing props and costumes and machines of Ceremonies were designed and built, saw more than 200 volunteers on a regular basis. Sequins that were applied individually to costumes, wire that was woven by hand into head-dresses, fabric that was painstakingly hand-painted, all this was done by volunteers – not just once but over and over again for weeks and months until the rehearsals began. And then the same volunteers rushed in to repair the costumes in time for the real show.

For Australians, the Olympic Ceremonies struck a chord of recognition, pride and confidence that have always been part of our character, but which perhaps has never before had an opportunity to be so publicly acknowledged. Our volunteers made that possible. To you all, my deep appreciation and a sense of wonder at everything you endured in order to bring such moments of pride to your fellow Australians.

You did us all proud.

(L to R) Jenny Parken, Lauren Burrows, Chloe Hislop, Vanessa Carr, Elise Souden, Jenna Skepper and Amanda Le Prevost (Year 8 Terrigal High School students) assisting at Opening Ceremony dress rehearsal

Students from Pittwater High School substitute as athletes for Kenya at the Opening Ceremony dress rehearsals

We hear stories of the volunteers who were so obvious as the 'Face of the Games', and people tend to think only of the 47,000 who were in the colourful uniforms designed deliberately to have them stand out in a crowd. However, there were four events which captured the hearts and imagination of Australians and the world – those being the Opening and Closing Ceremonies of both the Olympic and Paralympic Games.

While it is of course not possible to recognise every volunteer in these pages, I certainly hope that we have given due credit to the relevant areas in which you were each involved. Your praises have been sung through all forms of Australian and International media, but I hope we are able to enlighten more people to the sacrifices and dedication you all made to give the rest of us such warm and proud memories of those wonderful ceremonies.

We could only guess at the number of volunteer hours that went into ceremonies when we realise that just two Assistant Stage Managers, **Elizabeth Ellis** and **Jonathan Allott**, contributed hundreds of hours between them.

Let us also not forget that this was a magnificent team effort, led by unbelievably gifted and talented visionaries, who not only had the capacity to put thoughts into reality, but also to blend such a diverse group of performers into a 'World's Best Spectacular'.

'I was one of the lucky people, along with 40 other of my peers from mixed years at Terrigal High School, who received a letter of success saying we were to dance in the Olympic Ceremonies. However, although we were excited, it was hard to celebrate when many of our friends had missed out.

'The rehearsals seemed endless, including the opportunity to be "athlete stand-ins" for the dress rehearsals for the Opening Ceremony. We rehearsed what seemed like every day of the Olympic holidays, but finally the time came, and as I ran onto the arena with a large beach umbrella, all I remember seeing was an enormous sea of red sparkling lights, which along with Christine Anu all dressed up, was just plain amazing – Wow!

'When it was all over I just couldn't believe it. I was in shock mode; I really just couldn't believe it. This was one of the best moments of my life, and definitely something to remember forever.' ... **Elise Souden**

'It all started with an ad in several horse magazines, newspapers, newsletters and of course word of mouth. That 140 very special horses and riders were needed for an Olympic event. At this stage no one knew, or even could imagine, what was to come.

'In January 2000 tryouts were held around Australia. We had to be able to ride one-handed, ride over tarps and of course carry a flag. We then had to wait to see if we were in!! The letters arrived, Yeh, we're off to Scone (three hours north-west of Sydney) for the first boot-training camp.

'In March 140 riders, horses, helpers, partners and supporters converged on the small town of Scone. We made new friends, told tales about our riding skills, but in the long-run nothing would prepare us for the 110,000 people who would clap and cheer us into the Olympic Stadium.

THEY 'WERE' THE FIRST SCENE! PHOTO BY CHRIS WESTLAKE

'To start with we had to learn a thing called troop drill. Now, some had done this at pony club a long time ago, others had never done it, so needless to say, we looked like a train wreck! But as the weekend wore on we became better and started to feel we could do this. We left that camp with mixed emotions. Would we be at the next camp? Was I good enough? Would my horse rise to the occasion?

'The next letter turned up – we were off again. This time it was June and very cold (and I mean very cold), especially when you are from the Sunshine State! On the drive down we encountered rain that turned to hail, then to top things off – snow. The horses did not know what hit them. But we survived!

'The month of September came around and we had to be in Sydney two weeks before the Opening Ceremony. Our home for the next two weeks was the Castle Hill Showgrounds. Many of us had never been to Sydney before, so when we hit that traffic, it was a little scary!

'The training and yelling began. We had to get back to working as one of a team. Our days were pretty much breakfast at 8.00 am, saddle up for 9.00 am, then train until lunch, rest, then drive into the stadium for practice. We had to be checked for bombs and other nasties at the logistics centre, and this took one hour to get all the horse trucks through. Our practice time was 10.00 pm until about 2.00 am, so the nights were long for riders and horses. This went on for a week until our first dress rehearsal.

'The next day was Sunday – a day of rest for rider and mount (thank goodness) – we needed it! But this is where things started to go wrong. Some of the camp started to get sick – myself included. On the Monday a doctor had to come to the showgrounds and see 45 of us. That night in the stadium they only had half of the team to work with. What were we to do? We dropped like flies!

'Wednesday was the next dress rehearsal in front of a live audience again. Many of us were still sick, but got out of our sick beds and rode that night. Many of us don't remember much, because we were either too sick or had too much medication, but our friends the horses carried us through. We practised for another two days – then it was THE night.

'The atmosphere was so different. There was a much bigger buzz about the place. We rode, and did our best display we could, and as you all saw, either live or on television, I think we all did a pretty good job.' ... **Kym Johnson (Rider)**

Sergeant Don Eyb conducting the Scone training camp

Photo by Chris Westlake

Zoe Lackey and Bruce Moxey

(L to R) Chris Therlow and Fiona Wallace

Photo by Chris Westlake

Pat Kelly proved that having only one arm was no obstacle to carrying the Olympic flag!

PHOTO BY CHRIS WESTLAKE

Graham Yates and Dee Wilson

PHOTO BY CHRIS WESTLAKE

Riders and crew – Thank You

'Now that the Olympic fireworks have settled and most of us are back into our daily routine, I'd like to take this opportunity to express my gratitude to each and every person involved in our world-record-breaking equestrian display. The effort, expense and expertise that were offered by all have not gone unnoticed: the hardships encountered by some and sacrifices made by others more than appreciated.

'Our team was made up of many unsung heroes, both behind the scenes and in the thick of the action. I thank these selfless team workers; the crew, volunteers, riders, their family and friends, and of course the horses. It was a tough ask of the horses as they were expected to perform in a way many never had before and possibly won't again. It was a very unique experience, and above all, a monumental team effort. Thank You.' … **Tony Jablonski (Event Director/Horsemaster)**

'I enlisted as a ceremonies volunteer, and also signed up to help out in the Ceremonies Office at Stadium Australia. Let me tell you, those Ceremonies people worked HARD – some were on multiple tasks, with extra responsibilities added as the deadline drew nearer. Two people with whom I worked closely, who I would like to make special mention of are: **Pam Kekos** (Co-ordinator, Accreditation) and **Gisela Payne** (Volunteer Recruitment Assistant) – they were just unbelievable, I don't know when they ever got a chance to go home!

'My work as cast assistant, although sometimes repetitive, was still exciting and fun. The excitement was contagious, especially as we approached dress rehearsals, and then finally the Opening Ceremony.

I will never forget the elation – they were proud, they were happy, they were excited – all the months of hard work had paid off. It has been a real honour, helping such an enormous team of people – both volunteers and paid staff – to produce "the best Olympic Games ever"!' ... **Judy Dickinson**

AKA – What's an AKA? – It is an Audience Kit Assistant – Those fantastic dedicated people who crawled all over the Olympic Stadium on 15 September 2000 and 1 October 2000, placing suitcases and Eskies on every seat.

Karen Ritson recalls: 'I was excited to be offered a volunteer position with ceremonies as an Audience Kit Assistant, but I had no idea what it involved. One Sunday in late July we were invited to the Stadium for a preview. After being allocated into groups, we were taken up the huge spirals to the "nose-bleed" section. What a magnificent stadium! WE ARE GOING TO PLACE AN AUDIENCE KIT ON EVERY ONE OF THOSE SEATS – WOW!

'It turned out to be an adventure, and despite some UPS AND DOWNS, we really enjoyed it. Probably the biggest challenge was keeping the Eskies on the seats for the Closing Ceremony in a howling wind, but we found ways! It was an experience I wouldn't have given up for anything.'

'When we first got the news that we would be in the Opening and Closing Ceremonies we were on top of the world, we were so excited but we never knew, and I don't think anybody knows unless they were involved with the ceremonies, how much hard work went into their production. There were times when we would get to SIAC for rehearsal at 1.00 pm and not leave till 11.00 pm, or we would be at school in the rain and wind rehearsing at night, everything had to be perfect of course. In the end it was one of the best experiences of my life and I will never forget it.' ...
Rebecca Curtis (Deep Sea Dreaming and My Island Home)

THE FIRE WARDEN AND RUNNER TEAM FOR THE OPENING AND CLOSING CEREMONIES

PHOTO BY BRONWYN MURPHY

(L TO R) JACKIE SLAVIERO AND SALLY EDGE (FIELD OF PLAY MARSHALS)

(L TO R) LANA GERENDAS AND COURTNEY NICHOLSON (LEAD TAPPERS – ETERNITY SEGMENT)

DEEP SEA DREAMING – SEACLOTH PERFORMERS RETURNING FROM STADIUM

TIN SYMPHONY – 'BOXES' PERFORMERS WITH THEIR LAWNMOWERS

CEREMONIES VOLUNTEER – WENDY WHALE, SHOWS HER OLYMPIC TORCH AND UNIFORM TO FELLOW CEREMONIES WORKERS AND PERFORMERS

'The volunteering for the Games and specifically for Ceremonies (in my experience) was eye-opening and wonderful. It was also very hard work. The volunteers I dealt with were stalwarts. Our rehearsals were often out at Schofields, an out-of-the-way, desolate, disused airfield at Quakers Hill. Rain, freezing cold (remember it was winter) or searing shine, they went out there and seemed to enjoy the carnival atmosphere, which developed once the large colourful marquees, and tents were erected. Sometimes the call was 7.30 am and went on well after the sun had set. The performers had to wait for long periods of time, getting steps right or cues fine-tuned. Once we got to rehearsal at the Stadium, we had all become a well-run, confident "close-knit" team.

'We only had two rehearsals at the Stadium before the live show. On that night, everyone was very excited, but I really didn't see many nerves – everything moved too fast for us to worry about worrying! My particular team, the cast assistants, were deployed all over Sydney Olympic Park, and also at schools set up as bus hubs. We had some help with the horses and horse handlers, while most of us were at Sydney International Athletic Centre, which is connected to the Olympic Stadium by a tunnel. Others were across the precinct, making sure the cast moved efficiently from one place to another. Some cast assistants helped with the artists' costumes, hair and make-up. It is hard for people to realise the enormity of getting all those people in the right place, at the right time, in the right gear!

'This time has been unique. I want to congratulate everyone who helped so willingly. We couldn't have done it without you. It will remain in my heart and mind forever. Thank you.' ... **Gisela Payne (Volunteer Co-ordinator, Ceremonies)**

'I was one of seven members of the Rotary Club of Prospect who volunteered for positions in the Opening and Closing Ceremonies, the other six being: **Rita Adams, Marcia Boyd, Marcia Hampton-Taylor, Bernie Hussey, Ron Lopez** and **Kay Withers**. Parading as an Athlete Escort with the Romanian Team was an absolutely overwhelming experience. However, another special aspect of my volunteer experience was being part of a proud father and daughter combination, as my 74-year-old father Arthur Skinner, was a bus liaison/coordinator with ORTA. He was having so much fun, I thought he would burst if I did not ring him every day to share the experiences!' ... **Joy Weatherall**

Peter and Suzanne Williams became volunteer Fire Wardens for the Opening and Closing Ceremonies on the encouragement of their friends Hugh and Kathy Sykes. Peter recalls: 'The official areas to be manned by Fire Wardens were listed as: Smoke Shutters, Stores Areas, Compactors, Holding Areas, Fire Extinguishers and Hose Reels, bottom of Spirals and patrol our area of the Ring Road. As well as patrolling these areas, other duties included assessing potential hazards, maintaining clear egress through Fire Exits, being prepared for evacuation, and importantly, liaising with Police and Fire Brigade Officers.

'The camaraderie between all the volunteers and performers was wonderful to experience. It was awesome to see how a seeming melee of costumed performers, props and crew blended itself together to put on such a magnificent show that was the envy of the world. We are very proud in our humble way to be part of it. Thanks to Hugh and Kathy for passing on the opportunity.'

Michelle Daniel, and several of her fellow students at Bonnyrigg Heights Primary School, first got the opportunity to dance at the Pacific School Games, and from that were chosen to take part in the Opening Ceremony of the Olympic Games. Michelle recalls: 'There were hours of practice, travelling and a few sacrifices along the way. At times I was sick, but still went to every rehearsal and always on time. But it was not until that morning on Friday, 15 September 2000, that I had a different feeling I can't quite describe; I was excited, anxious, nervous, happy and proud.'

'I got to know my dance friends (Andrea, Yolla, Chloe and Amy) very well over the many long rehearsals for the Opening Ceremony. We had only been dancing together a little while before we were auditioned for the Olympic Games, now we are the best of friends. This will be one childhood experience we will never forget. To volunteer our time was such a small price to pay for such a wonderful experience.' ... **Bridget Zizza (Eternity)**

Linda Deutsch (flag and placard bearer assistant)

Dancers for 'Elle Macpherson Float' at rehearsal with Elle

Children, parents, teachers and drivers from all over NSW have endured long hours meeting the commitment to be part of the Sydney Olympic and Paralympic Games. One such group was the Dubbo and District Sing 2001 Choir, which consisted of students from the central western towns of Dubbo, Yeoval, Narromine, Coolah, Tullamore, Wellington and Dunedoo.

Some members of this group had to travel to Sydney 15 times, resulting in 150 hours of travelling. However, although a lot of time was spent away from home, the group had wonderful support from the Dubbo RSL and other local businesses, not only for their travel, but to assist with the week-long stay at Camp Mackay at Kurrajong, for the Dress Rehearsals and Opening Ceremony. This was a wonderful setting at the foot of the Blue Mountains west of Sydney, where the staff were extremely supportive of the children's needs.

Nicole Murphy was a determined 11-year-old who was so passionate about representing Dubbo in the Olympic Opening Ceremony, that when she had to undergo an urgent pacemaker replacement for her congenital heart blockage, she only missed one rehearsal. Just days after being discharged, Nicole was back in secret rehearsals with the rest of the cast, even though she could barely lift her arms over her head.

Nadia Mullavey is a 12-year-old member of the Sing 2001 Choir, who is very grateful for her parents' support in the family sacrifice which had to be made for her to realise her dream of being part of the Olympic Opening Ceremony. This was in addition to her older sister Trudi preparing hundreds of children for performances during the Torch Relay visit to Dubbo. Nadia recalls: 'The night of the opening ceremony was great. There I was on the floor of Stadium Australia, it was wonderful. All the torches and the stars glistening in the night as we sang "Under the Southern Skies", with lead singer Nikki Webster.

THE DUBBO AND DISTRICT SING 2001 CHOIR WITH CONDUCTOR MELANIE MEERS (CENTRE) IN THE COSTUMES WORN DURING THE OLYMPIC OPENING CEREMONY: (BACK, WHITE TOPS L TO R) CLARE GRIFFIN, JOANNA MALONE, CASSANDRA O'LEARY, KAITLYN WILSON, LAUREN BURKE, RYAN GEORGE, JACQUI GILBERT, KIM DOVER, SALLY WILSON, NATASHA COX, LINDSAY HADFIELD, LISA MCCOSKER, JOSEPH SIMONS; (MIDDLE, DARK TOPS) CHERISE JOHNSON, KATRINA MARRETT, LYNDALL WITTS, MARNIE STANBROOK, DAINIA MATHIESON, NICOLE MURPHY, NADIA MULLAVEY, JACQUI HUGHES; (FRONT) KATY MILLS, DANIELLE SHUTTLE, LOUISE COLLIE, ELA HYLAND, KIRSTY O'LEARY AND AMANDA PARISH

The energy started pumping and my stomach of nerves floated away. I guess the feeling may have been that I could show the world the true me, and that I could achieve anything that my heart set out to try.'

Mitchell Smith was a 'Tin Man' in the segment 'Tin Symphony' of the Olympic Opening Ceremony. Besides learning a lot as a performer, Mitchell also learned plenty about using public transport when travelling from Manly on Sydney's Northern Beaches to Schofields in the Western Suburbs.

'I'm 16 years old, and one of the younger ones in our segment, but we all had an absolute blast! We had stage management that was great, and our segment director Dougy was Awesome. On the night it was just so good because we knew what we were in for, but the roar on the way onto the field of play was the best.'

'I was one of the volunteer tap dancers in the Opening Ceremony finale – "Eternity". What an experience, I know I will never dance in front of a bigger audience. It was loads of fun, learning new steps and rhythms, also getting used to tapping in a new style of tap shoe – the Blundstone work boot. With the additional bit of sole and the taps, each boot could weigh about 2 kilos or more – depending on the size boot we needed.

'While learning the routine we tapped on the flat, but gee how the outlook changed when we started rehearsing on the ramps of the trucks – how would you go dancing on a slope of 11 degrees? It was very exciting, I especially had never done any sort of tap dance like this before. I really wanted to tell someone what we were doing at rehearsals – it was very hard to go home and get asked "How were rehearsals?" only to be able to answer "Good/great" etc.' ... **Shannon Mapstone**

'I am 17 years old, and have been dancing since I was four. I have danced in Disneyland, Disney World, Shopping Centres and Various Shows, but I have never had the experience like I had on the night of the Opening Ceremony, it was Exciting, Amazing – like a dream come true. I was in "Eternity Jazz", and I had so much fun at rehearsals. Dancing at the Opening Ceremony was an experience I won't forget for a lifetime.' ... **Melissa Byrne**

'I was one of 120 outriggers and dragon boaters who made up "The Waratahs" in the Nature segment of the Opening Ceremony. We were chosen for our team building skills and strength training. Each piece of the Waratah weighed around 60 kgs and required two people to operate them. There were some problems with breakages when we first had the actual props, but that was soon sorted out to finally produce the beautiful flowers you saw in the ceremony.' ... **Stephanie Powell**

Joy Gilmour nearly had second thoughts about her daughter Joanne participating in the Olympic Ceremonies when she saw the schedule of 34 rehearsals. The Gilmours live in Wagga Wagga, some ten hours return trip to Sydney. This mother and daughter spent nearly 350 hours driving time because being part of such a special event, was always going to be worth the effort.

These shoes were not made for dancing!

(L to R) Michelle Molyneux and Shannon Mapstone – 'Eternity' tap dancers

Performers from Bonnyrigg Heights Primary School who were part of the 'Southern Skies' segment

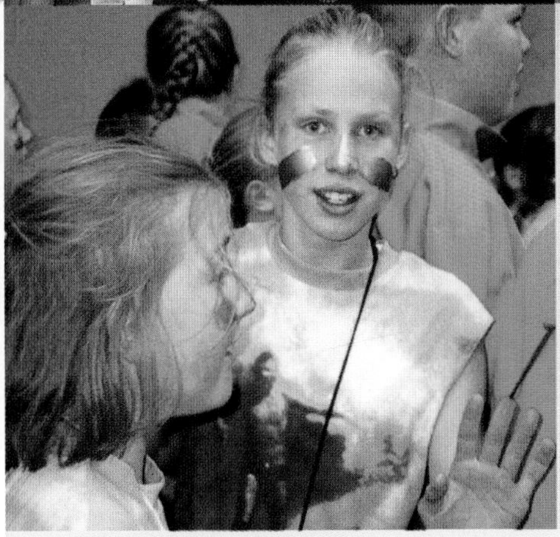

Erica Hansen, with other 'Southern Skies' performers, about to enter the stadium. Erica's family all became involved in the Olympic Games, in costume repair, costume dressing for mum (Judy), and dad (Mike) helped American broadcaster NBC on the marathon course

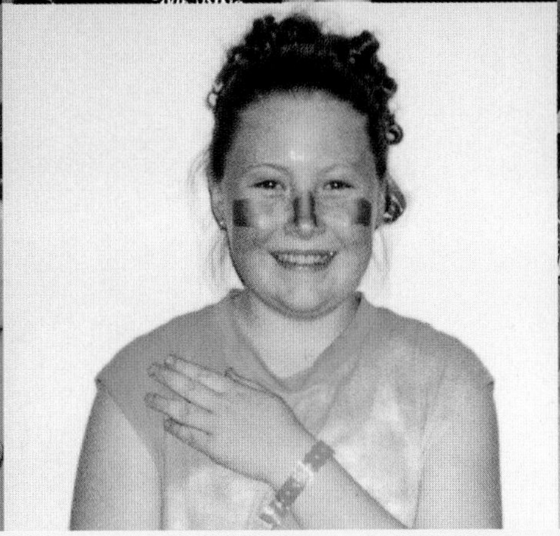

Emma Grills – Southern Skies segment. 'With all the rehearsals I learned to travel around Sydney by train and bus with the two teachers from Bonnyrigg Height's Primary School – Miss Madden and Miss Perin'

Samuel Terry Primary School performers – 'Southern Skies' segment. (L to R) back row – Jean Kirby, Emma Maestri, Laura Palmer, Carley Guernier, Courtney Talbot, Belinda Fenton and Megan Lofthouse. centre – Shane Waddell. front row – Chelsea Barnett, Natalie Layt and Julia Hiatt

WAITING FOR THE SURF PHOTO BY BRONWYN MURPHY

RACHEL LAFFAN (TEDDY IN THE LOLLY FOREST – PARALYMPIC CLOSING CEREMONY)

ANOTHER LONG WAIT AT REHEARSALS

Allison Fogg, 'Eternity' cast member, expressed much emotion about the preparation, friendships and sacrifices made to be part of this wonderful event, but the last verse of a poem she compiled summed it up well:

With that thought and the lights, music and scenery,
We tried our hardest, just like all of the rest.
To perform, smile and dance like never before,
To show the world that Sydney's the Best!

'Eternity' cast member, **Tiffany Dickens**, says: 'The reason I auditioned is because I thought that it would be a fantastic experience, and a great way to meet new people. Every time I think back to the rehearsals and the Ceremony it takes my breath away.'

'There was so much spirit, but lining up before we went on, when "Southern Skies" was playing and we could see the whole audience around us, all their lights and cameras flashing, it was just an unbelievable sight. The best part of the dance was when we were dancing in the aisles, right next to the audience, and all of our excitement fused with the audience's, we could see their faces and smiles. The dance was so much fun and the music was exciting, there was so much energy. It was a great experience, and it's great that so many people got the chance to be a part of, and experience the Olympics in special ways. You didn't have to be an athlete, but you could still be a part of it, you could use your talents, and contribute in ways that were within your reach.' ... **Rebecca Piplica (age 14)**

'I was excited that my school, McCarthy Catholic College, was chosen for the Closing Ceremony of the Sydney 2000 Olympic Games. My school was in the "Lawn Mower" segment. It was fun but the practices were very long. I would like to thank Mrs McMahon, our dance teacher, and the ceremonies crew.' ... **Jessica Barnett**

Expressions by Greenwich Public School performers:

'The best 30 minutes of my life.'... Nicole Braude
'I wish I could do it again.'... Hunter Monk
'I will never forget how happy all the athletes were.'... Alison Hanks
'The best day of my life.'... Karishma Bhandary
'I was filled with amazement, excitement and exhilaration.'... Emily Sutherland
'We worked really hard, but what a buzz.'... Ross McQuinn
'An amazing and unforgettable experience.'... Liz Oliver
'All the nerves rushed away, and the excitement rushed in.'... Chloe Want
'I carried out the Czech Republic ball.'... Danielle Norton-Smith
'I will keep it as a special memory forever.'... Erica Boucher
'I couldn't believe it when I got chosen.'... Gabriel Pender
'Totally wonderful show I'll never forget.'... Lucy Bowers

Andrew Clare was a member of the 2000-strong marching bands: 'We rehearsed every Sunday for four hours and put a lot of personal work into it as well. However, it was more than worth the effort, a magnificent experience.'

'If you want to be noticed, become a fire-breather. It was one man's vision to train as many people as possible to eat and breathe fire; that man was Charles Crawshaw. With the support of his brother Felix, Will Garwood and others, Charles inspired an ever-increasing number of fire-breathers to be part of a new world record group performing on the steps of the Opera House on 15 September each year from 1995. Continual lobbying resulted in the 1999 confirmation by SOCOG that we would be part of the Olympic Ceremonies.

'My wife Gina is also a fire-breather and was with me throughout all the meetings, training sessions, rehearsals and performances. We shared the lows (long hours of waiting, freezing, baking, early mornings, late nights, traffic delays, logistical problems and lost workdays, etc.) as well as the highs (15 minutes of fame, glory, a deep sense of pride and self-satisfaction, new friendships, unique photos and video) and will no doubt share our special story for decades to come with our children and grandchildren. Long may the spirit of the Olympics live to uplift and enrich the lives of future generations across the planet.' ... Martin Mitchell

Personal comments by fire-breathers

'I was eating fire, licking fire, blowing dragons and had no hair left on my arms.'... Alison Galvin
'I enjoyed the experience beyond anything I am likely to do again.'... Jill Rohloff
'With my son Brad, we will be giving it our best shot.'... Bruce Rigby

'Playing with fire is always fun, hot and exciting.'... **Leo Chen**

'Every time I fire-breathe I feel an exhilaration from doing something that few people ever get a chance to do.'... **Murray Henstock**

'I now consider myself the world's most conservative fire-breather.'...**Tony Fowler**

'Fire-breathing has given me back my self-confidence and personal power.'... **Lynn Watson**

'My participation in the Olympics was in memory of my parents.'... **Coral Barnes**

'There's a lot more to fire for me, it's about *living your fire* and taking risks.'... **Michele Goeldi**

'Here I was a middle-aged, middle of the road, Australian woman who thought she knew her goals in life.'... **Gail Hindman**

'That awesome sound, the proximity to the heat – it makes your chest heave.'... **Patrick Crane**

'We made the decision to join and haven't regretted it for a moment.'... **Identical twin brothers Marc and Paul Whittaker**

'It blew me away to think I could be part of such a great event.'... **David Mathews**

'Ironically the only time I have burned myself in the three months of training and rehearsals was on hot coffee.'... **Leslie Miller**

'Being part of the Olympic Opening Ceremony is a blast.'... **Jacqueline Hofste**

'My initial thought was, you have to be nuts to do something like that.'... **Farhad Haidari**

'My husband would call me a dragon (and get away with it!).'... **Mona Bedwany**

'The level of commitment turned out to be a lot more than expected, but this has contributed to the experience.'... **Dysz Gancewicz**

'I feel totally privileged to be involved and meet some of the best people.'... **Andrew Tattersall**

'I'll always remember this special day, and the special journey I took to get there.'... **Lexa Green**

'For me it was one of the proudest moments of my life.'... **Felix Crawshaw (Co-ordinator and Head Trainer)**

(L TO R) GINA, GLEN, FELIX AND MARTIN – READY TO 'FIRE-UP'

FIRE-BREATHER JILL ROHLOFF

FIRE-BREATHER MARTIN MITCHELL

'NATURE' SEGMENT PERFORMERS WITH FACES PAINTED READY FOR COSTUMES

SOME OF THE ACROBATIC TEAM

PHOTO BY BRONWYN MURPHY

(L TO R) MELISSA MITCHELL, KATIE BEST, EMMA RATCLIFF, KIRSTY PATTERSON AND KAREN THRUCHLY – 'NATURE' SEGMENT PERFORMERS AT SIAC BEFORE HEADING TO STADIUM AUSTRALIA

Kath O'Brien sums up her impression of being a volunteer in the Superdome for the congregation of athletes prior to the Olympic Opening Ceremony:

'The whole world in one room. At the same time.

Athletes everywhere. Sensational Oh Yeah!'

The Redfern bunker!

Julie Palmer sums up the clandestine activities surrounding the 'secret location' in Redfern where ceremonies props and costumes were being prepared. An unnoticed, low-profile group of dedicated volunteers put in thousands of hours making the scenery that stunned the world. 'I've never been a secretive person. Cloak and dagger is just not my style! My Olympic volunteering experience was in the beginning quite spooky.

'After answering the "no frills" ad in the newspaper, and receiving a very basic map by post, I found myself driving down the backstreets of Newtown to ancient and derelict railway yards. The rough road in showed no sign of life except a few parked cars. I felt that I was surely lost. I drove gingerly past a girl sitting on a plastic chair patting a sleepy dog. "What are you looking for?" she asked. "A place to do some sewing", I replied. "This is the place," she smiled back, "park wherever you can and come in".

'After picking my way through the mud and puddles, I entered a small room. It contained a desk and a lady attending to papers. No clues as to what was going on here! This was in fact as far as you got without signing the "Top Secret" paperwork.

'I was then taken into a very noisy room where they were welding, etc. – this was not for me! I was asked if I could use a sewing machine, and after a positive answer I was ushered to the inner sanctum, up the stairs, through the tearoom and up more stairs.

'At the top we came to an unmarked door with just a hole for a handle. It was like entering a bunker or a submarine with no windows or exits, but it was huge.

Pixel Kids in action

Pixel Kids (L to R) Jade Sciascia and MaryAnne Genco

Pixel Kids (L to R) Chris De Leon, Mona Kassouf, Rose Antoun and Afifah Daoud

'I spent three days working on various projects. Sadly I could do no more. I found out that my husband Ken was dying and would not come out of hospital. It pleased him to see me do my part. He worked as a driver on the weekend of Father's Day with the Brazilian Team, but did not survive to see the Closing Ceremony.

'I was proud to see some of my work and that of those other great volunteers displayed at the Powerhouse Museum.'

Jenny Burgess responded to a newspaper advertisement for volunteers to work in the Art Department at Redfern to glue, sew and paint the props and costumes for the Opening and Closing Ceremonies. 'Fabulous, I knew I had found my niche! This was like being a kid in a lolly shop, to a girl who enjoys anything arty/crafty.

'Come "show time", there were some special moments, like having the occasional opportunity to carry props out to the edge of the Field of Play during the show and trying to soak up the atmosphere before being ushered backstage again. Also seeing some of the props and costumes I had worked on … out on the field … and didn't they look fabulous!'

'I only worked for one month on making costumes and props at Redfern, but it was amazing to see the volunteers putting in so many hours, never knowing from day to day what they would be working on. I, like many, was not aware that this was not being done by paid employees, and it was interesting to see the skill of those involved. Some of them went on to be dressers on the night, but a few like myself just had the enjoyment of being part of such a wonderful experience.' … **Marian Denton**

Irene McCowan was a Performer Marshal for the Opening and Closing Ceremonies. However, as a receptionist at Santa Sabina College at Strathfield, she developed wonderful friendships with students from the school who were performing, as they kept their secrets about the ceremonies. It was not a problem for her to contact teachers to adjust homework assignments because rehearsals took weekend time. To quote Irene: 'It was a wonderful experience.'

Expressions by Santa Sabina College – Pixel Kids

'After walking out of the stadium listening to the bands,
Everyone got the chance to shake the athletes' hands.
As we left we saw the fire works blast,
I will remember this day forever even though it is now in the past.' ... Sarah Ramjan

'You all had fun watching us paint those scenes on the pixels and flying those kites. Many of those students were from Santa Sabina, and I, Helen, was one of them.' ... Helen Fernandez-Baca

'So dancing and painting in the ceremony may not be something I tell my grandchildren, but all those smiling faces beaming down on me as I ran out from under the stands is something I will never forget.' Lisa Farrel

'The stadium is where we were together,
A wonderful time we had.
Experience – one I will keep forever,
I am Australian.' ... Amanda Hoh

Standing around the pixels, applauding the athletes as they entered the stadium made me become more aware for those with disabilities. These athletes are role models to many people, being respected and admired for their courage and faith.' ... Elizabeth Sonego

'Overall, I will have and do have the joy of saying what a fabulous experience it was and for the rest of my life I will recount the story when I was 13, and was involved as a volunteer in the Paralympics. Thank you, organisers, teachers, my friends, fellow volunteers and everyone involved, especially the athletes for giving me that joy!' ... Marianna Lopert

'When it came to leaving the stadium, we sang and danced to Taxiride, and then started shaking hands with all the athletes. I was actually shaking hands with people who were going to go on and win medals! That was the best.' ... Emily Ofner

Pixel kids – Ben Mackay, Matthew Phipson and Matthew Greig from Carlingford High School

Paralympic opening ceremony performers from Greenwich Public School

(L to R) Alexander Winston, Ian Watts and Joel Sercombe from Greenwich Public School ready for the Paralympic opening ceremony

'By the time I'd settled down, my nerves vanished, and I started to enjoy myself. I watched and heard the singers, I saw the athletes parade past me, I waved and shook their hands and I saw the flame being lit. I had the best seat in the house!' ... **Sarah Carroll**

'This experience would not have been possible if it wasn't for the constant support of our teachers. Seven devoted members of staff came to every rehearsal and helped to teach us the dance steps. They gave up their time so that we would have this once-in-a-lifetime opportunity. I'd like to say thank you to the members of staff at Santa Sabina who made it possible for us to have the time of our lives.' ... **Margaret Moses**

'The only problem is, as The Seekers so very rightly put it – The Carnival is Over.' ... **Hannah Shiel**

'I was fortunate to gain a cross section of experiences during the Olympic Games by having the opportunity to not only have all the ups and downs and mishaps and wonderful association with the enthusiastic public as a Spectator Services Host, but by being a Performance Marshal for the Ceremonies. I was stimulated by the fantastic young kids who were performing and inspiring everyone, and this put me on an exuberant high for the entire two weeks.' ... **Jane Lurie**

'My name is **Lesley Fentiman**, I am a teacher and worked as a member of the Floating Team for the Ceremonies. This gave me exposure to a wide range of activities, including distribution of the Closing Ceremony Kits. However, nothing can replace the feeling of People! People! and more People on Opening Ceremony night when I was assigned to the Superdome. Only those who were there can imagine what it was like to be with the elite of the world's athletes in one building!'

'On Opening Ceremony night I was located in the large parking station next to the Superdome (known to the Ceremonies Team as P1). The "Awakening" segment comprised several hundred indigenous Australians from many parts of our country. While finishing touches to make-up were being made, a special visitor arrived to wish them all well – popular television presenter and actor,

THE WARATAHS

MOTHER AND DAUGHTER CHERIN PULLAR AND BROOKE MCNAMARA, WAITING FOR THEIR BUS TO SYDNEY FOR REHEARSAL AS TAP DANCERS IN THE 'ETERNITY' SEGMENT OF THE OPENING CEREMONY

'SOUTHERN SKIES' PERFORMERS AINSLIE DOWNES AND ELLA FISHER FROM DUNGOG, NSW

Shane Stubbs (field of play marshal) waiting with the multitude at SIAC

Diane Zagaglia in the VIP buggy

Alicia Dumlao-Dormitorio (audience kit assistant)

Ernie Dingo, moved around the groups telling them "The world is watching, go and do your people proud". Ernie's visit gave everyone a real lift.' ... **John Cameron (Assistant Stage Manager)**

'Sadly my husband died before he could realise his dream of being an Olympic volunteer, and for a while I had considered giving up. I did keep going though, as I wanted to do this for his memory. I am glad that I did, because the energy derived from the experience, and the friendships developed, have contributed to a stabilising effect for me, and even now I am arranging a reunion with new-found volunteer friends.' ... **Virginia Ryan (Horse Handler)**

'There is so much to relive about my experience as a Truck Segment Assistant in the Olympic Opening Ceremony. Yes, those massive vehicles, which formed the ramps for the Tap Dancers – there were some testing moments, long days and finally unbelievable emotions and memories.

'At the start I was an individual, unsure and curious; As the production developed I was part of a team. On The Night, there were no individuals, no teams, we were just one!' ... **Michael Rodrigues**

As can be appreciated by the stories which flow through this segment, participants for all aspects of the ceremonies have been sourced from nearly every conceivable organisation and club. Many Placard Bearers came from surf life saving clubs such as Cronulla SLSC – **Rachel Braine (Botswana), Stuart Braine (Benin), Tim Robinson (Rwanda), Chris Giles (Hong Kong) and Paul Wigg (Trinidad and Tobago).** Also from Coogee SLSC were – **Leigh Habler (Yugoslavia), Cameron Habler (Belarus), Shannon Habler (Barbados) and Carla Buntin (Brunai)**. Of course, those for whom we do not have details are just as much appreciated for their contribution.

Margaret Cliff worked at SOCOG HQ from mid-1999. This was an enjoyable time for Margaret, and the realisation of a dream. However, in the words of her daughter-in-law Sarah Cliff: 'While all this was occurring, Margaret was facing another life-changing experience – a serious battle with cancer, discovered just months before the Olympics were due to start.

'Her first course of chemotherapy was juggled around her SOCOG work.

'The second course was due during the first week of the Olympics – however it was postponed by her specialist so she could participate after all. Margaret took her place in the stadium as a volunteer for the Closing Ceremony, an incredibly long, exhausting yet exhilarating experience that she wouldn't have missed for anything in the world. The Driza-bone and Akubra she wore now hang in her wardrobe, and are worn with pride. Going straight back to the postponed chemotherapy unfortunately meant missing the Volunteers' Parade.

'Margaret has now completed three courses of chemotherapy, and things look good. This has been an unforgettable experience for an unforgettably brave, dedicated and honourable woman.'

'When I first informed friends that I would be carrying a placard and leading a country out into the stadium for the Olympic Opening Ceremony, my friends all started to make fun of me and tell me I was dreaming. At one of the very early rehearsals, we were informed of the country we would represent, and this made my story even seem more of a fairytale because I was given Egypt. Then everyone's reaction was, "So Owen, does that mean you have to walk like an Egyptian?" They would then start laughing at me, totally convinced that it was a silly story. My response was usually, "Okay then, watch me on television and work it out for yourselves." This of course made them laugh even harder. GUESS WHO HAD THE LAST LAUGH?' ... **Owen Eckersley**

Dominique Farago – placard bearer – Vietnam

placard bearers – (l to r) Trent Westerweller, Sarah Miles and Jane McFadden

placard bearers – (l to r) Tamara, Tim and Kate

Awakening performers with cast assistant Lorraine Vickery

(L to R) Leanne South, Debbie Coventry and Michelle Coventry (horse handlers and field of play marshals)

August Keskula migrated to Australia from Estonia in 1947, and passionately gives of his time in appreciation of what his new country has given him. August was a field of play marshal for ceremonies, and food service assistant in both the Olympic and Paralympic villages

Scuba divers from 'Deep Sea Dreaming'

Field of play marshals Werner and Lily Schulz with cast coordinator, Maree Sheehan, prior to the closing ceremony

sisters Lucinda (blue face) and Katrina Breen

Fire-breathing ladies.

Annette Dinning with Slim Dusty at the closing ceremony of the Olympic Games. Annette was not only an assistant stage manager for the ceremonies, but a St John Ambulance volunteer for both the Olympics and Paralympics

'Eternity' performers from 'Accent on Dance' and 'Gold Star' prior to the Olympic opening ceremony

VOM 6/7 props assistants – (back) Kay, Roz, Marine, David, Barbara, Carolyn, Jason, Tina, Elizabeth and Udo; (front) Simon, Caroline, Kimmy and Robert

Making ceremonies costumes – IOC protocol volunteer Robyn Findlay (right) and her mother, Margaret Findlay

Larissa Willson, Casey Hadfield, Shardie Johns, Louise Devlin, Kirby Darlington and Bes Ayre – 'Eternity' tap dancers – ready for final dress rehearsal

Volunteers Parade...

ORTA
NORTH RYDE

N.S.W. RURAL FIRE SERVICE

OPENING & CLOSING
CEREMONIES
VOLUNTEERS

INTERSTATE VENUES

Brisbane – Canberra – Melbourne – Adelaide

While the focus of the Olympic Games was in Sydney, the four Interstate Football Venues provided excitement and hospitality to the athletes and spectators, as well as enabling another dedicated group of volunteers in each location to enjoy their own unique Olympic Experience.

These people were no less important than their Sydney counterparts. They shared the same uniform, the same training, even participated in their city parades with the athletes, and of course provided the same high standard of friendly efficient service to their Olympic guests.

The following experiences express how fortunate most of these volunteers felt in also living in an Olympic Host City.

JERRY ZALDARRIAGA CAME TO AUSTRALIA FROM HIS NATIVE PHILIPPINES EARLY IN THE YEAR 2000, ONLY TO BE SWEPT UP IN THE EMOTION OF THE OLYMPIC GAMES. JERRY FELT THAT IT WAS A SPECIAL GIFT TO SHARE VOLUNTARILY, AND REALLY ENJOYED THE TEAMWORK AND DEDICATION OF HIS FELLOW VOLUNTEERS

SPECTATOR SERVICES HOSTS ERIC HORN AND LISA HOPES AT THE MCG

Eric Horn had his Olympic Spirit ignited while growing up in Los Angeles, and clearly remembers the summer of 1984. Eric immigrated to Australia in the mid-1990s, and was again caught up in Olympic fever, this time realising he could become more involved than just as a spectator.

The two things which were most special to Eric during his time as Spectator Services Host at the Melbourne Cricket Ground, were the friendships and the public support, especially as Eric recalls: 'On our last night all the volunteers were invited to line up and take a walk across the football field at halftime. The song "Heroes Live Forever" blasted through the stadium.'

Adelaide: A place to remember

'It is the small quirky things that make big events even more special and memorable! This is a little story from the Olympics in Adelaide. It is a story that occurs at the edges of "Protocol" but it is one that takes the Olympics in Adelaide, Australia to the streets of Brasilia!

'Mr Ferenc Szekely was one of eight football referees that came to Adelaide as part of the Olympics. Because he had heard that he could get them here, he came to Australia and Adelaide with his heart set on getting copper numbers for his house in Brasilia. As part of my work in Protocol (though referees are not strictly the responsibility of Protocol), I had met the referees at the airport and escorted them back to their hotel. We chatted, as you do. Having delivered them to the Hotel Hilton staff, and wished them a Great Games, I thought to myself that was the end of that!

'On my way to work the next morning I ran into Mr Szekely and a referee from Germany and we chatted some more. They were off to go shopping. I gave them directions and on they went. Later in the day Protocol gathered as a team to go down to the stadium for a final run-through of the set-up and our back-of-house role with the Olympic Family. As we waited to go to the stadium, Mr Szekely came into the foyer and asked me if I could help him. He especially wanted to buy copper house numbers – not brass, chrome, silver plated, ceramic, wood, glazed, simply copper – numbers 10 and 9.

'He hadn't been able to find them while out shopping and was not going to be able to get about much because of training and refereeing.

'Offering the money for the numbers and detailing the sizes he asked if I could get them for him no matter what the cost. I explained that I couldn't take the money, and that as far as I knew copper house numbers were not readily available. This was not going to be an over-the-counter purchase! I said I would do my best and get back to him. Next morning I set about the task. Preliminary phone calls to a couple of stores including an ostensibly "copper" specialist confirmed what I knew – there was no such thing as a commercially available copper house number. Next bet was local artists. A couple of calls to a university art school to see if there were any students working in copper and to a gallery with studios for artists and craft workers – no luck there! Next call was to a landscape architect friend and colleague at the University of South Australia. She had never seen copper house numbers in her work in Melbourne or Adelaide, even overseas, but she suggested a couple of companies that do specialist items for clients. A phone call to Melbourne and a fabulous person "who knew someone who knew someone else in Adelaide" who, even if they couldn't do this themselves, could probably put me onto someone. Sure enough, back in my hometown through someone who knew someone, I found Malcolm Lucadei of Associated Signs. Even though his business had never made copper numbers, and if Mr Szekely could get down to his business, he and the engraving manager, Phil, would get hold of some copper and make the numbers. I faxed all the information through to Mr Szekely and heard nothing more.

'In the foyer of the Hilton Hotel, on my very last shift and as Mr Szekely was about to fly to Brisbane to referee, he rushed over to shake my hand and to tell me that whenever he looked at the house numbers 9 and 10 he would think of the Olympics in Adelaide, of the fabulous city of Adelaide and that he would always bless the wonderful people of Adelaide and Australia! This, he said, he would do forever!

'On the fringes of the Sydney Olympics, an exceptional town produced exceptional results – a tangible part of the international Olympic connection will sit not in a photo album, as a pin on a hat or tucked away as a personal favourite memory. It will sit on the exterior of a house for all to see. I hope that the copper numbers will provide Mr Szekely with the opportunity to tell friends, visitors and family a small and warm story about the Olympics in Adelaide!

'After all, it *is* true! You can get copper house numbers in Adelaide, Australia!

'My personal lessons in this? First, it opened up for me the unheralded work of what must be thousands upon thousands of referees, judges, timekeepers, and the like working away in urban and remote Africa, South America, Asia, Europe, Scandinavia, the Pacific, Australia and all over, to support sport, and some of whom make it to the Olympics! I made sure that I looked for them on television and while I was at the Games in Sydney. Secondly and just as importantly, I know first-hand that out of the spotlight, ordinary people in their working lives, like Malcolm Lucadei and Phil, who didn't make it to Sydney or any Olympic event, often went out of their way and contributed to make the Games the huge success that they were. How special is that!' ... Vicki Crowley (Protocol Adelaide)

Jake Broadstock is a 20-year-old university student. He volunteered to work at Hindmarsh Stadium, Adelaide, for the Olympic Football. Jake couldn't believe his luck when he was allocated a position in Athlete Services, face-to-face with some of the world's highest-paid athletes, escorting them to buses, change-rooms and the field of battle. For Jake, the Olympics were an *adrenalin rush!!*

'In 1964 my father attended the Tokyo Olympics (as a spectator) and always raved about the whole Olympic Games thing. When I realised some of the Football would be played in Adelaide, I jumped at the chance to help out at the Olympic Games in my home state. I live 220 kilometres north of Adelaide, in Port Pirie, so it meant I had to spend almost two weeks with my sister in Adelaide to allow me to complete my volunteer duties. All my training was also in Adelaide so I travelled quite a few kilometres to and from Adelaide – I must admit, I asked myself a few times if it would really be worth it.

'Let me tell you, it was worth every second that I had to spend away from my family and every kilometre I drove to and from Adelaide in preparation. I think it was probably the most rewarding thing I have ever done.

'I was also lucky enough to travel to Sydney as a spectator to watch the Gold Medal Football Final. Anyway, the first thing that hit me after arriving at the railway station at Olympic Park was the helpful and friendly "vollies" who approached everyone and helped out. I felt so proud of them (although I had nothing at all to do with them!) when other people in my group commented how great they all were. I only hope people were saying the same about us in Adelaide!' ... **Andrea Mirra (Spectator Services Host)**

TRANSPORT VOLUNTEERS – GOVERNMENT HOUSE, ADELAIDE

NICOLA SMITH AND WARREN WEBB – 'THE KEYS TO YOUR DRIVING SATISFACTION!' – ADELAIDE HILTON HOTEL

SPORTS ATTENDANT MARK MCBRYDE, PROUDLY CARRIES THE AUSTRALIAN FLAG AS VOLUNTEERS MARCH THROUGH THE STREETS OF BRISBANE

John Rickter was hidden away in the Radio Distribution Centre of Hindmarsh Stadium in Adelaide during Olympic Football events. However, John would not have missed the camaraderie or challenge for anything.

'In 1956 I was a young child living on a sheep property in central Victoria. Dad took me to see the Olympic Torch changing hands from one runner to the next at Tatura, near Shepparton, and I was struck with Olympic Fever.

'When the opportunity arose to volunteer for the Sydney Olympic Games, I immediately applied for Spectator Services at the Aquatic Centre or the Olympic Stadium. When I was diagnosed with a serious illness early in 2000, I decided after treatment was completed, to change my venue to Brisbane in order to be closer to home and family. Unfortunately, in doing so I lost my chance for Spectator Services, but instead was offered the Accreditation Office at the Gabba in Brisbane, which turned out to be even better!

'Some of those who were accredited at the Gabba office included athletes from countries who had selected Queensland as their pre-Olympics training venue. These included: Jamaican Track and Field, Norwegian Fencing and Cycling, Great Britain Track and Field, Shooting and Rowing, Netherlands Diving, all the football teams playing their preliminary games in Brisbane, including Brazil and Cameroon, plus many Australian athletes.

'Those seven weeks were one of the best experiences of my life, assisted enormously in a final recuperation from my illness (I am now back at work full-time) and have given me many wonderful friendships and memories.' … **Caroline Byrne**

Lea Sruhan isn't quite sure how her name became involved with Olympic Torch Relay preparations prior to her Spectator Services role with Olympic Football at the Brisbane venue. However, while the early starts developed into extremely long days, the interest and excitement in working alongside SOCOG Staff, police, security and various event organisers was found to be very stimulating.

Lea recalls: 'I am very privileged to have been a small part of the Sydney 2000 Olympics by my participation in both the Torch Relay and Gabba Football. I was extremely lucky to work with a small, but dedicated and friendly team, and that is always what makes volunteering the fun that it is. I am now looking forward to the Goodwill Games being held in Brisbane in 2001.'

'I was a volunteer in the Spectator Services Section of Olympic Football at the Gabba in Brisbane. I became a volunteer in the main because I could not afford to go to Sydney, and the Gabba Stadium was not far from home.

'My experience enabled me to learn how to cope with different people and attitudes, and to be personally patient. The training I received at the Olympics was of great value when I did volunteer work at the Gold Coast Indy Car Races a few weeks after the Olympic Games.' ... **Phil Maddren**

All venues had daily competitions to stimulate volunteers into either sharing of themselves, or as mind teasers. An overwhelming endorsement as to why they had become involved as volunteers – '... wanted to contribute and be involved in this *once-in-a-lifetime experience* ...' by Gabba volunteers **Paul Gledhill, Beryl Renton, Judy Schulz, Ash Walmsley, Peter Hicks, Rose Lazar, Lilian Barajas, Trish Brennan, Wally Linderman, Tim Saxby, Brooke Fricker, Craig Hempstead, Jane Turner, Sebastian Tops, Bob Boyle, Jesse Orchard, Barrie Harvey and Christine Donaldson.**

When asked what his family and friends said when he told them he was working as a volunteer at the Olympic Games, **John McIntyre** responded: ' ... you're nuts, but good on you!'

To the Sydney 2000 workforce at the Brisbane Cricket Ground

'Tonight's game will be one of mixed emotions for our Gabba Workforce – elation and satisfaction for a job well done, yet a tinge of sadness that this is the last game.

'Over the past ten days, we have had six exceptionally successful event days, and tonight's full house, our total attendance will exceed 205,000.

'The fact that the whole event has gone so well is testament to the outstanding efforts of our Workforce.

'Led superbly by our Functional Area Managers, every team has delivered. You should be justifiably proud of your efforts. Whatever we do in the future, our lives will be richer for the friendships we have made and the unique experience we have gained as a member of the Olympic Games Workforce.

'On behalf of SOCOG and all Functional Area Managers, please accept my sincere gratitude and thanks for your contribution. We feel privileged to have worked with such a professional and dedicated team.' ... **Alan Graham (Venue Operations Manager)**

A Small but Meaningful Token

'I saw the Cameroon Delegation outside Gate 3 looking rather lost. I stopped to see if there was anything I could do to help. One of the delegates told me that they were not sure about where they were to meet their bus to go back to their hotel. I offered to accompany him to Gate 2 to speak with one of the Transport people. As we were heading round to Gate 2, the gentleman got a call on his mobile phone from the bus driver telling him that he would pick them up at Gate 2. Having found out where, I offered to go back and let the others know to go to Gate 2.

'The following week, when Cameroon played the Czech Republic, I was marshalling outside Corporate Gate 6 when some of the same group of Cameroon delegates came past, including the gentleman I had spoken to. He recognised me and beckoned me over to him. As I approached, he gave me a program for the Cameroon Olympic Team. He said it was to say "Thank You". I would not have been the only Games Force team member to receive one, but the fact that the gentleman remembered me has touched me very deeply, and will remain a lasting memory.' ... **Jane Turner (Spectator Services Host – Brisbane)**

Approximately ten months before the Olympic Games, the Australian Federal Police called for volunteers to be part of Olympic Volunteers In Policing (OVIP). **Bruce Lang** (Commander, Hall Emergency Service

ALPHA TEAM (MID LEVEL) – WOOLLOONGABBA FOOTBALL STADIUM

SPECTATOR SERVICES HOST ROSLYN ROBERTS JOINS THE STARS & STRIPES ENTHUSIASM

VOLUNTEERS WAITING FOR ASSIGNED DUTIES AT BRUCE STADIUM, CANBERRA

PROTOCOL ATTENDANT ANDREW SOKAC, WHO CONTRIBUTED MUCH IN THE AREAS OF VENUE STAFFING, UNIFORMS, SPECTATOR SERVICES, EVENT SERVICES, VENUE MANAGEMENT, TRANSPORT AND PRESS OPERATIONS IN THE LEAD-UP TO HIS GAMES-TIME ROLE IN IOC RELATIONS AND PROTOCOL AT THE OLYMPIC FOOTBALL VENUE – BRISBANE

DELTA TEAM – SPECTATOR SERVICES HOSTS – THE GABBA, BRISBANE

PERSONNEL FROM EMERGENCY SERVICES, AUSTRALIAN FEDERAL POLICE AND BUSH FIRE SERVICES BEING RECOGNISED BY THE ACT GOVERNMENT FOR THEIR SUPPORT FOR THE TORCH RELAY AND OVIP DUTIES

Unit) was one of approximately 120 respondents. Bruce recalls: "There was much excitement and experience to be gained through the whole exercise, and as we helped the Australian Federal Police with crowd control for both the Olympic and Paralympic Athletes parades in Canberra, it was a fitting end to the *fever* which overwhelmed Australia in 2000.'

'My first contact with anybody from SOCOG was at the "Get to Know You Night", and we were greeted by the Manager of Spectator Services, Kate Alexander – for such a young person with such a hugh responsibility she turned out to be the salt of the earth in times of need. From that moment on I felt we could handle anything, even though uniform collection tested them with somebody *vertically challenged* like me. But with the help of my friendly dressmaker the end result was tolerable, and oh boy did I feel proud!

'Over the 12 days of competition in Canberra I met and mingled with people from all over the world and from all walks of life – the man next door to the Nigerian High Commissioner. A special moment for me was when I was called to the Venue Control Office (stashed away in the corridors of the unknown where mere mortals didn't go) and asked to accompany an injured Nigerian player to hospital because the Protocol Officer in charge had already gone with an injured Norwegian.

'I was advised that I had been chosen to assist as they felt that I would represent Australia in a diplomatic and courteous manner, and that I could be relied upon to uphold the required protocol. How proud and honoured I was that this trust was given to me. I went home tired after a very late night at the hospital, but feeling good about my situation.

'Marching through the streets of Canberra with the athletes was a fitting and exciting way to end a great Olympic experience.' ... **Roslyn Roberts**

We hear of roller-coaster experiences that people endure in all aspects of life, and the Olympic/Paralympic experience was no different. However, the experiences of **Felicity Way** in the football host city of Canberra, could just about rival that of many folk at the heart of activities in Sydney.

Felicity was given a volunteer position at the International Press Help Desk, at the Venue Press Centre, Bruce Stadium, Canberra. It is well documented that Bruce Stadium went through some severe difficulties with the surface – to the point of threats that all matches could be taken away from the venue. While Felicity was not the individual having to face the media, this was hardly a high point in her Olympic experience.

Of course solutions were found, and Bruce Stadium became a very successful venue for competitors, spectators and staff. Felicity continues: 'We had a great group of people working in Press Operations. We enjoyed our late hours, and our diverse interests, we enjoyed each other, and most of all we enjoyed the experience.

'Highlights were many, but to me the Games were a lifetime high. I wrote a diary each night. I finished my diary entries by saying – *It was a pleasure, it was a privilege, it was a joy, it was THE GAMES*.'

ORTA

(OLYMPIC ROADS AND TRANSPORT AUTHORITY)

FOREWORD

By Bob Leece, Chief Executive Officer, ORTA

The Sydney 2000 Olympic and Paralympic Games involved Australia's biggest and most demanding transport operation. As expected, it placed enormous stress on both the machinery and the people involved in its delivery. What was not so widely expected was the level of success with which the operation unfolded. That success was due in no small part to the tireless commitment of volunteers.

ORTA's 9000 volunteers were not just bit players or part-timers. They played a critically important role day after day in the world-class transport system Sydney provided to athletes, officials, media and spectators.

ORTA's 6000 volunteer drivers collectively undertook more than 200,000 trips during the Olympic and Paralympic Games, covering more than ten million kilometres.

Another 3000 volunteers filled other transport-related positions. They included load zone officers, help desk personnel at venues and interchanges, administration staff who gave support to managers and staff at ORTA headquarters and road event marshals. On the eve of the Games, a further 600 volunteered to be navigators and provided great assistance in essential improvements to athlete bus services. Some particularly generous volunteers began work with ORTA years before the Games. Many others started weeks before the Olympic Games and stayed on for the Paralympic Games.

Like all people who attended the Games, I had first-hand experience of the dedication and enthusiasm of volunteers. All Olympic and Paralympic volunteers are to be congratulated for their efforts, and have rightly received loud public acclaim. But as Chief Executive Officer of the Olympic transport organisation, I want to particularly thank the volunteers who donned a purple-sleeved transport uniform during the Games.

You were all great.

'Having spent many years volunteering in Rotaract and Hockey Clubs, I was privileged to enjoy the hospitality of other countries as part of touring parties. The Sydney Olympic Games has now been my opportunity to return the hospitality and enhance other people's experiences.' ... **Allan Williams (Driver)**

Don Carter is one of the longest-serving volunteers to have worked with ORTA. Don started with the SOCOG Pioneer Volunteer Program, and transferred to ORTA in August 1997. By the conclusion of the Pioneer Volunteer Program, Don had worked over 3000 volunteer hours.

Don usually worked as the Fleet Officer at the Jones Street Depot of SOCOG, but was not averse to driving if the opportunity arose. This is evident in that he drove for the duration of the Australian segment of the Torch Relay.

The Car Pool commenced its existence on 30 March 1998, when **Stuart Ratcliffe** (Manager, ORTA Family Fleet) consulted with Pioneer Volunteers, **Bob Walder** and **George Nolan**. The Car Pool Office operated initially from a section of the ORTA area on the 9th floor at Jones Street. As ORTA and the car service grew, disruptions occurred to their operations, and in January 1999, the Car Pool Office was moved down to street level near the boom gate, and a drivers' lounge was provided in space nearby.

The first drivers 'off the rank' were **Joyce Walsh, Wal Troy, Roy Moore** and **John Damen**, with George, Bob and Don Carter (who joined in May) sharing the Fleet Officer duties. As demand increased, **Bill Shelley** and **Wim Drayer** joined the team. Of course the team of drivers also increased considerably.

'In the later part of last century, SOCOG called for volunteers for the Olympics. My future was set out to continue working until April 2001. For the Olympic period I would have the time to be a volunteer as TAFE advised there would be three weeks holidays during that time. So, I volunteered to drive and stated that I would like to be an NOC or T1 driver. With that settled, TAFE offered redundancies. Plans of mice and men?

DRIVERS BREAK AREA – JONES STREET CAR POOL

TEAM EFFORT – TRANSPORT AND PROTOCOL

Don Carter at the Jones Street depot of SOCOG

Drivers Lou Magritzer (right), his wife Judy Tang and Frank Meusburger – Frank boarded with Lou during the 1956 Melbourne Olympics

(L to R) supervisor Jeannine Barakat, Olympian Betty Cuthbert, load zone officers Ron Gorman and Peter McBride, supervisor Kumutha Srisivalingham

Mother and daughter drivers – (L to R) Elizabeth and Lorraine Milla, enjoyed sharing so many of the driving and emotional experiences, including sleeping on the streets of Sydney, to ensure they received complimentary tickets to the closing ceremony

Bev Conley (driver and community torch relay volunteer) who won a lunchtime outing with Dawn Fraser on the Olympic Show with the following poem:

A volunteer driver for ORTA
I'm not much good in the water
After lunch with Dawn,
Greatest Aussie born –
Maybe I'll get to transport her.

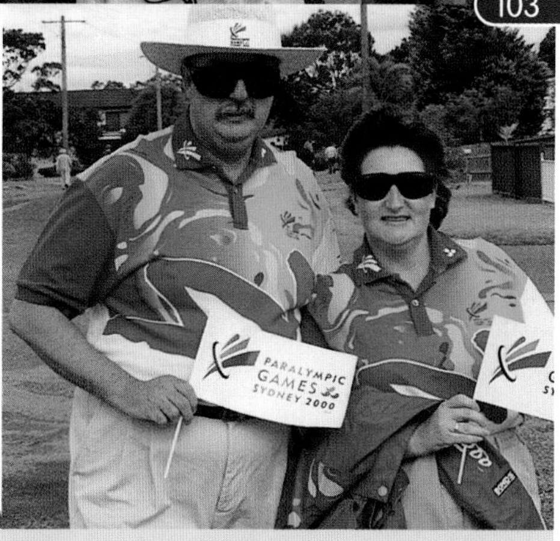

Ken and Donna Blenman, T3 drivers from Gorokan, NSW

Transport volunteers at Cecil Park Shooting Centre

Lester Pasley (load zone officer, stadium transport team)

'January saw me retired and the commencement of seven training modules, but with more flexibility of time. I was allocated the position of NOC Driver – the country, Ethiopia. This was a challenging but rewarding experience. The Ethiopians were friendly, although most athletes tended to be shy, with the exception of Haile Gebrselassie, a true gentleman and outstanding athlete.

'It was a wonderful experience, which I shall probably talk about for years to come. Every visitor to whom I spoke praised the whole event in all aspects. It has been an honour to be involved.' ... **John Davies**

NOC Driver **Lyn Whyte** has very special memories of her adventures driving for the El Salvador team, especially when they visited the Westmead Children's Hospital. Lyn recalls: 'The athletes put on a judo demonstration, and to see the look on those children's faces was reward enough. The El Salvador delegation presented some pictures of native birds from their country, which will be hung in the art gallery they have in the hospital. We were all given a bandaged bear cap. It is stories like this that we do not often hear about.'

'When I put my name down as a volunteer for the Olympics, I fully expected them to say I was too old (79), but the reply was positive.

'After the training period I was told I was to be a T1 driver, and ultimately allotted to look after an Olympic Family VIP, Mr Guiseppe Cinnirella.

'I was unable to get any information about my client because of security. All I could find out was that he would arrive by air from Milan in Italy on a certain date. I was told to be at the airport and given a new Statesman to cater for his needs. I duly attended the airport and spent five hours looking for my VIP, but he could not be located. Enquiries finally found Mr Cinnirella had arrived, but did not know that a driver and car had been allocated for his use, and so proceeded privately to his hotel.

'When I drove to his hotel for our first meeting I wondered what to expect. Would we be able to understand each other? Was he old or young? Would he be very formal? I need not have worried. Mr Cinnirella was indeed a friendly gentleman of middle age, a family man, and was not concerned about protocol.

'I enjoyed his company greatly, and he was most appreciative of everything Australia and its volunteers had achieved. When eventually I took my client back to the airport and said goodbye, I was sorry to see him go. But I was a very proud Australian.' ... Hugh McCarron

'I was handed my job allocation at the airport – destination – Long Bay Gaol! My passenger introduced himself as George, a minister of religion. He then requested his baggage be in the back seat with him rather than in the boot. Well, as we were driving along, he began tuning his banjo, and soon burst into song. He had a good voice, and I said to George that I love "Amazing Grace" and that I felt he would do it justice. So, "Amazing Grace" it was. When he finished, we were stopped at red lights on Anzac Parade, and it was 5.30 on a Friday afternoon surrounded by cars, and I burst into applause. It must have been loud, because after I settled down, I looked around and the other drivers were giving me odd looks. Their looks said – *what sort of nut is she?* Instead of shrinking in my seat, I smiled at them and felt pleased with myself.

'On arrival at Long Bay Gaol the guard looked at my uniform and accreditation and said, "You've made a mistake, you have the wrong address". Following an explanation, George was escorted to his meeting by the prison Chaplin.' ... Mary Lunn (Driver – Airport Cluster)

Glenda Olesen from Roleystone, Western Australia, spent ten days in Sydney in July 2000, volunteering at test events, and many people were saying she was mad. However, as the Games approached, they began to say how lucky she was.

Glenda actually stayed in Sydney for six weeks for both the Olympics and Paralympics with her niece at Bondi, in order to perform her duties as Load Zone Officer at the Sailing events. 'It certainly was worth the effort,' said Glenda.

'The Year 2000 is going to take a lot of beating, what with the Celebration of the New Millennium, my 50th birthday and of course the Olympic and Paralympic Games. It was only April 2000 that my 19-year-old son Kel (who made an impulse decision to come) and I drove from Wollongong to Sydney for an initial interview with ORTA. Then a few days later we were advised that we had been accepted, and that we could commence our training modules.

'It was great to share the Olympic experience with Kel as T3 drivers based at Darling Harbour. I continued on to be an NPC Driver attached to the Malaysian Team for the Paralympics, an experience that just continued to develop cultural understanding for our guests and me. While extending additional hospitality on "un-rostered days" by taking our guests to Manly and the Blue Mountains was part of having pride in our country, this has now resulted in having accepted an invitation by the Malaysian delegates to be their guests later in 2001.' ... Phil Murray

Cathie Tozer (NOC Driver for Liberia) was another person who gained much pleasure out of taking members of her delegation on excursions away from the normal competition venues. On a ferry trip across the Hawkesbury River Cathie recalls: 'The guys had a blast – the looks on their faces told the story.'

'I certainly enjoyed my experiences in accreditation at the Homebush Arrival and Accreditation Centre, and as driver for Botswana during the Olympics and Jamaica during the Paralympics. However, we all had to go through our training and familiarisation, which often highlighted our shortcomings, as it did for me when I was a navigator out of North Ryde Depot during a test event. After trying to answer the phone in the dashboard console without any success, I decided to show some initiative by phoning base to ask if they could advise who may be trying to contact us. The operator said she didn't know who called, but would make a note that I had phoned in. As I was about to hang up, and still with the phone in my hand, the call tone came again, but it was coming from the dashboard console!

'The sound I thought had been the phone call signal proved to be the alarm in the car advising the driver that he was exceeding the 80 km/h and not the phone at all!' ... **Neville Merrell**

Although **Marion Goard** lived most of her life in Sydney, she now lives at Narooma on the NSW south coast. Marion was pleased as punch when Australia won the bid to host the 2000 Olympic and Paralympic Games, and despite a deal of negative criticism about the event, she decided to put her years of city driving experience to good use by volunteering as a driver.

Marion's Olympic experience was a variety of driving for the National Olympic Committees of Zambia, Azerbaijan and Samoa – a mix of cultural experiences to be treasured for all time, including attending the Sunday service at a Samoan Church at Ingleburn.

Marion finally laments: 'Then came the drive home, with everything appearing back to normal. Did it all really happen or was it part of the Dreamtime? Well, now it's back to gardening, painting, and classes ...'

Ian Warlters volunteered because he carried the Olympic Torch in 1956, and felt that he would not have much of a chance of carrying it in 2000.

Ian recalls: 'I did the whole Driving Training modules at TAFE and volunteered as a driver for a National Olympic Committee (NOC) and was allocated to Romania and also later to Austria.

'One afternoon I was walking past the NOC office for Ukraine and talking (which is just so out of character for a "ave-a-chat" such as I) when a bloke ran out of the NOC office saying, quite loudly, "I

DRIVER GJ LEE (THIRD FROM RIGHT) WITH NEWLY ACQUIRED FRIENDS OVER THE PREVIOUS FIVE HOURS WHILE QUEUING FOR CLOSING CEREMONY TICKETS

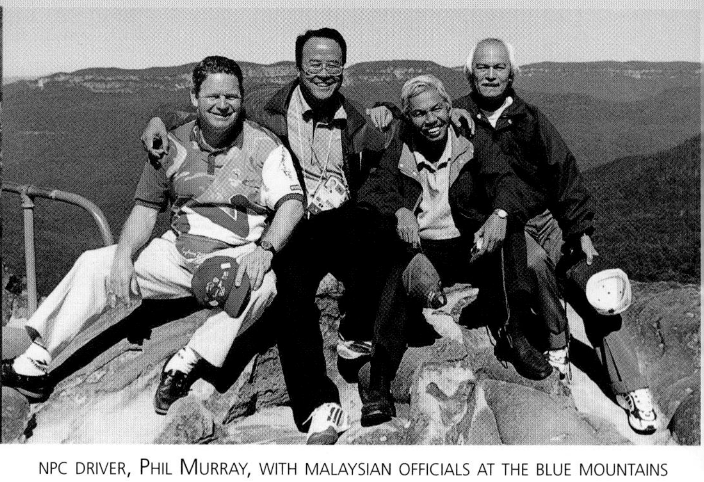

NPC DRIVER, PHIL MURRAY, WITH MALAYSIAN OFFICIALS AT THE BLUE MOUNTAINS

NOC VOLUNTEERS WITH MEMBERS OF THE RUSSIAN DELEGATION

CAN WE HELP YOU? (ADRIAN & VERA)

LOAD ZONE OFFICERS BARBARA, SUZANNE AND ANNE

know that voice – you're Ian Warlters." He grabbed up my accreditation and congratulated himself. His accreditation declared that he was **Peter Tymoc**. What it didn't show was that he had been a National Serviceman in Wewak in Papua New Guinea during 1969, nor that the last time he had heard my voice was back then when I was a Captain and his direct supervisor.

'Isn't it good to see that some things just never change? Obviously we've exchanged addresses and phone numbers, and will get together and remind each other of various experiences!'

'My first reaction to being a volunteer was a real feeling of wanting the Olympic and Paralympic Games to be a great success, and if I could help make this happen by taking a role, I could then take my own flag and carry it with pride.

'I would become a T3 Driver for the car pool at North Ryde, but as we were to be flexible, and of course not everything went as per the training manual, so I even went along for a ride as navigator. As many are aware, allocating driving duties required a control mechanism, and so the DELI ticket system made fairer job allocation.

'Once I moved on to the Paralympics and to see these athletes, gave me such a humble look at all around me. I was so inspired by their tenacity to get over the finish line, success at whatever position they finish.

'I can still relive all these past months, weeks, days, knowing every one of us volunteers made our 2000 Olympic and Paralympic Games THE BEST EVER.' ... **MJM**

Adrian Gilderdale was a 19-year-old NOC driver for the Samoan Team, who enjoyed sharing the emotional highs and lows of team members as he drove them round Sydney. One of his most enjoyable days was when Samoan and Swiss athletes shared his vehicle. Adrian recalls: 'Whilst waiting for some Samoan athletes at the main entry to the Olympic Village I noticed two rather disoriented young athletes in the bus bay. I approached the two girls asking them where they were going. They replied "to Darling Harbour, but we have missed our bus." I informed the girls they could come with me, as I had two vacant seats and was bound for Darling Harbour. They were thankful and came on board.

OLYMPIC FAMILY TRANSPORT DESK,
QANTAS DOMESTIC TERMINAL

DRIVER DAVE JEANES FROM TWEED HEADS

EILA DIFFLEY FROM THIRLMERE, NSW

'During our journey one of the Swiss athletes by the name of Sophie Lamon produced her Silver Medal she had won in fencing. As a way of saying thank you, Sophie was sharing her medal with us as I negotiated peak hour traffic. This was an uplifting experience, and a true indication of the trust between athletes and volunteers. As I continued the journey, my carload of young clients all sang along to Triple M tunes.'

'I was allocated the position of NOC driver for the Danish Team, and when I found out we would be operating from inside the Olympic Village I was stoked! I always remember that just about every Olympian I'd heard speak had said that for them being in the Olympic Village was just the best experience when competing at an Olympic Games, and now I had a chance to be a part of that and see what it was like from the inside.

'The Danish were a great team to be with, including the other drivers and NOC Assistants. It really was one of the best times of my life, two and a bit weeks of driving around the best city in the world and having a great time doing it. It's something I'll never forget, and can really only thank Matt for introducing me to the ORTA program.' ... **Rob Thomson**

Morag Sutton was a Load Zone Officer at Sydney Olympic Park, and recalls one of those special moments, which bring out the spirit of Olympism. 'I had helped the Chef de Mission for Dominica purchase hip bags similar to the one I was wearing, and while he was waiting for his transport we looked up information on his country in my Mini World Factfile. He was interested in buying a copy of the book, so I gave him the name of bookshops plus my business card and away he went.

'The next day I received a call – "Mrs Morag it is the Chef de Mission for Dominica, I cannot find such a book and my day is full. I return to Dominica tomorrow morning!" I said leave it to me, will you be at the Stadium this afternoon? The answer was affirmative. I could not get the exact book, but he was very happy with the alternative.

'About 10.30 pm a call on my mobile checking I would be there in half an hour. Around 11.00 pm a car pulled up, and out stepped the gentleman and handed me a beautiful leather keyring inscribed

Dominica Olympic Committee. He shook my hand and thanked me for all I had done to help him, said goodbye and got back in the car.

'It was then that I realised that the sport at the Olympic Games is only part of this global meeting of people from all walks of life and all corners of the world. A meeting that enriches the host city and its dwellers in such a profound and lasting manner.'

'Being from Brisbane some people thought I was mad to volunteer to become a driver in Sydney, because of the stories you hear about the traffic and the drivers! However, I excel when presented with such a challenge. When I arrived in Sydney for my training the dream was close to reality. I decided to do all my training in one week so I attended the different modules from Monday to Saturday from 3 to 8 July 2000. The reason that I left my training until the last possible moment was so I could really take it all in and remember most of the routes, because I was coming back to Sydney in the last week of August.

'My association with fellow volunteers was a positive and rewarding aspect of my Olympic experience; this included protocol assistants **Robyn Gerber, Christina Kazan** and **Keith Davies**. It was all over too quickly, but I must say that in spite of the financial cost, it was the time of my life, and I would do it all again tomorrow if at all possible.' … **Cameron Smith**

Helen Armstrong was not a volunteer – she was the *stay home support* for husband **Jeff** (NOC Driver) and daughter **Katherine** (Opening Ceremony – Eternity Tap). Her sister **Erica** and brother-in-law **Klaus** were also NOC drivers, but her other daughter **Rosemary**, a trained stiltwalker, was warming up at the audition when she had her first fall in five years, breaking her wrist.

Helen recalls the beginning of the family's Olympic Games Affair: 'Ten years ago our family of two adults and three small children travelled to Greece. At the time, Athens was bidding for the 1996 Olympic Games, so more than usual the topic of Olympic Games, modern and ancient, was a strong focus. On a tour of ancient cities we visited Olympia and enjoyed exploring the ruins and museum. The life, both mythological and modern, fascinated us, and we felt as if part of our souls were captured by the land of ancient Greece. If Athens won the centenary games we were going back.

RELAXING AFTER A HARD DAY AT THE EQUESTRIAN CENTRE

DRIVERS GAYL AND MIKE WEST

TRANSPORT INFORMATION BOOTH, MAIN DINING AREA, ATHLETES VILLAGE

NOC DRIVERS AND ASSISTANTS FOR GERMAN DELEGATION

NOC DRIVER JENNIFER ILTER, WEARING THE SILVER MEDAL WON BY JAMAICAN ATHLETE SANDY RICHARDS

VOLUNTEER DRIVERS JEAN AND BRUCE ROGERSON DID NOT GET TO DRIVE VISITORS IN THEIR VINTAGE 1928 WHIPPET

'But it was not to be. We watched while Atlanta triumphed in its bid, and then excitement grew – could it be Sydney in 2000?

'As history has it, the Olympic Games came to Sydney, and so our family passionately became involved. Preparation for the Games was all consuming, with driving modules for Jeff and ceremonies rehearsals for Katherine. When Jeff was notified that he would be driving for the Jamaican Team I bought him a Rastafarian hat, complete with crocheted dreadlocks! I just had to get in the Spirit!

'I can see on my desk the photo of our family in Greece, squinting into the golden light at the Temple of Athena in the ancient ruins of Olympia. At the very spot where we stood, at the site of the ancient Olympic Games, the Olympic Flame is kindled by the sun's rays using a polished cauldron. This year, the flame blazed on Sydney's skyline, a tribute to athletes, officials and visitors from around the world. We welcome them all as a nation and as a family. After all, we are all part of the Family of Man, and the Olympic Games are a celebration of that.

'And in four years' time, maybe we will be in Athens, following our Olympic Dream.'

'There were the knockers and constant rubbishing from the media. I stood firm, no one was going to make me think that Sydney couldn't do it, or that it was a waste of money. I still remember the times as a child, when I was driven past the stadium used in the first Modern Olympics in Athens, Greece.

'My wife and I were generously given two tickets to the Closing Ceremony from someone I had driven for one day. Oh, what a wonderful world! I had tears in my eyes when the F1-11 swept over us and the cauldron, and stole the flame that Australians had taken to be their own.

'I thank everyone involved, from the venue construction teams to *The most dedicated and wonderful volunteers ever*. I shall never forget those magical September days when Sydney hosted the 2000 Olympic Games, and I was part of it!' ... **Grant Baker (Transport)**

Last minute volunteer

Jo Anne Deady became a volunteer navigator only two days before the Games started, after seeing an advertisement on television. 'A rushed training program, and all of a sudden I was navigating buses round Sydney Olympic Park, Sydney Airport, Blacktown, Bondi Beach, Meadowbank, Lakemba, Warriewood and Rushcutters Bay. Long hours and tiring, but worth every minute of this exciting experience.'

My treasured memories

'The Olympic and Paralympic Games have been the most challenging and exciting events in my life. Firstly, I had the challenging task of training the ORTA volunteer drivers, non-drivers, bus drivers, truck drivers, lollipop people, load zone operators, and luggage handlers for both the Games.

'I have had the most wonderful experiences meeting people from all walks of life. The enthusiasm and keenness of the volunteers who attended the training sessions was like a disease. I was so sad when the Olympic training ended. A few months prior to the Games I rang ORTA and SOCOG to get in as a volunteer and was so disappointed because they didn't need me. I felt that everything had ended for me too suddenly and I wanted so badly to continue to be part of the Olympic fever.

'A week before the Olympics my husband passed away which dampened my spirit more. However, a week before the Paralympic Games commenced I was called to deliver some more training for bus drivers and I felt rejuvenated again. This time my determination to become a volunteer was very strong and I tried every possible means to get in.

'My perseverance finally paid off and I'm so thankful for becoming a fleet driver volunteer. I was on cloud nine! I met a lot of the drivers I had trained and many Paralympians, officials and coaches. This is one experience I will always treasure and even though I gave up so much of my own work hours to be part of these Games, I don't have any regrets.' ... **Rosemary Lim**

'I was asked to leave school at age 14 years to go out and work for the family, being migrants from Malta in 1957. In 1992 I decided to enter Sydney TAFE to complete high school. This I did, and it allowed me to achieve my Marketing Certificate at University.

'When I heard about the signing up of volunteers for the Olympic Games, I was ecstatic. I saw an opportunity to give back to my country something for allowing me to have such a high standard of living.

'My biggest support in all my endeavours was my wife with whom I have shared my life for 33 years. I'm sure all we volunteers had someone to support us through all this. Now back to reality, work that is, it's time to remember, enjoy and pass on the goodwill from the Games to whoever I touch. It has made me a better man because now I talk to strangers.' ... **Edward Zammit (Driver)**

'I was lucky enough to be an NOC driver assigned to Belgium during both the Olympic and Paralympic Games, based in the Athletes Village. The friendships I formed, both with the teams and other volunteers will remain a lifelong tribute to the power of the Games to bring people from every corner of the globe together.

'My experience throughout both Games was an amazing, life-changing experience which I would not have missed for the world, and I am incredibly proud to have been part of.' ... **Skye Lever (NOC Driver)**

'To the very kind and thoughtful person who handed my reading glasses in to the Coward Street Depot at Sydney Airport, *a very big thank you*. The tapestry case, which the glasses were in, is very special to me. I did not expect to receive the glasses back, and only asked at the depot on the off-chance that they may be there. Again, a very grateful Thank You!' ... **Valmai Kelaita (T3 Driver)**

Those wonderful years – 1997–2000

'My earliest memories of the Olympics go back to Melbourne in 1956, when my brother, James Rixon, was selected to carry the Olympic Torch on the Far North Coast of NSW. I was only eight years old at the time, and watching him run seemed like a good way to get a day off school!

'Moving forward to 1997, my daughter heard about people volunteering for the Olympic Games and said "Mum, you would like to do that!" So began my wonderful pre-Olympic experiences as a Pioneer Volunteer with the Amsterdam Team (Pioneer Volunteers were placed in teams named after former host Olympic and Paralympic cities). The excitement of working in the Hive (Volunteer base) at SOCOG, test events and promotional campaigns for volunteer recruitment, all made the journey to the Olympic and Paralympic Games a time to cherish.

'For several years I had been a volunteer driver with the NSW Tennis Open at White City, so when the Transport Fleet was developed at SOCOG I was asked to be part of it. One thing led to another, and I was included in the campaign to recruit drivers. This included bus, pamphlet and newspaper promotions, something my husband had to come to grips with, as he found it unnerving to drive the length of South Dowling Street with me on the back of a bus in front of him. After a newspaper promotion, he did create a stir when he went into work and announced "I slept with the page 2 girl!"

'The biggest honour of all my pre-Games activities was to be given the privilege of carrying the Paralympic Torch. My training for that "event" should have made me feel like one of the athletes, but I soon realised I was more suited to cheering them on!

'Now the Games are over, the wonderful memories of these last few years and the new friends I made will remain with me always. The Sydney Thank-You Parade through the city streets was a most amazing way for us all to be recognised, but knowing we had all helped to make the Sydney 2000 Games "the most successful ever" was sufficient reward.' ... **Joye Walsh**

'Okay, so there were mishaps involving some of the drivers, but wouldn't you expect that with the numbers involved, and the kilometres driven? Let's overlook these things for fear of embarrassing the offenders, and recognise the overwhelming success of the Transport Program.' ... **Dorothy Miller**

'Participating as a volunteer presents an intangible and valuable reward – the appreciation given by the person/s one is selflessly assisting. As a result, one hopes to become a better person and have a richer world worth living in and sharing. This has been my main motivation for being involved as an Olympic volunteer, and it has contributed to my admiration of the selfless contributions of other volunteer organisations – in particular the firefighters who helped save my parents' home in the bushfires of 1994.' **Raphael Sy**

Patricia MacDonald and George Sachse were part of the grassroots ORTA volunteers who helped out in the office at SOCOG, as well as test events involving visiting dignitaries. George became a Pioneer Volunteer in 1996, and prior to the formation of ORTA found himself in a variety of activities, of which he recalls: 'The oddest day I have had was planting trees in Sydney Park in pouring rain. We worked for about seven hours soaking wet and covered in mud. A more sorry looking mob you never saw, but we got the job done and laughed at each other's soggy appearance.'

Both Patricia and George relate to the most satisfying part of the whole experience as being the friendships and relationships developed. New acquaintances and old friendships renewed, particularly for Patricia who caught up with several former work colleagues from the Department of Motor Transport during the 1950s.

Patricia believes we are all better for the experience.

Patricia MacDonald and George Sachse

driver Joye Walsh – on the buses!

Neil Barnachea (customer services officer, transport mall, Olympic Village)

Alan and Karen Walsh had a 'parade' on 5 October 2000, to celebrate their 15th wedding anniversary!

Dora Lenane (centre) at 81 years was the oldest driver at the Jones Street depot

T1 Driver Experiences

'After being extremely well cared for during training by both TAFE staff and ORTA staff, the experience of collecting my car was a major drama – if I hadn't been so determined to see this through I would have gone home and called it off. However, the trauma of getting into Sydney Olympic Park for the first time was overcome, and I settled into an enjoyable driving experience.

'Everything was going fine until unfortunately, during my days off, a relief driver whilst stopped at a red light, was hit by a bus – "Millie" was written off. "My Millie" – brand-new, shiny, gone. Minor panic that night as a replacement vehicle was located and then delivered to my home. Thank you to both SOP and the Ryde Depot for their willingness to make this transition an easy one for me. Another Maroon Statesman – although this one was an "OLY" with Holden markings, still brand new with only 50 kilometres on the clock. My son was impressed, as "OLY" had a supercharged engine.

'"OLY" and I worked the next two weeks without any mishaps. Dropping off, picking up and parking (which I did very cautiously). I became very attached to "OLY" and felt sad for "Millie". I can tell you it was a culture shock getting back into my own car at the end of the games.' ... **Lyn Gaddes**

Special Moments for an Olympic/Paralympic Driver

'Two weeks before the Olympic Games began, I delivered the Spanish Team's grooms to the Equestrian Centre around midnight on one of western Sydney's chilliest nights. I took the lady member of the trio to her room. The first thing I noticed in the room were the heaters – her attention was taken by a child's painting "Sunset over Uluru" with the greeting "Welcome to Australia". The visitor longingly stroked a corner of the picture and said "You have spent millions of dollars on venues, you have recruited fifty thousand volunteers, but this is what I will treasure, the memory of a child's painting!"' ... **Damian Keane**

Can't drive! – Don't let that stop you!

'I live in a small country village called Binalong, which has a population of approximately 250 people. It is about four hours' drive from Sydney. When I got the opportunity for an appointment with ORTA, my partner offered to drive me to Sydney. What should have been a leisurely drive, turned out to be a frantic rush at the end due to a terrible smash on the freeway.

'Once I had been offered the position of Load Zone Operator I then had to fit into training schedules, which did not disrupt my business too much. For these sessions I caught a coach to Sydney. It passed through our village at 9.00am. Change at Yass, and then a half-hour stop at Goulburn, arriving in Sydney at 2.10 pm. The coach company was doing well out of me over the coming months, and I think I'd seen most of their videos.

'I was enjoying the build-up and the friendships being developed, but when I attended uniform and accreditation collection I nearly died – "Fleet Driver" on my accreditation. Excuse me, I don't and can't drive a car! Fortunately that was resolved, and I went on to experience one of the most thrilling periods of my life. Most of all I will not forget the people, especially those who allowed me to "house-sit" for them. Roll on the next Olympics.' ... Ms Lindsay McDonald

'I have said to my family and many friends, that I did not know the meaning of the word OVERWHELMED until I became a volunteer.' ... Lorraine Lambert (ORTA)

Paralympians and the Aussie public

'On the Tuesday after the Closing Ceremony, the NPC Drivers and Assistants looking after Mexico, took them on a sightseeing trip. First it was a tour of Waratah Park for some "bonding" with our wildlife, then off to Manly for lunch.

'Feeling a little dry, we called into the New Brighton Hotel for a small ale. As the Mexicans entered, the entire "bar" applauded. Not long after, a man came over with a big platter of food and presented it to the Mexicans. His words were: "My mates and I chipped in for this to say thank you for helping make our Games as good as they were." When the Mexicans tried to thank him, he said: "We are only brickies, but we have to thank you, not you thank us."

'To me this showed the Australian attitude and friendship that we like to think we all have. We all as volunteers did our job and enjoyed it. But we must not forget the wonderful Australian public and the way they opened their hearts.' ... Peter Mason (Fleet Driver)

'I travelled down and back from Newcastle by train and bus, which meant some six hours of travel each day. Including interviews, training, uniform issue and accreditation, Volunteers' Parade and 23 days of rostered duty, I spent over 220 hours of travel time during the 11 months.

'I do remember my tears of emotion, the boredom of waiting around, my anger at being denied entry to events to be with my passengers when there were hundreds of empty seats, and the frustration of being sent on trips where the passengers had already left before I arrived.

'However, I found the whole experience most exciting and uplifting. It is something I will never forget, and remains one of my proudest moments.' ... **David Winkelmann (T3 Driver – North Ryde)**

'When seeing an advertisement in a magazine for volunteer drivers for the Olympic Games, I couldn't help but say, *that's something I'd really love to do.* So, even though we live in Bathurst (a few hours' drive west of Sydney), with my husband and children's blessing I separated myself from them for four weeks, for an adventure that was far beyond all my expectations. Sure, the family missed me, but they were so proud of their wife and mother. Thanks to ORTA for your great organisation of everything.' ... **Linda Corner**

'The atmosphere and exuberance of the people involved in the Sydney 2000 Olympic and Paralympic Games was amazing, and something I will cherish for the rest of my life, something I will never forget.' ... **Donato Tomei (Driver)**

Not all Olympic experiences were as fulfilling as we would have hoped, and one NOC Driver who deserved better was **Yvonne Sayers**. Yvonne had the passion to help, but the delegation to which she was assigned did not give her any driving, and in most situations did not even show any interest in speaking with her. Finally, when no other driver was available, Yvonne was given a driving duty, but on arrival back at the Village, they tried to refuse her entry. After several other unpleasant experiences, Yvonne QUIT!

However, come the Paralympics, Yvonne was prepared to give it another try because she did not want to let anybody down. Yvonne explains: 'My experience this time was amazing. The first day made up for all the bad times with the other team. I could not believe that my 12 shifts just flew by. There were

PETER BOSEVSKI, NOC DRIVER, MACEDONIAN TEAM

T1 DRIVERS ATTACHED TO COCA-COLA

days when I was glad to get home though, especially after doing a shift from 1.00 pm to 1.30 am. But I didn't mind because they treated us so well.

'I have been a doer, rather than leave it to someone else, but after you see an athlete with no arms swim in a race and do it for their country, my problems are small in comparison. I would do it all again.

The joy and experience of volunteering were all that it was meant to be. It gave one self-respect and a sense of achievement in the knowledge that you were giving of your best. The whole experience can perhaps be encapsulated in what the late John F Kennedy once said: "Ask not what your country can do for you, but what you can do for your country." ... Elvan Tong (T3 Driver – North Ryde)

'Children can put us all in our place, as my 11-year-old grandson Mitchell did. He entered the accreditation area, and up to the front doors of the Downes Pavilion where he tried to pass Noel, our security person, a few police and Spectator Services volunteers who were stationed there.

'He asked Noel could he see his Pop. Noel asked Mitchell, "What does he look like?" He told Noel that his Pop was old, had grey hair and floppy ears. Thanks Mitchell!!!' ... Jim Stanley (Load Zone Officer)

'The 22 shifts I spent with Colombian Team and the volunteers in the Athletes Village were filled with drama, fun, sadness, highs, lows and I think I felt every emotion possible.

'I happened to be working dayshift on my birthday, the same day the Colombians were officially welcomed into the Village. The NOC assistants organised a cake. The Colombians and their official guests sang "Happy Birthday" in English and then in Spanish. It was a very special day, one I will cherish forever.' ... Sharon Gaha (NOC Driver)

A night to remember at the IBC

'It was a cold windy night midway through the Games – heavy rain lashed Sydney Olympic Park, accompanied by thunder and lightning. I arrived to work the graveyard shift at 10.00 pm, in my capacity as Load Zone Officer.

'The day supervisor told me that the night manager had taken sick, and that I would be in charge. This left just one other volunteer and myself, and although the weather worsened, we were managing. However, he decided at 1.00 am that he needed to go home!

'Well, the IBC had thousands of people working there, and at all hours they were coming and going. Fortunately I found a trusted ally in Michael Sykes, a bus driver from Toronto, NSW. Michael was of enormous help, and together we pulled off *A Night to Remember!* Thanks Michael – and that was just a part of a huge team effort put in by my supervisors and teammates which made that fortnight in September 2000 *Unforgettable!*' ... Philip Ellis

'Whilst on the job, what struck me most was the humanity displayed in everyone I met. For a complete fortnight, all barriers were broken, and instead of living in a society where everybody was relatively lifeless and unwilling to communicate, I found myself talking to strangers with brimming joy and energy. There may be language and cultural barriers, but nobody noticed. We communicate and share the Olympic spirit in whichever way we can. It is just the way the world ought to be, and it is great for us to be leading the rest of the world, with our evermore welcoming, reconciliating and embracing of multiple cultures. All the best for all my comrades, and may we meet again in the near future.' ... **Jeffrey Szeto (T3 Fleet Driver – North Ryde Depot)**

Thank You

'I did not have the opportunity to thank all the Driver Team Leaders at NOC Drivers' Headquarters in the Village, for the support and friendship during the Games. We all had such a fun time.

'To **Trudy, Lesley, Jan** and **Alan**, thank you for your guidance and leadership during some difficult situations.

'Although we all only met for such a short period of time, the love and compassion given to me on my last shift (2 October) when I received the sad news that my dear Dad had passed away, will be something that I will always treasure. 'God bless you all and may we all meet again.' ... **Beverley Roberts**

Even with the best of intentions, a part-time country school bus driver coming to Sydney for the first time in 20 years was going to find driving a city Olympic bus route a challenge! However, NOC Driver **Brian Ford** chose to see the funny side of his experience.

DRIVER MARGARET OSMAN SHARES THE SPIRIT WITH MEMBERS OF THE MARCHING BAND

THE LEWIS FAMILY – NEIL, SUE (TORCHBEARER) AND GLORIA

'Early one morning the bus at Lidcombe Station was in total darkness although half a load of volunteers had felt their way into seats. "Do you know where this bus is going?" a small, timid voice asked at the door. "The Olympic Village," offered a volunteer up front. "Yes, but which way?" asked the lost one. A chorus of helpful directions and comments were offered until one passenger called out, "Don't worry mate, the driver will be here in a moment and he will know where to go!" "I am the bus driver," was the pained reply.

'Trying to be helpful, in the best Australian tradition, the new chum was directed to the village by a route chosen for its directness rather than the authorised one.'

We were of all ages

'The queue at the IBC tuckshop was slower than normal. I looked at the girl assisting, and she was refusing to take the money from the customer. He was trying to pay with an old paper $2 note. I assured the lass it was legal tender, but she had to call her supervisor, she was too young to know!' ... Judith Duffy

'The fireworks were booming overhead at the conclusion to the Opening Ceremony when a fellow walked up to me and said his driver should have been here 30 minutes earlier. I said *no worries mate, I'll take you*. As we drove along, and got talking, I realised my passenger was Sergey Bubka, the famous Ukrainian pole-vaulter and Olympic Champion from Seoul 1988. We had a wonderful discussion all the way to the Regent Hotel, and I parted from him absolutely elated. Another great Olympic experience!' ... Ian Cook (T3 pool Driver)

'On reporting for duty on Sunday, 10 September, I was told that I would be taking the Mini Bus with six Nigerian Team members and officials to the airport, to meet and pick up one of their athletes. With the Nigerians still in a very sombre mood after the death of one of their athletes, I was told it was Glory Alozie, the fiancée of the deceased.

'There were a few challenges at the airport, and as I began to depart the airport with the media surrounding the vehicle, shouting questions and photographers' lights flashing – the only comment made as we were leaving was by one of the Nigerian officials that they "were only doing their job".

'I was to be with the Nigerians for the next four hours, as we had to go to the HAAC first for Glory to pick up her accreditation and then wait there, as all she wanted to see was her European coach.

'The experience of all of this has shown me how people from other countries handle the loss of a person so close.

'It was great to see later in the Olympics that Glory competed and received the Silver Medal in her event.' ... Jim Gilhooly (NOC Driver – Nigerian Olympic Team)

'As I said goodbye to one of the athletes at the airport she said: "The world says thank you, that's not enough, the whole universe says thank you." I felt humble.' ... **Janette Dive (Driver)**

'The clients I had for the Olympics and Paralympics were very interesting and exciting. It was a pleasure to drive them. But, to see their faces when they saw a kangaroo, koala, snake, etc. for the first time was priceless.' ... **Catherine Westley (T1 Driver)**

'The highest honour I received was when the Deputy Chef de Mission presented me with a Medallion from Moscow, which was his own. It was a midnight shift, and I was on the go all afternoon, he only needed to ask if I could do one more run and the last job, well of course I said yes, and then he handed me the keys and the Medallion. I didn't know what to say except thank you – *spasiba*.' ... **Virginia Hatzsy (NOC Driver – Russian Federation)**

Mrs Thea Archinal travelled from the town of Casino on the far north coast of NSW to be one of the NOC drivers for the small African country of Cote d'Ivoire (formerly Ivory Coast). Thea explains: 'They were a small team of just 25 members – ten officials and 15 athletes. I gained a more intimate understanding and appreciation of people who live in a far less affluent country than we do. One of the athletes brought with him to Australia 25 pieces of his own artwork; with the aim of selling them so he could pay his expenses. I managed to buy three pieces, and I feel I have not only got special souvenirs, but I have helped somebody else.'

'I was an ORTA driver based at Darling Harbour – my involvement was a last-minute one as a suggestion from my mother, **Marj Lynton**, who had been volunteering in sports entries at SOCOG since March. During my fast-forward training in August my father died (I was called out of a training day to attend his last moments in hospital) at which my mother almost decided to call it a day for her

CAN WE HELP YOU?

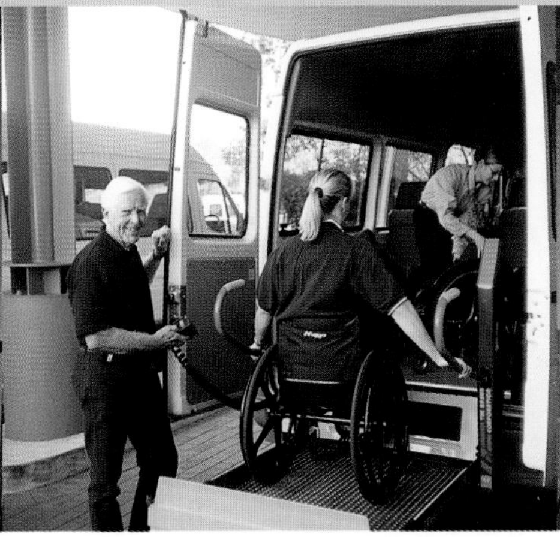

RAY HOSKIN TRYING OUT THE WHEELCHAIR LIFT

FLEET DRIVER JOHN PINCOTT

The support behind the volunteers – Bob Norrington (right) hosted Rob Nickalls (NOC driver) from Canberra

Mavis Booth (ORTA and Pioneer volunteer) receives award pin from Claire Houston (manager, Games Event Training)

volunteering. We managed to talk her back into it, and her Olympic experience (and mine as well) was memorable, amazing and therapeutic.

'Another big plus for my Olympic experience was that I met many lovely people through driving – drivers and passengers.' ... **Anne Lynton**

Dedicated ORTA and Pioneer Volunteer, **Mavis Booth**, helped in the early co-ordination of The Hive (level 5 – Jones Street), used her previous travel agency skills to arrange bookings for the Torch Relay, helped arrange the 'Two Years to Go and One Year to Go' functions conducted by her local Pioneer Volunteer team, drove for the Jones Street Car Pool, as well as participating in many test events.

During the Olympic Games, Mavis was well utilised as a T1 Driver with the IOC Marketing Team, based at the Regent Hotel. Then during the Paralympics, she drove one of the Deputy Mayors of the Athletes Village, and the Director of TAFE Campuses of the Hunter Valley. Mavis concludes: 'The whole experience of the last seven years has made an indelible watermark on my river of life forever.'

Doug and Gwen Gay of Penrith attended the first meeting for prospective volunteers held at the Penrith Council Chambers. They had the added interest in that their grandson, Aaron Bourne, is a wheelchair fencer. After working at test events, Gwen says: 'Volunteering has given thousands of eager and enthusiastic people memories that will last all their lives. They have helped Australia to put on the best Olympics/Paralympics ever, to show the world that people from all walks of Australian life are behind our SOCOG organisers, so that athletes from many countries can realise their dreams of competing in an Olympic/Paralympic Games. We have made friends among other volunteers that we hope will continue for many years. At the end of a day's work many of us are bone tired and footsore, but fully satisfied with the job we have done.'

Lucky Darling Harbour

ORTA kindly provided the opportunity for two lucky volunteers to win their very own Holden Commodore – one from the Olympic volunteers and one from the Paralympic volunteers. Both winners, **Grahame Small** and **Trish Sylvester**, were based at Darling Harbour. Thank you both for your contribution to the success of the Olympic and Paralympic Games.

'My second Olympic experience began with some frustrations in trying to offer my services as a volunteer as far back as 1994. It was not until 1999, that I got signed up, and commenced pre-Games duties as an ORTA tour guide. This was an absolutely wonderful lead-up to the Games, and I remember thinking that if I missed out on the Games I would still feel part of it. I met lots of interesting, enthusiastic and thoughtful people who kept the flame of Olympic desire alight. Also by chance I met my bridesmaid, Christine Martin, whom I had not seen for 30 years, and who also was a driver in 1956. That was my pre-Games highlight!

'In August 2000, I contracted Legionnaire's disease and was hospitalised. During the worst of this illness I thought my Olympic dreams were gone. I recovered sufficiently to be driving four weeks after discharge from hospital. One highlight was picking up Steve Redman, the British oarsman who had just won his fifth gold medal at five different Olympic Games, and taking him to a city destination where he was to be honoured for his achievement.

'In 1956 my experience as a volunteer "lady driver" was very different. It had to be, as I saw those Games through the eyes of a 19-year-old. I remember the French Count who gave me boxes of "candy", which were really chocolates. I remember the police who gave us right of way if we were flying our "standard", which indicated there was an official on board. I drove a 1936 Vauxhall tourer from Sydney to Melbourne to get there. It took two days, which was considerably quicker than the year before when I rode a pushbike from Sydney to Melbourne.

Dorene Schafferius (right) – Melbourne 1956

Dorene Schafferius – Sydney 2000

Paralympic Village, Transport Mall, Information Desk

PATRICIA AND FRED DEBNAM

NOC DRIVERS FOR POLISH OLYMPIC TEAM
(L TO R) MARK, BRUCE, ED, BARBARA, THERESA AND KERRY

FATHER AND SON DRIVERS IAN AND DAVID MANN

'The 1956 and 2000 Olympic Games have given me so many wonderful and exciting stories to tell my grandchildren, that I will have to maintain good health to buy the time it will take to relate them all.' ... **Dorene Schafferius**

Patricia and Fred Debnam enjoyed a busier pre-Games period than most as they gradually worked their way into full-time volunteer ORTA positions. Between them, Patricia and Fred have participated in test events for Shooting, Equestrian, Rowing, Wheelchair Tennis, plus attending many fairs, functions and fetes putting out the word about Olympic volunteering and seeking people to volunteer their services.

Fred drove over 20,000 kilometres with prospective Paralympians promoting the (LEAP) Link Elite Athlete Program, visiting schools and other venues.

During the Olympic and Paralympic Games, Fred was a T1 Driver for members of the Olympic Family, while Patricia was stationed at the Renaissance Hotel co-ordinating transport for the worldwide marketing arm of the Olympic Games. Both agree they would not have missed this experience for the world.

'It has been a momentous period since I sat up all night in September 1993, till I was asked to travel out to Sydney Olympic Park on the night of the Closing Ceremony to act as navigator for drivers unfamiliar with Sydney, bringing visitors back to the city.' ... **Geoff Sallis (T3 – Driver)**

Sally Liebowitz, Joan Allan, Peter Wilson, Athena Tzigeras, John Cullen, Peter Salier, Joe Minney, Peter Galle, Michael Sourjah, Danny Mok, Filomena Lay, Marguerite McNeill, David Soames, Phil Watts, Lynette Connor, Ian Conway-Powles, Sudeep Prakash and Neville Wenban were ORTA volunteers who expressed pride and satisfaction in their involvement. Your efforts are widely appreciated, especially by those who had direct contact with you.

A common thread in the attitude of volunteers is that nothing will stand in their way of becoming involved in the Sydney 2000 Olympic and Paralympic Games. Some of us even push ourselves to the limit, and that can be said of **Ken Palmer**, an ORTA driver attached to the Brazilian Team, and based in the Olympic Village. Ken had not been in good health for six weeks, but still began his driving commitment on Saturday, 2 September 2000; the day athletes would begin arriving in the Village.

Three days later Ken went into hospital, and two days later had an operation for bowel cancer. The concerned Brazilian Delegation sent flowers to Ken as their sincere appreciation of his effort to contribute to their Olympic experience. Ken's wife Julie rang to say how emotional and appreciative he was of the Brazilians' thoughts. She said, 'Ken just keeps looking at the flowers saying "At least I made the Olympic Games."' **Kenneth Palmer** died before the Sydney 2000 Olympic Games concluded, but he became an *Olympic Volunteer*.

The team of volunteers working with Ken, and who deeply respect his commitment were: **NOC Drivers – Jim Begley, Kevin Whalan, Gary Schloss, Geoff Rowell, Bob Bates, Lal Byers, Colleen Kime, Robyn O'Connor, Robyn Newberry, Graham Edgar, Christina Basta, Lee Klomp, Nicholas Cummings, Deidra Groppenbacher, Malcolm Halligan, Geoff Martin, Javier Fernandez and Ramon Fernandez, plus NOC Assistants – Julia Bonzi Fachini Gomes, Milton Da Rocha Netto, Conceicao Maria Da Costa Santos and Laurie Smith.**

'I was lounging around at the Athletes village entry when I was told my next assignment would be driving car number two of the Chad Olympic Delegation. Claude, our local interpreter, introduced me to the "President of Chad"– "No, no, I am the President of the Chad Olympic Committee", the tall, black administrator explained. The group consisted of two athletes, including a man and a woman runner, and six administrative staff. When I was told that their only male athlete was sick at the Royal North Shore Hospital it dawned upon me that this was an awkward situation for the President. All

For many, the journey was just as important and rewarding as the 'main event'. Here (L to R) Kevin Hudson, Danielle Sherry (ORTA staff), Geena Davis (archer), Marie Rumsey and George Sachse share the moment at the archery test event

Marcus Hiam from Warragul, Victoria

NORTH RYDE DRIVERS LOUNGE

(L TO R) MARGARET CHANEY, WINTER OLYMPIAN ZALI STEGGELL, GEORGE SACHSE AND JOHN CHANEY AT IMAX THEATRE

these administrators and their one male athlete out of action! We were soon off to visit him!

'Three days later, when I was back at the village, who should I see but Claude and the Chad delegation. I rushed up to them to enquire how their sick athlete was doing. "Ask him yourself!" volunteered Claude. I turned round to see a young, shining, happy face. "How are you?" I asked shaking the athlete's hand. "Fine, just fine." He said. I was so pleased another of our visiting delegations enjoyed a happy outcome.' ... **Tim Hookins (T3 Driver)**

Long lost friends

'Unbeknown to each other, we both decided to be volunteers for the Olympic and Paralympic Games, so we could be part of the *experience of a lifetime.*

'It was during the Paralympics that **Sue Williamson** and I met up again, 33 years after completing our nurses training at the Royal Alexandra Hospital for Children at Camperdown. I was a driver completing my third shift and as I went to sign off, I was surprised to see Sue working behind the desk! We had lost contact over the years, but when we met it was just like old times – thanks to volunteering!' ... **Dawn Howell**

'My most challenging trip was when I transported to the airport under time pressure, an official who had been responsible for broadcasting technology at one of the western venues. His car booking was somehow mislaid and I collected him at Westmead just before 10 am, for a noon flight to Los Angeles. He demanded I get him to Mascot in four minutes, or let him drive! Neither was possible, but I delivered him (via the Eastern Distributor) safely to the International terminal before 11am – good enough time. I helped carry his bags (which were too heavy for one person) into the Departure lounge and passed him to another transport volunteer, but narrowly escaped being booked for not remaining with my vehicle on the Departure ramp. My passenger stormed off without a glance or further word! We may have stumbled, but we did not let him down!' ... **Ken Broadhead**

ORTA volunteer Sophia Hendel broadcasting on community radio.

(L to R) John Brilman, John Damon, Wim Drayer, Jack Nieuwlind and Hermann Steenhouwer – pre-games drivers

Sophia Hendel was very happy to be accepted as an ORTA Driver based at North Ryde Depot. However, her driving was cut short by illness. Sophia was not prepared to sit at home and feel sorry for herself, instead she came into North Ryde Depot and used her Community Radio skills to interview volunteers based there. Following are brief extracts of what some of those volunteers shared with Sophia:

Amy Hewiston is studying Travel and Tourism, and saw this experience as an extension of her studies.

Karl and June Ritar live on 1000 acres near Mudgee in central western NSW, where they grow sheep, lavender plants and the NSW State Flower – Waratah. June remembers watching the Melbourne Olympics through shop windows, and while in her position at North Ryde Depot did not get to any events at the Sydney Olympic Games, she lived the event through the experiences of others, including husband Karl who was a T1 Driver for the Austrian IOC member Dr Leopold Wallner.

Janet Porter was very happy to have also worked at UDAC (Uniform Distribution and Accreditation Centre) – such an efficient and friendly location.

Ross Jacob met a fellow volunteer he had not seen for 30 years, and was glad this event brought them together to share so many memories.

Barbara Sanders sometimes had problems understanding where her guests wanted to go, but always got there and departed friends!

Don Anderson at 67 years is a retired bulldozer driver, but assured us that his past career was not a criterion for driving Commodores.

John Edwards enjoyed the diverse nationalities he had the pleasure of driving.

Shiv Gopalia migrated from the United Kingdom only six months before the Olympic Games, and enjoyed the multicultural aspect of the whole event.

Lawrie Merrigan is a retired Victorian Police Officer who 'just had to be part of the whole event'.

Sue Hurndell sang in clubs and on cruise ships for 20 years, but now had a very supportive family behind her involvement as an ORTA driver.

Mervyn Ritzrod was a T1 Driver for the Danish Delegation, and believes this project has added years to some people's lives.

Marion Goord was tired of people knocking the Games, so decided to help make it happen.

John Cowin (from Perth) – early in the year was 1200 kilometres north of Perth, when his son rang and suggested he come and stay with him in Sydney to be a volunteer!

Adrian Trothe moved to Sydney years ago from Nyngan in north-western NSW. No real reason for volunteering, except the job had to be done, so lets do it!

Joe Khoury's normal occupation is a plumber, but here he enjoyed driving Royalty, IOC Members, and the Mayor of Athens.

Emmanuel Mifsud spent four years driving semi-trailers in Europe, but enjoyed helping fellow volunteers in making their lives easier as Transport Despatcher.

Mohamed Zuhaia is a registered Male Nurse, but volunteered to return something to Australia.

Bill Howden made his first contact with Australian Olympians in 1952 while working in a cycle factory in Birmingham, England. 'We built wheels for them, and after they won gold in Helsinki, they came back to thank us.' Bill's second Olympic experience was as a T2 Driver, but one of his most interesting experiences was during the Paralympics when given the job of driving a Dutch official and his wife from the Novotel Brighton Beach to the velodrome. The official was blind, so asked Bill to describe the suburbs through which they were travelling. Bill was amazed at the keen perception of the man, and really enjoyed sharing the surrounds with him. However, on his return home, Bill's wife wasn't sure what he had been drinking when he said that he had taken a blind man on a sightseeing tour!

DRIVER MATTHEW LLOYD

ESTHER DEAN REGISTERING DRIVERS – PARALYMPIC VILLAGE

CRAIG HAWKE – 'THE BEST SIX WEEKS OF MY LIFE!'

Jan Potapof has a Christmas message – December 1999

Banner made by Margaret Dunn for the volunteers parade

(L to R) Carrol Reynolds (Adelaide), Lionel Barral (Sydney) and Margaret Dunn (Orange)

Transport volunteers relax after a long day at the Equestrian Centre

Geoff Scott and Lizzie Kornhaber – T1 drivers for IBM delegates and German IOC delegate Dr Thomas Bach, respectively

Margaret Donnelly (Venue Staffing) and Barbara Sanders (NOC Transport) renewed friendship at the Athletes Village after meeting on a ship to England in 1970

KENYAN NOC DRIVERS AT VOLUNTEERS PARADE

TRANSPORT VOLUNTEERS AT STATE HOCKEY CENTRE AND STATE SPORTS CENTRE

DEDICATED ORTA VOLUNTEERS BACK AT NORTH RYDE DEPOT IN LATE NOVEMBER 2000, HELPING WITH DISTRIBUTION OF THE FINAL *TRANSPORTA* MAGAZINE

INAUGURAL DRIVERS' LUNCHEON AFTER VOLUNTEERS PARADE

Volunteers Parade...

RYDE AQUATIC CENTRE
TAFE

CONGRATULATIONS VOLUNTEERS!
TRAINED BY
TAFE

LANGUAGE SERVICES

If ever there was a segment that reflected the multicultural aspect of Australia, it is Language Services.

While more and more second and third generation Australians are beginning to learn a second language, it is the more recent immigrants who have stepped forward to share their skills in providing a very necessary communication link with the world's visitors.

Not all volunteers enjoyed an easy lifestyle prior to coming to this country, and for that reason **Frederick Shaliapin** saw the Olympic volunteer experience as an extension of his contribution back to the country which gave him a new life.

Born in The Peoples Republic of China in 1931 to a French mother and Russian father, Frederick found himself in a prisoner of war camp in the early 1940s because his father had moved to Australia. Upon his release Frederick was fortunate enough to join his father in Australia, and some years later commenced his community contribution as a member of the Bondi Surf Life Saving Club.

Frederick's Olympic and Paralympic experience has not only given him the satisfaction of contributing to the communication of the world's people, but provided him with friendships for a lifetime.

Albert Alegre is not particularly a sports fan. However, Albert is backing up for his second Olympic Games, having volunteered in Barcelona in 1992. Albert is fluent in Catalan, Spanish, French and English, and holds a professional level interpreting accreditation.

So many good aspects of Albert's Barcelona experience ensured he would not let the opportunity pass him by now that he is living in Australia.

Linkio Pekka, a native of Finland, did not have large demands for his Finnish and Swedish language skills due to the good English skills of the Nordic countries. However, Linkio was an enthusiastic supporter for Australia gaining the Olympic/Paralympic nomination by gathering names from the Australian/Finnish community.

MANDARIN INTERPRETER JOY LU

MARIANNE BARRY AT THE OLYMPIC VILLAGE MULTILINGUAL SWITCHBOARD

Linkio became a Pioneer Volunteer in 1997 as part of the London Team based in the Eastern Suburbs of Sydney, and was honoured to have the privilege of carrying the Olympic Torch on Day 79 at Maclean on the New South Wales north coast.

Spanish language specialist **Luis Lopez** gives a big THANK YOU to his wife and children for their support and understanding in allowing him the time to participate in a total of 22 shifts. Luis and his family live at Wollongong, south of Sydney, and his travel time could vary from 90 minutes by car to three hours by public transport each way.

Originally putting his name down as a volunteer in 1993 to support Australia's bid, Luis has taken every opportunity to contribute, and owes his allocation to the Blacktown Aquilina Centre to the fact that he spent five days as a volunteer for the Baseball Intercontinental Cup in November 1999. Luis enjoyed his association with the Cuban Baseball and Softball Teams as friendly happy-go-lucky people. It was worth the long drives.

'I am a teacher of languages, so naturally enough I joined Language Services. I met other "wannabe" interpreters, wide-eyed amateurs like myself, swept up in the Olympic spirit. They were of all ages and backgrounds. There were University students doing it as part of their course, there were elderly couples keen to add to their already rich tapestry of life's experiences, but we all had one thing in common: we all enlisted with the innocent enthusiasm of ANZAC recruits.' ...
Brian Doughan

Nordic-Scandinavian Interpreters at the Multilingual Switchboard

Valentina (Tina) Thomas (German interpreter) 'I couldn't believe my luck when the German silver medal winner threw his bouquet into the audience, and I caught it

Quotes from the Language Services Daily

A volunteer's perspective of the Games.

'Working in the Language Services section I feel like I'm on a sea voyage or in the United Nations. Or, more to the point, in the Tower of Babel. So many people, each with a different story, a different language and yet all moved by a peculiar sense of achievement to help these Olympics even if the contribution is seemingly minimal. Personally, I was very honoured when approached a year ago to work as a volunteer in the Olympic Games. Well, sprinter I am not, nor a swimmer, but yes, I do interpreting and translating in Polish. Now after travelling in the dark, I am almost a sprinter, almost a jumper, etc. I jump on the bus, sprint to the train, no gold medals for that. But the most rewarding thing for me is the feeling of camaraderie, belonging to the vast group of blue-coated Olympians and the smiles we exchanged and the looks we get as early as 5 am on the trains. Whatever moments I will cherish, I will remember most of all the change from silent train commuters to extrovert and happy fellow Olympian Sydneysiders. Long live my memories.' ... **Henryka Bochenek**

The end of Shooting!

'JOY, SADNESS, UNREAL OR JUST PLAIN PROUD.'
These are the words of **John Kapos**, Language Manager at the shooting venue.

'... to see the great Michael Diamond shoot for gold. Russell Mark ... take the silver ... is only the beginning. To help athletes with language problems, and have a great team put it all together. Seeing a great team of Language Service volunteers escort medal winners to doping control and see the faces of the athletes with a sigh of relief when someone is there to help them ... watching the joy on the athletes' faces when we tell them that they have to follow us to the medal ceremonies ... The biggest thrill is the end of the day when we have a venue team debrief and they constantly thank Language Services for a great day's work.

'All this wouldn't and couldn't have happened without my great team of Language Service volunteers. I would like to thank them for all their hard and vigilant work.'

Olivia Ristovska is very appreciative of her family in Macedonia supporting her to attend college in Australia. Little did she know that this would lead to being a Language Specialist at the Olympic Games.

However her Olympic experience would not have happened if friends Kirsten and Bret had not looked after her son Christian. Like many volunteers, Olivia owes much gratitude to the 'invisible volunteer brigade'; people like her friends Vlado, Sandra, Michael, Maria, Angie, Luisa and Dr Michael Payton. Olivia says, 'their support made me become stronger and more confident in a foreign country.'

'As long as I can remember, I always wanted to work at the Olympic Games, but I thought that I would not be able to. So just imagine my surprise when I saw an advertisement in the *Sunday Mail*

(Adelaide) for volunteers. I had the opportunity to see many events during my role as Greek Language Specialist, and I have developed many friendships while in Sydney.

'I am definitely glad to have taken up this opportunity to volunteer at the Games and I am fortunate to have come all the way from Adelaide in order to give of my services at the heart of the action – in Sydney.' … **Vicki Savvas**

'Being a Gemini I am forever ready for adventure. Moreover, I lost my husband in 1999, and decided that volunteering for the Olympic Games would be a panacea. And so it proved to be.

'As Hungarian Language Specialist my main venues were the Pavilions and the Dome. However, being allocated the position of marshal at the Superdome for the Opening Ceremonies was something special. The Ceremony was also a family affair in that my daughter **Linda Deutsch** was also involved as flag and placard bearer assistant.

'On deeper reflection, the sights and sounds which filled the enormous Superdome and the endless concourse on opening night left me with the most enduring images.

'A surging tide of colour was rising on the huge staircase leading up to the top level, where I stood waiting for "my" athletes and officials from Japan and Jordan. Within minutes a kaleidoscope of faces and uniforms filled the concourse to capacity, visual flashes of tricolours, bright turbans, dazzling silver and gold beads on national costumes, the mottled tempera of the Japanese capes.

'The Sydney Superdome became the centre of the world. Its great spaces echoed the hubbub of many tongues as athletes were swapping greetings and Olympic pins. I felt quite dizzy from the sensations around me. My throat swelled then as it did a fortnight later when all those wonderful people lining the route said "Thank You" for something that I enjoyed doing so much.' … **Ily Benedek**

'I was stationed at the Whitewater Stadium in Penrith on the day of the Men's C2 Final. The Polish team had just completed its run and the two athletes were on the far side of the mixed zone, just

Velella Timmony (second from left at back) says 'we at Language Services had just the best time'

Estonian Language Specialists with Olympic mascots Syd, Millie and Olly. (Standing L to R) Olav Pihlak, Lea Holm, Marika McLachlan, Tiina Iismaa. (Kneeling) Vella Pihlak and Siiri Iismaa

close enough for me to hear them. They were very happy with their performance and thought they came in sixth or at best fourth, not realising they already had the Bronze Medal. When the French team missed the last gate and incurred a huge penalty, the Poles were catapulted to Silver medal position. An official informed them of their standing. At first there was utter disbelief, more discussion and then that magic joy of athletes who feel they have achieved the impossible and have gained the ultimate reward of a medal. I felt truly privileged to witness their joy and later interpret their jubilation for the Olympic reporter.' ... **Yolanda Seach, Language Specialist (Polish)**

Tongue Twister was the newsletter produced by SOCOG to keep language specialists up to date on activities in their area. Italian Language Specialist **Rosa Cavallaro** is a volunteer who owes her Olympic experience to this newsletter. Seeing a friend reading the newsletter in mid-1999, Rosa expressed an interest in becoming a volunteer. Her contact with SOCOG led to a stimulating interpreting course followed by the thrill of being in the thick of activity at the Main Press Centre and the Baseball and Softball venue at Blacktown.

While Rosa was able to take annual leave for the duration of the Olympic Games, she spent the first two weeks of September working her regular job and volunteering at the Main Press Centre on weekends. Rosa says: 'This volunteering was the greatest experience of my life.'

'Although there was not much need for my German interpreting skills at the venues I was allocated, I had a fantastic time and am so glad that I have done it.' ... **Barbara Addison-Weiss**

Helen Caudullo was a Language Specialist in the Olympic Village and at Sydney Olympic Park. Like many others she had a dream to carry the Olympic Torch. It was not to be, but she felt privileged to be able to at least hold the unlit Torch. 'It does not matter to me, the fire lives within me. It represents so many things, Love, Peace, Courage, Power of all spirits in one, Hope and Eternity and the will to carry on no matter what.'

NUMBER OF LANGUAGE SPECIALISTS PER LANGUAGE

Albanian	3	Farsi	10	Lithuanian	6	Slovenian	1
Amharic	3	Finnish	6	Macedonian	4	Spanish	85
Arabic	43	French	83	Maltese	1	Swahili	2
Armenian	3	German	43	Mandarin	75	Swedish	4
Azen	1	Greek	29	Mongolian	2	Tagalog	3
Bahasa	12	Hebrew	3	Nepali	2	Thai	3
Bosnian	1	Hindi	8	Norwegian	2	Turkish	9
Bulgarian	11	Hungarian	32	Polish	29	Ukrainian	14
Cantonese	7	Italian	59	Portuguese	35	Urdu	1
Croatian	7	Japanese	73	Romanian	12	Vietnamese	3
Czech	20	Kazakh	1	Russian	65		
Danish	2	Khmer	2	Serbian	15		
Dutch	3	Korean	47	Sinhala	1		
Estonian	5	Latvian	6	Slovak	9	**TOTAL**	**906**

THE CLOCKWORK OLYMPICS

Oh wonder of wonders
How great is this clock
That ticks with precision
Yet solid as rock

With dozens of levers
And hundreds of springs
Each knowing their movement
Each coiling their swings

And thousands of cog wheels
With thousands of teeth
Each measuring so truly
Above and beneath

Yet all these are people
With feelings and thought
Their skills and their service
So willingly brought

If sitting or standing
Or static or not
Each ticking in union
With time running hot

There's people with rosters
And schedules and lists
And those at computers
With so many twists

And language frustrating
With such acronyms
So hard to remember
What penance for sins

Talk never to strangers
My Mother had said
May God rest her dear soul
She'd surely see red

With strangers so friendly
How can one not talk
As towards a venue
Together you walk

For all of a sudden
You find that you've got
New brothers and sisters
Of whom you knew not

All linked by an outfit
That binds and that bonds
So coloured, so stylish
Supplied all by BONDS

With sleeves that are labelled
Like parts made for clocks
The sleeves that distinguish
Who ticks and who tocks

Our fear was the transport
How long will one wait
At stations and bus stop
But no worries mate

The clock face of Sydney
With clock works behind
The time is soon coming
When we can unwind

These feel-good Olympics
The best we are told
Hooray for Australia
The great Green and Gold

CITIUS ALTIUS and FORTIUS
Mean doing one's best
You've done us proud Sydney
And now we can rest.

Extract from verse by
Don Zerafa (Volunteer,
Language Services)

'Throughout the parade the atmosphere was electrifying, people from different cultures were socialising. I renewed my old friendships and made new ones.' …
Antoinette Awad – language specialist (Arabic)

Helen Caudullo dreamed of carrying the Olympic torch

SPECTATOR SERVICES

While no group of volunteers were more important than others, the group that were more *in the faces* of the public, athletes and media, were the *yellow sleeve brigade,* Spectator Services. They directed you, advised you, answered questions, entertained you, and knew everything (or sent you to the next *yellow sleeve* if they didn't). They were outside every venue, inside every venue, and at just about every point in between. Their stories of passion, dedication, excitement, and of the wonderful emotional experiences, could fill thousands of pages.

'We met in our first year at Willoughby High School in 1942. In the following five years we competed with one another in House Sports. In those days, which were War Years, SPORT was the highlight of our school lives. We also realised that if we ran fast enough and made the team we had two days or more off school for Interschool Competition — so we ran! Our friendship continued over the years, we shared the joys and tribulations of marriage, children, holidays and trips.

'On reaching my 69th year, I decided to volunteer for the Olympic Games. I quietly went off and did just that, and then told everyone. I asked **Alyson** to join me as it would be so much more fun to do it together. So there we were in the year 2000 at the tender ages of 70 and 71 donning our uniforms and rising at the crack of dawn to do our best. It has been such a lot of fun.' ... **Nell Wright.**

Does it get any better than this?

'From our part of the Stadium, the views of the track and field events are breath-taking. What other job in the world provides the fringe benefit of witnessing such amazing athletes representing their countries?

'At the end of my shift, the train is crowded and I have to stand all the way to Central Station. My feet are aching, I just miss my connecting train, and so have to wait for the next one. If this happened to me at any other time, I would have been fuming, but, today, it doesn't seem to matter. I am in "dreamland", waiting with a smile on my face, when a lady stands beside me and says "You look like you have had a good day." "Yes", I reply. "It doesn't get any better than this."' ... **Douglas Cairns (Spectator Services Host)**

'I wanted to write and tell you how proud I am of my family. My mum is a volunteer for both the Olympics and Paralympics. She has two sisters, a brother and a brother-in-law who are also volunteers. They have come from everywhere to be part of the Olympic Games. They are all staying together in Concord West, and this is the first time all siblings have resided under the one roof together since they started leaving

Anne and Tony Nastasi put on hold their tenth wedding anniversary celebrations and Tony's 37th birthday celebrations as they were celebrating something bigger – Sydney's Olympic Games! Here they are seen relaxing in the Domain after the volunteers parade

Margaret and Earl Gray – 'like having a wedding anniversary every day'

(L to R) Judith Kane, Ray Kane, Bev Hyett, Keith Meredith and Helen Spier

Eighty-year-old Joy Wallman was thrilled to receive a letter from the CEO of SOCOG, Sandy Hollway, thanking her for her contribution

(L to R) Linda Restuccia, Cecelia Tesoriero and Christine Rocca together by chance after being given free tickets

home about 35 years ago! My grandmother who resides in a hostel in Taree (four hours north of Sydney) has come down to stay as well to share the Olympic spirit with them. The house is like Central Station! Each person is volunteering in a different area; one in the Athletes Village, one in the Superdome, one at the Hockey Venue, and ushering and another driving; and all are on different shifts. Needless to say the front door key has been duplicated several times over! They have given up their holidays, their families, paid their own fares, etc. to come, and they are having a ball doing it. It has been so good to see them all together again. Without the Olympics in Sydney, this would never have happened and it will probably be the last time that their mother sees them together. The names of these wonderful family members are … **Helen Spier** (nee Meredith) from Wingham, NSW, **Beverley Hyett** (nee Meredith) from Woodvale, WA, **Judith Kane** (nee Meredith) and **Ray Kane** from Concord West, NSW and **Keith Meredith** from Victoria. You have made me so proud.' … **Suzanne Wallace.**

'On Saturday, 30 September I arrived at 6.00 am and met up with my cousin **Cecelia** to start our day's work. Soon after we both met my sister **Linda** who was from the South Gate area, allocated inside the Stadium to assist the spectators. We decided to try to meet up later in the day.

'Cecelia and I were rostered on together for the first time in front of the Olympic Stadium. We enjoyed greeting the early workers and spectators. At about 12.30 pm a lady and her son approached Cecelia and I with a dilemma, she had been given two tickets for the soccer final, but had already bought two tickets to the basketball finals. So therefore, she offered us the two soccer final tickets. We were so pleased as we had finished our last shift.

'As we slowly made our way into the Stadium and reached our seats, to our astonishment and amazement, Linda was seated next to us. Linda received her ticket from a stranger who thought she was doing a wonderful job on the megaphone and assisting others, that he thought she deserved the ticket.

'Can you believe the three free tickets, 110,000 people and we ended up sitting right next to each other. We could not have planned it better, we feel like it was a thank you for all our voluntary work.' … **Christine Rocca (Spectator Services Host)**

Family affair and unexpected meeting

Sue Air was thrilled that her husband, son and daughter would all join her in the Olympic experience. Her husband **Dennis** was involved at the International Broadcast Centre, her daughter **Georgina** carried the Olympic Torch in the test event at Nowra on the NSW south coast, while her son Hamish was a tour guide.

Sue was based at the Equestrian Centre, and relates this story: 'My son was a tour guide for one of the major sponsors, Panasonic, and told me that the Equestrian Centre was not on his itinerary. Halfway through the first Cross Country day at a road access point I was swapping team members to new positions and out of the blue I heard "Mum I'm here!" and there was **Hamish**. He knew I was out there, but in the 25 kilometres of course had no idea where. He said his mission was to find me in 50,000 people!

'Some of the American tourists wanted to see this event at short notice, and he had no way of letting me know. He said his guests would be really happy to know he'd been successful. It made my day. He was the only person I knew in all that crowd!'

A different challenge for the boy from Western Australia

Before taking up his role as a Spectator Services Host at the Main Press Centre, **Andrew Curtis** from WA was a Performer Marshal at the Opening Ceremony, and it is in this capacity that he relates the following anecdote:

'Due to the secrecy surrounding the artistic content of the ceremony, there was heightened interest from the media for a glimpse of any performer/costume, etc. which could have provided some clue or insight of what was to come in the Opening Ceremony.

'A group of us were therefore given instructions to prevent the exit of any performer who was wearing any body make-up or pieces of costume. Whilst carrying out this role, I was approached by an attractive young lady (18 or 19 years old I guess) who was most insistent that she be allowed outside of the venue.

'I reiterated my instructions but she still wanted to speak to my supervisor. Unfortunately for her – the message was repeated, and she left disappointed. As we were walking back to my initial post, I asked her why she was so desperate to leave.

'She said "I need my underwear." My response was, "Excuse me" (hoping I had misheard her!) She replied, "You don't understand, I need my underwear to perform."

'To which I countered , "I'm sure you do!"

'She then explained that her role in the Nature section had been changed from a Blue Leschenaultia

Joy and Voula Fotopoulos – 'the sisters' as they became affectionately known. Their shifts in ticketing, ushering, marshalling and access monitoring were identical

Members of the West Epping Uniting Church in Sydney covered a variety of volunteer roles

In training for 2016 (wherever that may be!) Mavis Hall with two-year-old granddaughter Kirstie

Table tennis crew Matty Padley, Max Steel and Kirsten Millerd relax at the break-up party

The Sowter family (L to R) Jason, Rosy and Trent. The Sowter family of Blakehurst NSW have always done things together, and volunteering at the Sydney Olympic Games was no exception

Hatch (formerly BHP Engineering) volunteers (L to R) Peter Seward, Hulusi Ozdemir, Arun Mukhopadhyay, Andrew Curtis, Kaye Metaxas and Wendy Diver

to a Water Lily and the only underwear she had with her was black. Given that her costume was relatively sheer and lighter in colour, she now needed natural or "nude" coloured lingerie. Upon hearing her plight, I explained that I was sympathetic to her problem and that although she wasn't permitted to exit the venue, I could possibly assist.

'With this news her demeanour changed and she quickly phoned her mum advising her that a man named Andrew would be coming to meet her to collect "The Package".

'Armed with a brief description of her mum's car and rego number, I headed off to the hastily arranged meeting point.

'Upon reaching the location, I was greeted by her mum who arrived shortly afterwards, with a plastic bag in her hand. With pleasantries exchanged, she sent me on my way with the comment "Tell my daughter they are clean" – frankly I thought this was a little too much information.

'When I returned with the package, the young lady said, "Think yourself honoured – it isn't every day that my mum gives my underwear to a strange man." With that she gave me a peck on the cheek, thanked me and headed back to the arena.

'And this was Day 1!!!!'

'I continued working in my full-time job and volunteered on my rostered days off, but the enjoyment and satisfaction that I gained overtook the tired feelings easily.' ... **Fiona McLennan (Spectator Services Host – Aquatic Centre)**

'I wanted to be a volunteer as I love Sydney and wanted to "show off" our city – I also thought that if there were enough volunteers it would save SOCOG and the State of NSW money. Another reason was the fact that my father had really wanted to take us to the 1956 Melbourne Olympic Games, but having four children less than ten years of age, it was financially not possible; so I was also doing it for him.

'I was very pleased that no matter what shift I was on, or what day it was, the volunteers looked smart – it was a great uniform, and we were proud to wear it.' ... **Elizabeth Gibson (Spectator Services Host)**

'We would like to thank all those people who made this event happen, and enabled us to give back to our City and Country our small token of gratitude for living and growing up in the best place in the world.' ... **Ian and Gwen Jarratt (Spectator Services Hosts – Aquatic Centre)**

'I went to Melbourne in 1956 for the Olympic Games. I was 16 years old and had just completed my Leaving Certificate. It was such a wonderful experience in my life that I vowed and declared I would attend every Olympic Games from then on. Needless to say I haven't!

'However I became a volunteer for Sydney and I met some lovely people, we all had our own stories to tell. I even met one lady whom I did my pathology training with 40 years ago. I was amazed at the number of people who came from outside Sydney to volunteer, paying their own expenses. I have been greatly surprised and thrilled by the response of everyone to us.' ... **Jill Greene**

'I first volunteered in 1998 when I was still living in my hometown of Hobart. My main motivation was the fact that my grandfather, Tom Darcey, was in the Australian Rowing Team at the 1948 London Olympic Games. I knew I would never compete as an athlete, but still wanted to have my own Olympic experience, to follow in his footsteps in some small way. I was very excited once we moved to Sydney, to know I would be involved more than the passive observer.' ... **Jane Green**

SPECTATOR SERVICES HOSTS ROBERT AND SUZANNE DON'T LET WET WEATHER DETER THEIR CHEERFUL GREETINGS FOR GUESTS TO THE MILLENNIUM MARQUEE

JUBILANT VOLUNTEERS AND STAFF CUTTING THE 'THANKS FOR THE MEMORIES' CAKE AT THE CONCLUSION OF ACTIVITIES AT THE AQUATIC CENTRE

ASSISTING SPECTATORS IN SYDNEY OLYMPIC PARK (L TO R) – FELIPE CANO, DELMAR GABRIEL AND PATRICK TAM

IRENE MACMORRAN (SPECTATOR SERVICES HOST)

LURDES SOUSA LEMOS (SPECTATOR SERVICES HOST)

'After the Closing Ceremony it was very hard to say "goodbye", but on 5 October 2000, we found each other again at the Volunteers Parade. The emotion was incredible: Tears, hugging, laughing, we were like happy children, it was such a good feeling. I was on cloud nine, ten feet tall and tried to savour every single moment.

'I close my eyes and I'm there – Hear the Buzz, the noisy people, the laughter. The spectacular lighting at night, the Cauldron – The Flame. The sweet experience will live in my heart till I die. It was like a different world, a fairytale.' ... **Julia Jaksa**

'The whole experience of the Games was life-altering, mainly because of the friendships that developed along the way, and the different people I met from around the world. It was incredible listening to everybody's stories and finding out what it was that compelled them to become volunteers. It was interesting to find that most of us were there for similar reasons, to have fun and to be part of the Olympic experience, and at the same time witness history in the making.' ... **Diane Karalis (Spectator Services Host – Aquatic Centre)**

Reason for volunteering – 'Well, I am a cancer survivor; wanted to say thanks for my "bonus" time (The Here and Now). 'My Olympic journey began the day I sat and faithfully filled in the application form from *The Sunday Telegraph*, answering every question and hoping to be accepted, being an older person (then 63 years).

'Best memory of initial interview at Parramatta – did I have any questions – Yes! "Am I too old?" Answer – "Only if you want to be." WHAT A BLAST – I felt 28 and at the starting blocks!' ...
Shirlee Wicht (Spectator Services Host – Olympic Stadium)

'The most amusing situation was when I was put in charge of the *blue* no standing zone, and who do you think I asked to move on, unbeknown to me, their Royal Highnesses the King and Queen of Sweden, but they were cool about it, they were just like anyone else enjoying the Games.

'It was my 50th birthday the day of the Opening Ceremony, and it was 51 years ago when my family arrived in Australia as Russian immigrants from China. This is also to say Thank You Australia for having us as your citizens.' ... **Irene Macmorran (Spectator Services)**

The 'coat and arms' theory

PERSON TYPE 1: BOTH ARMS LOOPED THROUGH STRAPS

This person will have a need for security and will enjoy being in control. Normally armed with a clipboard and will assess all situations exceedingly carefully.

PERSON TYPE 2: ONE ARM IN STRAP AND ONE OUT

An unstable personality liable to changes of mind/opinion and therefore will have a radio in order to inform others of his/her brilliant new ideas.

PERSON TYPE 3: BOTH ARMS OUT

A free-floating soul who goes wherever life takes them, accepts any challenge. This type may well have both clipboard and radio, often leaving them in odd places whilst seeking new and wonderful experiences.

Yours neurotically, ... **Gill Amos (Spectator Services)**

'The Paralympics was one of the most amazing experiences I have had in my life. It was wonderful to see all the spectators (including the school children) leaving the Tennis Centre with smiles and looks of amazement on their faces. I would even hear people talking of the admiration they had for the athletes, and how inspirational they were – some even telling me that they planned to take up sporting activities (including tap dancing) again.' ...
Katharine Barker (Spectator Services – Tennis Centre)

John Henderson said that despite being advised in the RAAF never to volunteer for anything, he derived a great deal of pleasure as a volunteer for the Olympic Games

(L to R) Gordon White, Richard Benjamin, Jackie Morling, Lisa Guillemot and Barb Jankovic (Equestrian Centre)

Helen Shaw (Spectator Services) – 'I feel much richer in my life now for this experience'

'My venue, the Equestrian Centre, was the most beautiful setting. Those early mornings, the mist rising, the horses and riders cantering around the stables, the friendly riders always so ready to give us a cheery wave … Coming to work to this was like entering another world!' …
Betty Fleming (Spectator Services)

The first time Yvonne Boekestein-Hay went to collect a uniform, it resulted in mixed emotions, she had just turned 18 years of age, and she like many of her time were happy to join the WRANS. However, at that very time the War finished, and they were advised to stay home and pick apples.

'The news of being accepted as a Volunteer was a prayer answered – to be at Rushcutters Bay a miracle. To be presented with a UNIFORM another miracle. How marvellous! Waiting impatiently for commencement of my rosters proved definitely one does not grow more patient with the passing years!

'That special bond – THE OLYMPIC BOND – was forged very deeply in our Colonial hearts. I can never thank enough the entire Olympics Organisation and all concerned with it for the most enjoyable and exciting days of my long life.' … **Yvonne Boekestein-Hay (Spectator Services)**

'Serving the keen spectators in all respects and meeting the athletes as well as other dedicated volunteers who did their jobs happily and professionally, gave me the boost of confidence and pride in my achievement that I never felt before. It changed me from a shy and reserved person to a calmer, more confident self, having developed a highly positive attitude towards life and people.

'The satisfaction I gained from participating was as good as winning a gold medal at the end of the day.'
Alfred De Carlo (Spectator Services Host)

'It was a great experience to be part of the team out at the Sydney Football Stadium. We felt this was the forgotten venue of the Olympics. We were a much smaller group than Sydney Olympic Park, but I believe we had just as much fun.' … **Sarah-Jane Becroft**

Spectator Services host Marlene Kleemeyer with her cheer squad – daughter Trudi, son-in-law Robert, and grandchildren Alexandra, Robert and Brittany at Sydney Olympic Park

Mathew Hrycyk (Spectator Services host – Sydney Olympic Park)

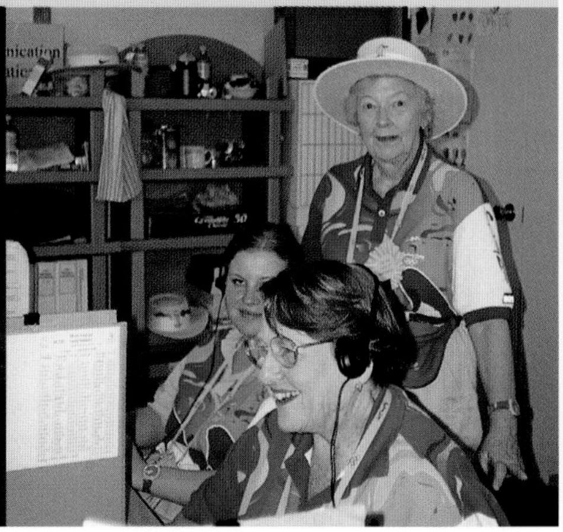

Katherine Leo, Colleen Carter (standing) and Erin Lewington (with earphones) at the venue command and control centre – Sydney International Shooting Centre

'I must say that initially I had a few reservations after I volunteered for the Olympics, particularly when I announced to my family that I intended taking my annual holidays so I could participate. However, once the Olympics had started and they were caught up in the euphoria of the event, they gave me overwhelming support. My husband said later he was sorry that he didn't make the effort to be involved.

'One afternoon during the gymnastics, I was positioned near a Chinese family – the event contained participants from many countries including Australia and China. I said to the young Chinese boy, "who are you supporting?" He replied in a broad Australian accent, "Australia of course." It really brought a tear to my eye.' ... **Elizabeth Steell (Spectator Services Host – Superdome)**

'I signed up as a volunteer in December 1998, but it wasn't until I put on my uniform a week before the Games I felt this was really going to happen to me.

'I commuted from the Central Coast to work on ten of the 16 days, and I think the thing I enjoyed most was the children on the trains and at the Games who wanted to talk to me as if I was someone special, and I did feel special in the uniform.' ... **Fay Harle (Spectator Services Host – Baseball Stadium)**

'I can't remember ever being in a place before where everybody around me was happy, excited and pleased to be there. I met some wonderful locals and people who had travelled for days just to get here, and they had great stories to tell about the journey.' ...
Patricia Parker (Spectator Services Host – Sydney Olympic Park)

Highs and Lows

'After two days working nine-hour shifts (with everyone new to the job and a lot of learning as we went along) followed by a twelve-and-a-half-hour shift which ended with me being covered in dust and exhausted, I started questioning myself about continuing.

'After the day's competition (Australia won the Gold Medal) while travelling on the bus from the Equestrian Centre back to the car park at Wonderland, I sat next to the father of an Australian team member at the Atlanta Olympic Games, and had a conversation with him that turned everything around for me. I knew then I would carry on and feel good about what I was doing (as a volunteer) and enjoy the rest of the Games.

'This person I spoke with on the bus couldn't praise the overall running of the equestrian events enough. To hear the comparisons from people who had been to other very large international events, people who were talking from personal experiences, I realised that the problems I had been coming up against were nothing when the volunteers got together as a team and supported each other.' ...
Shirley Allan (Spectator Services Host)

'Words can not adequately convey how I feel about this experience, which has greatly boosted my low self-esteem. I am a much more confident person, and this confidence is such that I now have my name listed to perform volunteer work to assist others.' …

Amy Bate (Spectator Services Host)

'Working in Olympic Boulevard, every time the message about thanking the volunteers was broadcast, the people walking past would all cheer, clap and say thank you. It gave me goose bumps and I was overwhelmed with a sense of pride.

'At the bus gate, if you were asked a question, you practically had to walk with the person to answer them because they didn't want to stop; they just wanted to get their bus. People commented on our perpetual smiles (as they ran for their bus) but they were just as happy, we were all happy, how could you not be, this was the Olympic Games, here in Sydney.' …

Tracey Clark (Spectator Services Host – Sydney Olympic Park)

'We find it impossible to describe the experience of volunteering at the Olympic Games to anyone who did not share this magical experience. It is as if those of us who experienced it moved into a private world. Other people share three dimensions of that world, but did not share the fourth.

'The pay was terrible (none) the hours were terrible (5.30 am starts and 1.30 am finishes) and the working conditions were extremely difficult (standing up to nine hours at a time). We got a thrill when the supervisor would bring us some barley sugar lollies and a bottle of water.

SPECTATOR SERVICES HOST HELENA DEBEVEC WITH BRONZE MEDALLIST ALEX CORRETJA FROM SPAIN

NICOLE WILLIAMS (SPECTATOR SERVICES – RYDE AQUATIC LEISURE CENTRE)

GLENN DICK WITH PARALYMPIC GOLD MEDAL

'Work was the only way we had to show our love for the Olympics and Sydney.' ...
Robert and Margaret Creswick (Spectator Services Hosts – Central Sector – Sydney Olympic Park)

'Our most memorable night was when **Patrice** and I had been to "The Brewery" and had a really fun night. We had to catch our bus from the Northern Terminal, and it was a 1.5 kilometre walk from the Stadium. At 3.00 am that walk was a long way!!! We were just deciding whether to take the high road or the low road when a chance to get transport came, to get to the terminal ... the garbage truck appeared ... we pleaded we had no energy left, and the nice young men doing the garbage round let us in the trailer with the garbage, and delivered us to the Bus Terminal. It beat walking! We laughed all the way and still do have a laugh about it.

'Being a volunteer at the Olympic Games was the most memorable experience I have ever had. My whole family was involved in various ways through the Games. My husband **Keith** was a volunteer driver based in the Olympic Village driving for the Ivory Coast Team. My daughter **Fiona** was a manager with the McDonald's Store at the International Broadcast Centre, and my son **Stuart** was involved in production of fireworks and laser shows in the city and the Paralympic Closing Ceremony.

'We were truly an Olympic Family.' ... **Heather Bensley (Spectator Services Host)**

'I am a widow, and with the push from two dear friends who said "this is what you need to go for", I became an Olympic/Paralympic volunteer. I will never forget or regret doing it.' ...
Lorna Duke (Spectator Services Host)

SPECTATOR SERVICES HOSTS – SOUTH SECTOR, PREPARING FOR THEIR NIGHT SHIFT ON SOUTHGATE DEPARTURES

PATRICE MANN AND HEATHER BENSLEY 'A GREAT WAY TO TRAVEL'

Spectator Services host Bill Levantrosser collects a ticket from another spectator at Sydney Olympic Park

Spectator Services hosts Lee Ann Tseung from Sydney and April Welch from Chicago,

Max Pember (Spectator Services host)

Creating a smile for Everyone

'I was standing outside in the public area when a young Korean boy came up to me and asked what was happening inside. I told him Judo and Boxing, so he asked me if he could go in and have a look at the Boxing. As I was telling him that he required a ticket, an elderly Asian gentleman, who was walking past, stopped and gave him two tickets. He asked the gentleman how much for the tickets, and the man said he could have them for free. I checked the tickets and told the boy they were for Judo that was currently in session, and that there was still about one-and-a-half hours in the session. The smile on the boy's face really made my day. He went in with his mother, and as he passed security he told them how he got the tickets. The smile on their faces matched the boy's and mine for the rest of the shift – created by a *giving man!*' ... **Jim Solman (Spectator Services Host – Darling Harbour)**

'I was so lucky to be allocated to the "Mobile Operations Support Team", as it gave me the chance to work in many venues and positions, I got to see many more sports and people than a lot of my fellow volunteers.' ... **Sharon Davis (Spectator Services Host)**

'My name is **Barbara Coburn**, and I live on the south coast of NSW in a little village called Fisherman's Paradise. I was not a volunteer, but a paid Team Leader. While I had some medical challenges prior to commencing, I would like to say that I met some extraordinary volunteers. I may not remember their names, but I will remember their faces and generous and caring ways. Like the gentleman who had cancer who never failed to help or never complained about the long periods in the hot sun; the lady in her eighties who worked every day with a happy cheery smile on her face; and the young Asian people who were such keen workers and did not miss a day. This was the Spirit of the Olympics.'

Some enthusiastic Australians spent frustrating months and in some cases years, trying to offer their services from the time Sydney was granted the right to host the 2000 Olympic/Paralympic Games. One of those people was **Fran Rogers**, who, through persistence, commenced volunteering with SOCOG in August 1999. Fran performed many volunteer hours at SOCOG Headquarters in the year leading up to the commencement of the Olympic Games. She was also joined by her daughter **Michelle** working at test events as new venues were being put through their paces. Finally, her granddaughter **Marnie** became involved in the 'Southern Skies' segment of the Opening Ceremony through her school at Gymea Bay, making three generations of family involvement – something they will always share and cherish.

A Taekwondo Ticket

'Once again as a gold-sleeved volunteer each day brought still another Olympic sector location and this time it was Dawn Fraser Avenue and Olympic Stadium. A very small lady approached me for directions, in her tiny hand was a Taekwondo ticket. Producing my Olympic Park map I tried to show her the way to the States Sports Centre, but it was no use, her language – Chinese – and the instructions I was giving her, I just knew she wouldn't make it. So I set off with her beside me to go the entire way to her venue. I found a ticket taker who could help, and speaking Mandarin, said a few words to the lady. Well that signalled hugs all around, such a tiny lady, but could she hug. I will never know what was said, but I do know the great excitement once the spectator knew she had arrived at her intended venue. What a wonderful day in the life of a volunteer.' ... **Jan (Janice) Sullivan (Spectator Services Host, Sydney Olympic Park)**

Shirley Allan at the scenic equestrian centre

'I liken my experience as a spectator services host in the south sector of the common domain, to being on playground duty at school, but with a loudhailer!' ... Beth Brand

'I volunteered to thank Australia, my new country, for accepting so many people from around the world on humanitarian basis, which included me.' ... Ilija Kamenjas

'Wow! Wow! Wow! – what an amazing 16 days in September in Sydney, having just experienced the Olympic Games as a volunteer at the Aquatic Centre. From the lighting of the Ring of Fire by Cathy Freeman (having the added significance that it was designed by engineers at my place of employment), through rubbing shoulders with the world's finest athletes and sharing their highs and lows, to the emotional conclusion when Mr Juan Antonio Samaranch declared that these were the best Olympic Games ever – and I was part of it!' ... **Wayne Godfrey (Spectator Services Host)**

'My father attended the 1956 Melbourne Olympic Games, and until he died in 1977, spoke of the special feeling that comes with the Olympics as people of all attending countries come together, REALLY COME TOGETHER.

'I have done lots of volunteering in my time and always enjoyed the experience, but this has been volunteering with passion that just flowed. Dad was correct in saying the coming together of people of many nations for the Olympic Games is something one has to experience. Wow!' ...
Gloria Cox (Spectator Services Host)

No excuses

'After three x 1200-kilometre round trips from our home in Warren, central NSW, the big day finally arrived and we started our first day at Blacktown Olympic Centre for Baseball and Softball. I worked the morning shift at Mag & Bag, and my wife **Karon** worked the afternoon shift at what became her favourite position – access point and accessible lift operator at the Baseball arena. We were worried about Karon being able to cope as she was seven months pregnant at the time, but everyone she had anything to do with was great and helped to ensure that she would last the distance.

Karon and I volunteered to help, so as everyone has everlasting memories of their Olympic experience.'

Footnote

'We are pleased to announce the safe arrival of William Thomas on 22 October 2000.' ... **Michael Fuller**

'I was amazed at the diversity of people from all cultures and age groups who volunteered. People who had limited English or were confined to wheelchairs, but with the same commitment to making the Games the super success they were.

'A lady who touched my heart was **Rose Johns**, who is confined to a wheelchair. Rose arrived at the sign-on desk in the mornings with a beaming smile ready to work. She has a great personality and does not let her disability stop her from contributing.

'Rose, and so many others, inspired me and the people they came in contact with, to make this whole experience that bit extra special.' ... **Anne Nelson.**

Betty Lewis travelled from Newcastle every day, catching either the 2.30 am or 5.15 am train. Her family were concerned that a lady in her 60s was taking on something beyond her, and many people commented that she would not stick it out. Well history shows that Betty was very sad when it was all over, and cherishes every minute of her Olympic/Paralympic experience.

'I will never forget the first morning I walked over the hill and saw the cauldron and the flame for the first time. It brought a tear to my eye, as I realised that I was about to be part of a two-week journey that would be creating history.

'Every volunteer could stand proud as it was announced at the Closing Ceremony that "*Sydney was the best Games ever*", but nothing prepared me for what was waiting back in Queensland for me.

'I received nothing short of a hero's welcome when I returned to work. I served as a volunteer yet I was welcomed as a gold medal winner.' … **Katrina Kickbush (Caloundra, Queensland)**

'Living in Australia, I was glad to get involved in the XXVII Olympiad because it reminded me of the proverb "when drinking water, remember the source". As a humble Australian of Vietnamese origin, I was also able to help, and let the world know that this country is no longer known as Australia "down under" but "up under".' … **Tuyet Nguyen (Spectator Services Host – Equestrian Centre)**

Dianne Johnson came from Ballina on the NSW north coast, and stayed with her cousin at Frenchs Forest on the north side of Sydney for the duration of the Olympic Games.

Dianne says: 'I feel I was very privileged in my volunteer work having such a variety of roles around Olympic Park. This put me in a position to share both the highs and lows of athletes and spectators

SPECTATOR SERVICES HOSTS – INTERNATIONAL BROADCAST CENTRE

'I SUFFERED SEVERE SLEEP DEPRIVATION AND MILD LARYNGITIS, BUT IT WAS ALL WORTH IT.' … MARIAN GRIMA (SPECTATOR SERVICES HOST) – IN FRONT OF SYDNEY OLYMPIC PARK TRAIN STATION

'The Olympic Games were made of special moments.' ... Chris Pike (Spectator Services host – Olympic Stadium)

Spectator Services hosts getting in the 'mood' at the SuperDome

'We sometimes confused people by appearing to be in two places at once!' ... twins Katherine and Leanne Garth (Spectator Services hosts – Olympic Stadium)

Three generations (l to r) Fran Rogers, daughter Michelle Woodhouse (Spectator Services) and granddaughter Marnie Rogers (Ceremonies)

'Kilo – the dream team' came from near and far – (l to r) Rose Taylor (Sydney), Marilyn Ritchings (Qld), Bob Wood (Vic), Sonya Wilson (South Australia), Debbie McMillan (Sydney), Regan Bunny (Vic), Margaret Simpson (Sydney) and Estelle Grady (Canberra) in front

alike – from having a gold medal placed around my neck to assisting a distraught spectator who was having an allergic reaction to something he had eaten.

'This experience has given me more of an understanding of all races of people – remember the words to the song – "We are one – but we are many". I am really proud to say I have been part of it.'

Shirley Marrington came from Queensland to volunteer at the Olympic and Paralympic Games. Shirley has a long history of volunteering, which is incorporated with having five children, 16 grandchildren and one great grandchild. Besides the personal friendships developed between volunteers, one of Shirley's highlights was meeting the many international visitors, and agreeing to their requests for photos with volunteers. At 70 years of age, Shirley was so moved by the atmosphere and friendships she developed during her stay in Sydney, she has made it known that she will be making herself available to volunteer in Athens in 2004, if the opportunity arises.

Lauren Webb says: 'It was well worth the plane trip from Tasmania, and the three weeks I took off University. However, my highlight was the appreciation of children of the volunteer contribution, like when a little girl, probably 11 years old, saw me wearing my accreditation and asked whether I had something to do with the Games. She later came back to ask for my autograph. I graciously obliged.'

Mal MacDonald travelled from Canberra to participate as a Spectator Services Host, and relates here to 'a day on the job':

'It was off to Darling Harbour to the Entertainment Centre to the Volleyball. This shift didn't start until 4 pm so I wandered around Sydney and Darling Harbour absorbing the Olympic feel. Imagine my joy when they were handing out our assignments for the night and gave me a megaphone and allowed me to sit in an umpires chair and rev up, sorry provide assistance to, the audience on their way into the venue. My natural shyness was put to one side and just how much fun can one person have with a captive audience and a megaphone. I, in true humility, believe I was able to act as a counsellor to a number of families and young couples and provide the advice usually only associated with great sages!'

Lost (Volunteer) at Olympic Park

'I was to meet up with my daughter Louise and grandson Daniel at North Gate to Olympic Park. Somehow we missed each other, but ten-year-old grandson knew what to do.

'He went up to a Police Officer and asked: "Excuse me, have you seen my grandfather? He's wearing a white hat and a blue jacket and his name is Ken." Unbelievably, even with this good description, the Police Officer could not help!' ... **Ken Laycock (Spectator Services Host)**

SPECTATOR SERVICES HOST – ASTRID SCHUSTER FROM MUNICH, GERMANY

(L TO R) ANDREA ZAMBOLT AND KYLIE YAHL (SPECTATOR SERVICES HOSTS – SYDNEY ENTERTAINMENT CENTRE)

SPECTATOR SERVICES HOSTS – ANNE NELSON STANDING) AND ROSE JOHNS

Can you relate to this?

John Elliott and Freda Matthews describe the adventure of travelling some distance for uniform collection. Living in Cowra in central western NSW, they decided to stay overnight in Lithgow: 'What time is it? … 3.45 am, and the train leaves here at Lithgow at 4.39 am! Up, showered, dressed and to the station, nicely in time for the train, in which we take our seats and are lulled into a light sleep safe in the knowledge that we were warm and comfortable until we arrive at Strathfield.

'WRONG!

'The announcer shattered our complacency by telling us that owing to track-work we had to alight at Lidcombe and catch a bus, and it was RAINING!

'So we did – ALMOST!

'We alighted at Lidcombe – up the stairs – following the signs to the bus – only to be told by a railway employee that we could catch a train to Redfern on platform 1. That we did, and eventually made it to the Uniform Distribution and Accreditation Centre, at Redfern.

'This was efficient, friendly and well run, but we can all remember:

'Follow the green line; follow the yellow line; collect accreditation over there; ladies this way – men that way; please try on this top; what size pants; the dressing room is over there; please try on a jacket; do you wish to buy another shirt; try on a hat; pick up a carry-bag with a water bottle, hip bag, rain poncho and two pairs of socks; checkout is through there … wow!

'There was less trauma on the train trip back to Lithgow, where we paid for our accommodation, then climbed into the car for the long uneventful drive to Cowra.'

'I was an incredibly honoured volunteer to come all the way from Dubbo in central western NSW. I would never have missed the experience of doing something as HUGE as working for the Olympic Games. I would have paid to be part of this wonderful tradition that has stemmed over centuries.' …
Penny Trakosas (Spectator Services Host – Darling Harbour)

'Sydney has been a life-changing experience for me, and I will forever be grateful in having been selected to serve my country with such a dedicated and passionate group of people. We definitely celebrated humanity.' … Paul Kleores (Spectator Services Host – Olympic Stadium)

'I come from Tamworth, NSW, but attend university in Sydney. I decided to spend my university holidays soaking up the whole Olympic experience as a volunteer, and it ended up being one of the best decisions of my life.' … Melisa Davis (Spectator Services Host – Sydney Olympic Park)

'It surprised me on every occasion I met or passed an athlete how humble and human they were, the world's best athletes were just ordinary people!! To be part of something where everyone is equal, and no forms of discrimination exist, was for myself the Olympic Spirit.' … Ron Hignett (Spectator Services Host – Superdome) from Adelaide

'Coming from Perth, WA, having two children living in Sydney at least took care of my accommodation. Also having a very understanding husband, allowed me five weeks to enjoy and be part of this once-in-a-lifetime event.' …
Denise Chaplin (Spectator Services Host – Tennis Centre)

'Born and raised in Sydney, I moved to Tasmania in 1970. I had been in Sydney for Bicentennial Day in 1988, and experienced the exhilaration of the city that day. Sydneysiders, like those in most big cities I guess, normally act remote among strangers in the streets. On Bicentennial Day, however, they made eye contact, grinned and laughed and shared the excitement.

'I expected that the city would be the same during the Olympics. I was wrong. It was better.' …
Dick Burns (Spectator Services Host – Sydney Entertainment Centre)

'If I could do it all again, I would, in a second. I leave the Sydney Games with thousands of memories and many friends. I know that I won't forget my Games experience for as long as I live. I reflect on

the Games of the XXVII Olympiad with delight in the knowledge that I was part of the success. The Winner is Sydney, and the winners are the volunteers!' ...
Robert Old (Spectator Services Host) from Sarina Beach, Queensland

'Saturday, 30 September 2000, I was walking up the main street of Blaxland (west of Sydney) on the way to the train at 4 am. I could see a lady ahead of me at the post box. She waited until I got to her and she said to me: "I couldn't let you go by without thanking you for all your help at the Games." I told her it was my pleasure doing so.

'This was typical of people's attitude, and I received comments similar to this both from international tourists and locals alike.' ... **Madeline Inglis (Spectator Services Host)**

'I worked as a Spectator Services Host at the Hockey Centre. Living in Valentine, Newcastle, I was unable to find accommodation in Sydney. I travelled by train from Cardiff; this took me three hours each way, sometimes longer getting home because of the crowds. I alighted at Concord West and had a quick 30-minute stroll to the Hockey Centre. On my way I met some wonderful people. One gentleman I met at Strathfield Station late at night said I looked exhausted (nice guy). We discovered we were both getting off at Cardiff, I expressed my fear of falling asleep and missing my station. The gentleman informed me he had an alarm clock and would wake me. Consequently I did sleep, and sure enough he woke me just before Cardiff. I wish to thank him immensely.' ... **Keri Miller**

ENTRY TEAM – SYDNEY INTERNATIONAL REGATTA CENTRE

SPECTATOR SERVICES HOST CATHY CONVEY FROM MELBOURNE WITH ONE OF HER NON-OLYMPIC SPORTING HEROES, FORMER AUSTRALIAN TEST CRICKETER IAN HEALY

RELAXING WITHOUT THE CROWDS AT THE HOCKEY CENTRE

ALL THE WAY FROM QUEENSLAND – MIKE QUINLAN

Spectator Services Host **Sue Booth** provided the following article for *COOEE News from the Common Domain:* 'On my way home on the train a gentleman from Los Angeles asked for directions to Doonside Station so he could go to see the baseball match that was on that night.

'After giving him directions, I told the gentleman how I loved to watch baseball on Fox Sports, and saw the Cuba vs South Africa match last Sunday at the Baseball Centre. The gentleman was amazed at my knowledge of the sport.

'When I said I'd just about give anything to see the USA vs Cuba game on Saturday, 23 September, he pulled a ticket for the game out of his pocket, and told me he was unfortunately on his way home to the USA tomorrow due to work problems, and gave me the ticket.

'Many thanks to my Supervisor who sent me home early as the whole thing would not have happened otherwise.'

'This was the most exciting time of my life because:

1. I was part of an Australian success story that will perhaps never be equalled;

2. Close contact with the world's elite sports men and women in all fields;

3. A chance opportunity to assist the family of Ian Thorpe on the night he won Australia's first gold medal;

4. Friendships that have provided me with life-long memories.'…

Peter Lynskey (Spectator Services Host) from Queensland

Valuable experience
Olympic commitment
Lots of laughs
Unbelievable weather
Nice people
Team spirit
Energetic shifts
Endless smiles
Remember the sunscreen and water…

Jenny Lake (Spectator Services Host)

Once in a lifetime opportunity
Living and sharing 'The Dream'
You had to be there
Many new friends and experiences
Pinnacle of sport
I will treasure for life
Ceremonies – a highlight

Gold, Silver, Bronze: not the only champions
Australia's 100th Gold: Thanks Cathy
Memorable hours
Energy to burn – despite tired legs
Sporting excellence, an honour to witness

So proud of my city: showcase to the world
Years of planning and personal expectations
Definitely a proud moment
Never doubted such success
Every moment so special
Yellow and Green: glowing brightly

2000; start of the new millennium
Oh, such a privilege for Sydney and Australia
Our sporting teams did us so proud
Only to turn back time; to do it all again.

Marian Osgood (Spectator Services Host)

The person behind the people who were the face of the games

'Although recruited as a Spectator Services Host, I was assigned to the Equipment Support Team, not that I knew what that was. It turns out that I was a part of a small group of people (two to three per shift) whose job it was to ensure that all the hosts, team leaders and supervisors in Spectator Services have all the equipment they needed to do *their* jobs.

'Our job included the distribution and collection of the radio units (as well as the maintenance of the batteries), ticket aprons, water, sunscreen, barriers, megaphones, umpires' chairs and even sticky tape, as well as the tracking and locating of wheelchairs inside our venue (Superdome). It meant that we began our work before the majority of the staff and finished well after the hosts had gone home.

'I would like to thank the Supervisors and Team Leaders for being patient and understanding that we could not be everywhere every minute of the day, and the Hosts for letting us commandeer you to push wheelchairs. But most of all I would like to thank the rest of the Equipment Support Team.

'It was wonderful to know that I was an important part in making sure that the volunteers themselves had an easier time of doing their jobs. So I guess that made me the person behind the people who were the face of the Games.' ... Melissa Molenaar

'The Ibis Hotel, Homebush, is where the excitement began for me. I was given a loudhailer and was told to give spectators and athletes directions to the railway station and other venues. The caring side of people was evident during the Games; shown especially by a lovely Dee Why family I met on the bus one day. On finding out that I was coming from the Central Coast every day, they insisted that I stay with them for the remaining eight days – *thank you.'* ... Alex Zoric (Spectator Services Host)

'Yes we had the real VIPs; Prime Ministers, Premiers, Presidents, Royalty, Diplomats, TV Stars, etc. However, it was the ordinary people as well who were our VIPs, everyone deserved the best experience they could have and we tried to give it to them.

'At 62 years of age, retired and a grandmother, it was great to be actively working for my country, but my husband was the volunteer to the volunteer – *the wind beneath my wings.'* ... Barbara Humphrey (Spectator Services Host)

'Sometimes any job can become tiresome, and it was probably this which maybe caused me to mumble the words, because an American spectator very excitedly grabbed me and said "Wow, you are the first Aussie I've met who has said *Gidday* without being prompted." I didn't have the heart to tell him I was saying Gate A and not Gidday.' ... Jenni Landor (Spectator Services Host)

'I found every day to be exciting as a volunteer because, as a member of Spectator Services in the Pavilion and Dome venues, no two days were the same, and as time progressed the public and volunteers became more and more involved in the day-to-day events. Just to be included in a full-house of 10,000 people in the Dome, for example, in the heat of battle for a medal chance between two countries which, under other circumstances would have been at each other's throats in a different kind of war, was absolutely magic.' ... **Nigel Wright**

Peter Bentley made his decision to *head off to Jones Street* (SOCOG Headquarters) *armed with a brief CV, despite lack of encouragement from friends and acquaintances.* While not every aspect of his early volunteering experience, especially test events, could be described as satisfying, the development of teamwork and relationships between volunteers at the various venues resulted in his time at Archery Park for the Paralympics being the pinnacle of his Sydney 2000 experience.

Although it was an environment of international competition, the humour and good nature of the volunteers highlighted this worthwhile experience.

'If we looked hazy, then that is how we were at 5.00 am at the Regatta Centre! However, there was a wonderful interaction we had with our spectator guests and fellow volunteers in those early hours.' ... **Judy Giles (Spectator Services Host)**

So many Spectator Services Volunteers expressed similar emotions about similar experiences – *representing my country; meeting the world's elite athletes; developing new friendships; seeing people from all over the world together in peace; the appreciation shown to volunteers by All, especially the Sydney Public.* **Kerrie Walsh, Michael Learnihan, Helen Shaw, Lorraine Clowes, David Diamond, Leone Nowfel, Margaret Knight, Nivedita Gupta, Danielle Gambetta, Sue Cole, Ngai Mee Chow, Eddie Fan, Katharine Barker, James Phillips, Melinda Hyland, Marcelle Fitzgerald, Bev Museth, Kate Howell, Jasper Hutabarat, Frances Bluhdorn, Heather Kemsley, Paul Benson, Alan Brown, Gill Thane, Helen Naudin, Fred Strassberg and Erwin Willems.**

Spectator Services Host **Alan McGowan's** most humbling experience was when two parents with two small boys arrived at North Gate. 'Just after passing us, the Dad stopped and told the youngsters "You see these people in uniform? Well they are good people, so if you get lost, look for one of them." It brought home how much trust the visitors put in the volunteers.'

'I guess the most memorable experience would have been when Cathy Freeman won her race. Being an Indigenous Australian, I was proud of her anyway, but being a volunteer while she was running her race gave me the biggest thrill of all. I realised that not only was I here representing myself, but I was also representing my people as well. I was fortunate enough to meet three other Indigenous Volunteers, who like me, were having the time of their lives.' ... **Lisa Jackson (Spectator Services Host – South Sector)**

'At the conclusion of the Closing Ceremony, we were attempting to guide the athletes back to the Village. However, many of them wanted to know how to get into the City. So we were directing them LEFT to the buses to the Village, RIGHT to the trains to the City, and those athletes with Surf Boards from the Ceremony, ABOUT TURN and head to Bondi. Athletes with Greg Norman Golf Clubs head to the nearest Golf Course, and the athlete who was riding the bicycle SHOE, to head for the Opera House!!!' ... **Georgina Day (Spectator Services Host)**

'Jolly Volley Vollies'

'Time flies when you are having fun! And I'm sure everyone who worked at the Sydney Entertainment Centre will agree with me when I say that the 16 days of the Olympic Games felt more like 16 seconds. The Entertainment Centre proudly hosted the Olympic Volleyball competition, and we had matches on every day. We volleyball volunteers had an absolute ball (no pun intended) and became affectionately known as the "jolly volley vollies!" Even though we did not work at a high-profile venue like the Stadium, or get to witness any world records being broken like at the Aquatic Centre, none of us would have swapped venues for all the pins in Sydney.' ... **Vanessa Pedley-Smith (Spectator Services Host)**

Jacinta Blencowe had a burning desire to be part of the Sydney Olympic Games, and like thousands of other Australians who did not live in Sydney, it required that little bit more planning. First choice was Spectator Services Host at the Regatta Centre, and that is what Jacinta was lucky enough to secure, although a warm bed in Melbourne was probably looking good at 2.30 am each day when Jacinta had to rise to be at the venue on time as a Team Leader.

While the excitement and atmosphere of the venue and the event maintained a stimulating adrenalin rush, Jacinta particularly enjoyed the interaction and camaraderie developed amongst her fellow interstate volunteers within the team from Queensland, Victoria, Western Australia and Country NSW.

SPECTATOR SERVICES HOSTS – MILLENNIUM MARQUE

NEVER FAR FROM THE FUN – (L TO R) MARGARET CHILDS, SANDY HOLLWAY AND LEAH ARMSTRONG

One of our oldest volunteers, Kath Pennefather – when asked how old, Kath replied 'too old!'

Norman Snowden (Spectator Services Host)

enjoying the shared experiences

Many volunteers attribute their enhanced skills and confidence to the Olympic/Paralympic volunteering experience. Spectator Services Host **Jennifer Quinlin** states: 'I had never really had a frontline "meet and greet" type of role before, and it scared me to death initially! I know that I learned a great deal about dealing with people, handling pressure and being confident, over those two and a half weeks.'

'The night of the first Dress Rehearsal held many memorable moments, but it was at the end of the evening, when the crowd was leaving, a total stranger came up to me, looked me straight in the face and said, "I want to thank you for becoming a volunteer." I can't find the words to describe how that made me feel. Tears came to my eyes at the same time as I felt my face beam with a smile.

'I was going home and a companion said "another day, another dollar, but there is no dollar for us volunteers." I replied that I had received tonight something more valuable than money. I had received a sincere thank you from a heart full of appreciation. Absolutely priceless. A moment I will never forget.' ... **Catherine Williams (Spectator Services Host)**

'One particular day I had tried without success to have a media person move from a spectator area as he did not speak English. The following day, when I was working on "Mag and Bag" I happened to see him; he was setting up his tripod and taking photos of the crowds, etc. I didn't think for a minute that he would recognise me, as I looked a little different, now wearing a hat and sunglasses. However after about 15 minutes, he just came over and stood beside me. He casually said, in English, "and how are you?" Then he said "and did you enjoy the weightlifting yesterday?" I couldn't help laughing at the subtle way he let me know that he won.' ... **Lynne Blackman**

Margaret Ashton had gone out of her way to take a Malaysian Team Manager shopping. Margaret recalls: 'The next day when I arrived back at the shooting range, she gave me a beautiful gift, plus her personal business card, which indicated she was a retired Assistant Police Commissioner with a lot of letters after her name, and I thought how lovely that she went out with Margaret from Casula (near Liverpool)!'

'After that fantastic Opening Ceremony I presented myself as a volunteer the next morning. It was still dark as I made my way, somewhat nervously, through the now empty streets of the city. But as I crossed the quay at Darling Harbour, I felt the excitement again at the thrill of walking through that beautiful bay, all brilliantly alight.

'There was that sense of pride welling up in me, that I belonged to such a beautiful place, and my step quickened in my new uniform that proclaimed that I was, and am, a part of all this.' ... **Fran Aroney**

'The experience that I have had over the last 16 days will never be equalled. It wasn't simply the joy of being close to some of the finest athletes in the world from a number of different countries; it was the camaraderie and the "can do" attitude that we all shared.

'I have made friends with people of varying ages and of varying backgrounds; a bond that will never be broken. This is one of the greatest legacies of the games!' ... **Alexandra Bohr (Mobile Operations Support Team)**

'The most often asked question by spectators of volunteers is; "Where can I buy a beer?" One spectator said to me; "You would have to be just the right person to tell me where I can buy a beer" as he looked at my accreditation showing the surname BREW!' ... **Cynthia Brew (Spectator Services Host)**

(L to R) Ann Abbott, Mark Cahill and Anne Cobcroft (McIntosh pavilion)

Spectator services hosts – Common Domain

Would anybody try to get past these two?

Sonia D'alessandro, Luned Clement and Lara Elam (spectator services hosts – olympic stadium)

Robynne Yeates (spectator services – tennis centre) meets one of her heroes Mark Woodforde

Marion and Trefor Jones

relaxation time for superdome spectator services hosts

Michelle Pearce (left) and Lynette Baxter (spectator services hosts – olympic stadium)

volunteers at sydney olympic park (central sector common domain) captured by a *Daily Telegraph* photographer. back row (l to r) Decha Pataramas (thailand), Hyesun Kwak (sydney), Christine Chuang (taiwan), Jenny Jamieson (brisbane), front row (l to r) Hiroko Onari (sydney), Nellie Papworth (jiggi via lismore), Karen Nicol (sydney)

Leslie (centre) with lifelong friends Nell Wright (left) and Alyson Mullane

No wonder some spectators were more than a little confused as to which way to go at Sydney Olympic Park!

Spectator services hosts – Sydney International Aquatic Centre

Barbara Cameron 'checking' husband Bruce

Volunteers Parade...

VOLUNTEERS PARADE
BONDS
TAFE
The Sun-Herald
Panasonic

SEE YOU
IN ATHENS
IN 2004!!

Thank you Everyone!!
It's been a pleasure
be a Volunteer,
You were wonderful!!

ST JOHN AMBULANCE

FOREWORD

by JOHN SPENCER
Chief Operations Officer, St John Ambulance Australia

The Olympic Games in Sydney in September 2000 have been described by HRH The Duke of Gloucester (Grand Prior of the Order of St John) as the largest single peacetime duty ever undertaken by St John. The medical response for the Games was extremely successful and St John volunteers can be proud of their part in making the Games the best ever!

St John had some 800 personnel accredited for Sydney Olympic Games venues and some 300 for the Paralympic Games. In addition, in Sydney a further 300 members provided the first aid services in the urban domain of the Sydney CBD and some other locations in the suburbs. The Torch Relay around Australia over 100 days saw 1838 members provide over 10,500 hours of duty as the Torch made its way around Australia. These duties covered a period in excess of three months and over 15,000 patients were treated by St John. We were pleased indeed to have volunteers from St John in England, Canada, New Zealand, South Africa and Hong Kong join their Australian counterparts for the event.

Interstate members provided the first aid services for soccer conducted in Adelaide, Brisbane, Canberra and Melbourne.

The book will provide a valuable record of the volunteer commitment to the 2000 Olympic and Paralympic Games and I commend the author for undertaking such a mammoth task. In particular, St John members can be proud of their achievements during these events. No other organisation could have carried out the role of providing spectator first aid services for all Olympic and Paralympic events around Australia. My compliments to all members who were involved on a job well done!

Each St John Ambulance volunteer had their own reasons for wanting to be part of Sydney 2000, and each went home with unique special memories of The Games.

Those coming from outside the Newcastle – Wollongong – Blue Mountains area were provided with accommodation at no cost in one of three locations, Glengarry Guide Camp at North Turramurra, Lane Cove River Caravan Park near North Ryde and Mt St Benedict School at Pennant Hills. Many new friendships were forged at these locations, and the hospitality was appreciated in these homes away from home.

The fifth floor of St John House in Surry Hills was converted into a St John Club for the duration of the Olympics/Paralympics. Members were able to gather and relax and socialise with members from interstate and overseas. The Club was free to members, and provided television, internet and email facilities together with a tourist 'help' desk. Sandwiches, tea and coffee were available free all day. This facility provided an environment for relaxation and friendship-building away from the pace of the Olympic City.

While this was a high-profile occasion, it must not be forgotten that these people did not come together for just this one event. During the past 12 months, 11,000 St John first aid volunteers treated 96,000 casualties across Australia, giving almost 700,000 hours to the Australian community.

'In real life, I am a Registered Nurse. I have worked in a variety of areas, but currently work on contracts of four to eight weeks at a time in the Arctic as a Community Health Nurse. I really enjoy my Arctic travels and have had the opportunity to work from Pangnirtung on Baffin Island in Canada's newest territory of Nunavut to Tuktoyaktuk in the Northwest Terrirories.

THE ST JOHN TEAM AT BLACKTOWN SOFTBALL STADIUM

DEBORAH COMANIUK FROM VANCOUVER ISLAND IN CANADA, PREPARING FOR THE MEN'S CYCLING ROAD RACE

IT WAS COLD IN ARMIDALE FOR THE TORCH RELAY – (L TO R) BARRY AND JENNY DAVIS AND FAY GLEAVE

ST JOHN VOLUNTEERS AT PYRMONT BAY PARK

ST JOHN CADET LUKE PARKER

'In 1976, I was to go to the Montreal Olympics as a fencing scorekeeper. Ultimately I did not go, and was very disappointed. Then in 1997, a rather benign copy of an invitation to apply for the Olympics came to the Division 1076 Brigade in Campbell River. I put in an application with no serious hope of being one of the five accepted. On return home from a contract in the Arctic in January 1998, I found the letter stating that I had been chosen to participate with St John Ambulance Australia. I was so excited, as this was the second time I was chosen to go to the Olympics, and by gosh I was not going to miss out this time. The Campbell River Branch of St John Ambulance was very supportive.

'Upon my arrival in Sydney, the warmth and genuine interest displayed by all members of St John Ambulance was immediate. I just knew this was going to be a wonderful experience. The experience and hospitality was overwhelming, from when NSW member, Faye, took me under her wing at the Opening Ceremony, to the exposure of Beach Volleyball, Road Cycling, Equestrian Cross Country and Handball.

'There was a lot of interest in the shoulder flashes on my St John Ambulance coat. The Canadian shoulder flash is unique with the dash of red in the maple leaf. A lot of people asked me about the printing on it: "Saint John Ambulance Saint Jean". People wanted to know who Jean was. I explained that Canada is bilingual, and Jean is the French version of John. I used that explanation until I met Marcia, an Australian St John Ambulance member from the state of Victoria. She suggested I tell people that Jean is John's wife. We both had a lot of fun with that line. This just characterised the Aussie spirit, and another reason I will never forget this wonderful experience.' ... **Deborah Comaniuk.**

'Coming from the coastal town of Bega (six hours south of Sydney) was a long and tiring process. In fact, by going through accreditation and other familiarisation processes on arrival in Sydney, our 6.30 am start in Bega did not finish till we arrived at our accommodation at Lane Cove Caravan Park at 8.00 pm.

'The atmosphere in Sydney was amazing! What an experience! The days were long, your legs and feet ached, but the atmosphere, the people and the casualties kept you going. You just had to be there!' ... **Sandra Crowe**

At the volunteers parade – author, Laurie Smith, with St John Ambulance volunteers Stephen, Darren, Warren, Janine and Marty

A special day

'While we never like to see people in trouble medically, we are there for that very purpose should the situation arise. On this particular day I was required to attend to an elderly lady high up in the Centre Court Tennis Stadium. She was seriously ill, and to make matters worse, her elderly husband went into shock due to her condition. To cut a long story short, a wonderful team effort of cooperation between St John Ambulance, Spectator Services and Medical volunteers resulted in successfully having both patients transferred to hospital.

'Later that day I was asked by my commander to go to the staff area with my fellow first aiders. To my surprise, there was Mr Juan Antonio Samaranch and Mr Michael Knight, thanking volunteers for all their efforts. Mr Samaranch handed me the Sydney 2000 Thank you Badge – my emotions were mixed, as I pondered what Mr Samaranch was going through with the recent death of his wife. A special day!' ... **Janine Marzulli (Manly/Warringah Division)**

Peter Connell and Justin Tippett were both surprised when they were accepted to be part of the Olympic Experience in Sydney – the only problem was, they hadn't really given any thought to how they could afford to go! Devonport, Tasmania was more than a 'short walk' from Sydney, but in the true spirit of the local community, 15 organisations raised sufficient funds to make the trip a reality.

Justin recalls: 'We were so appreciative of the local support, and it was a relief when we finally commenced our adventure. However, Sydney was SOMETHING ELSE, having never been there before, let alone at Olympic time. I was just overwhelmed by the size of the place and the amount of people. But we need not have worried, everyone was so friendly and in party mode! The St John Ambulance people made us so welcome.'

'I worked at many different venues, both competition and non-competition, and most of our first aid was of the sunburn and blister type. I left for home knowing that I had been a small part of the most organised and well-trained group of people I have ever met. I found people so dedicated and focused, they were full of Olympic Spirit at every venue.

'I was talking with another St John Ambulance volunteer, discussing our sore feet, when we saw two people in wheelchairs coming out of the Superdome after an evening event, pushed by their carers. Both were dependent on oxygen (oxygen bottle holders built into the wheelchair design).

'Our feet stopped hurting and we both went on completing our duty for that night, realising how privileged we were in being able to work with them. Their motto for the Paralympic Games – "Set No Limits" – certainly was appropriate.' ... **Denise Lewis**

Annette Dinning volunteered in different areas for the Olympics and Paralympics, including Ceremonies staff and St John Ambulance. Annette summarises: 'All positions were fulfilling, exciting, rewarding but demanding. I had the opportunity to work with teams of people that were dedicated, friendly, supportive, happy and most of all, they had the spirit that was infectious ... this I think was the very characteristic that made the Games the success they were.'

Justin Tippett (in vehicle) and Peter Connell – St John Ambulance volunteers from Devonport, Tasmania

(L to R) Lesley McEwan (Glebe Division) and Delores Heares (Bankstown Division) at the synchronised swimming test event in April 2000

MEDICAL TEAM – WHITE-WATER STADIUM

ANYONE FOR GOLF! – AT THE CHINESE GARDENS – DARLING HARBOUR PHOTO BY JOHN CHAMBERLAIN

CREW AT RAILWAY MEDICAL TENT – SYDNEY OLYMPIC PARK

(L TO R) ALISON GARDINER (RICHMOND DIVISION), LIZ COOPER (MANLY DIVISION) AND CHRIS CLARKE (TAMWORTH DIVISION) PHOTO BY JOHN CHAMBERLAIN

(L TO R) KEITH CARDEN, MRS IRENE ROGERS, JEAN CARDEN, FRANCIS CHAPMAN, KAREN SAULS, KATE BUCHNER, PETER CRAWSHAW, KAYDN GRIFFIN AND ROBERT DALE

ST JOHN VOLUNTEERS AT THE OLYMPIC STADIUM

THE PREPARATION

'MEET YOU THERE!'

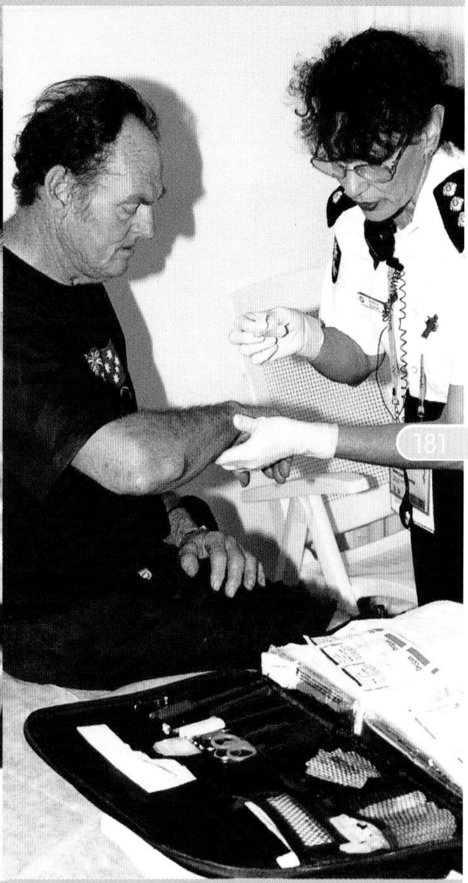

ST JOHN AMBULANCE VOLUNTEER ILAN LOWBEER AND IBM IT SPECIALIST TECH SUPPORT VOLUNTEER MICHELLE TUCH

VITAL COMMUNICATION

PROFESSIONAL CARE

Contributing to emotional health

'I was looking after our St John team at North Head for the Olympic sailing. In the team were **Karen Sauls** and **Kate Buchner** from South Africa, **Francis Chapman** from Queensland, **Peter Crawshaw** from Victoria, **Robert Dale** from South Australia and **Marty Van Der Wallen** and myself from Manly-Warringah Division.

'There was a suggestion that it was Karen's birthday, so my wife, Denise, baked a batch of muffins and sent them with a pink candle. Alas, it was not Karen's birthday, but on my rounds of the spectators I helped an elderly lady into a chair and was proudly told by her that it was her 89th birthday today!

'So, making use of resources, we put the pink candle in a muffin, and six of the team went and presented Mrs Irene Rogers with her "birthday cake", lit the candle and sang "Happy Birthday". She was absolutely thrilled, as were her daughter and son-in-law, Jean and Keith Carden.' ... **Kaydn Griffin**

'I became involved in St John Ambulance and subsequently the Paralympics because it is important to me, and I have Cerebral Palsy. During this time I was not judged on my disability, as there were many people with varying disabilities themselves. I have made so many friends within the St John ranks, and I hope that my efforts and involvement will lead to bigger and better things.' ... **Nicole Kerley**

'On a crowded train coming home from Olympic Park a ten-year-old boy asked his mother "What goes black white black white black white black white?" ... a penguin falling down the stairs!" A man on the other side of the carriage shouted: "No! A St John Ambulance man falling down the stairs." This will be one of my lasting impressions of the Games – complete strangers talking and joking with each other.' ... **Greg Bateman, ACT**

'When I arrived in Australia in 1967 with my husband and daughter, pregnant with my son and speaking no English, I could not have imagined that 33 years later I would stand on the winners' podium at the Beach Volleyball with the autograph of one of the Australian Golden Girls. What a glorious experience – four days on duty at the sailing with views to die for and five days at the beach volleyball. I think I was in heaven. If Australia ever hosts the Games again, I'll be there.' ... **Inge Vezer, Victoria**

'The highlight of the Games was the enthusiasm of all the volunteers – both St John and SOCOG. Everyone worked so well together and there was a natural rapport, which built up with people from all over the world. Every day I was working with someone different which was so interesting, and travelling each day on the train and talking with positive, happy spectators was fun too.' ... **Patricia Burgess, Queensland**

Peter Lorimer enjoyed the variety of Sailing, Athletics, Tennis and Football in his role with St John Ambulance. He and his wife Jan drove from their home in South Australia, towing a caravan, in preparation for their stay in the Lane Cove Caravan Park. 'It was worth every bit of the effort, for the opportunity to contribute, and meet people from across Australia and the world,' said Peter.

POUNDING THE BEAT!

OUT OF TOWN VOLUNTEERS

It was interesting how from 1999 onwards, the volunteer contribution was no longer the domain of Sydney or even NSW enthusiasts! Nor was it ever meant to be! However, once the launch of Volunteers 2000 was made in the latter part of 1998, and test events began to take place, the influx of interstate volunteers was not just encouraging but huge! Nobody could overlook the passion and commitment of volunteers who sacrificed time and finances to travel from country NSW and interstate. There were even the few international visitors who came during this period for orientation.

One could sense that this was becoming an Australia-wide contribution, and that Australians were embracing the Olympic and Paralympic Games as THEIRS!

Suzie Szalay from Mt Gambier, South Australia and Bruce Peel welcome a guest to the Information Centre in the Athletes Village

Georgina Pickers (centre) from Queensland, with colleagues Josie and Tim at the Main Press Centre

Just as no volunteer was ever rated more important than another, nor should one's commitment to be involved, be rated more highly than others. However, through the following pages it is hoped that we will all have a better appreciation of the commitment, passion and sacrifice that brought our volunteer force together.

Judy Docksey lives in Armidale in the New England District of northern NSW, and was volunteer co-ordinator for the Olympic Torch Relay celebrations in Armidale, before going to Sydney as a volunteer. Judy recalls: 'I have volunteered in countless sporting and community groups over the past 30 years, but being part of the euphoria of an Olympic City was something for which one could never be prepared. I have been asked many times "what was the highlight?" but the experience was a highlight! The essence of volunteering is serving, so the simple act of providing an Indian hockey player with a cup of tea rated with other more visual roles. Of course, attending a major event such as the second Opening Ceremony Dress Rehearsal was a bonus only attained by having put oneself in the environment by volunteering!'

Graham Webb's Olympic commitment began as Liaison Officer for the Olympic Torch Relay in the Burdekin Shire Council District in Far North Queensland. He then went to Sydney, where he recalls: 'My experience at the Uniform Distribution and Accreditation Centre (UDAC) at Redfern, and in Spectator Services at Olympic events will remain in my memory as one of my greatest achievements as a volunteer. Special moments which resulted from just being there were, attending the final Dress Rehearsal for the Opening Ceremony, witnessing my niece Karrie Webb (the World's number 1 Woman Golfer) light a cauldron at Sydney Town Hall, and generally mixing and associating with the greatest bunch of Australian and overseas volunteers I have had the pleasure of being associated with.'

Not all volunteers who contributed to the success of the Olympic and Paralympic Games actually attended the Games. **Don Williams** of Oregon, USA, has vast experience as a competitor, coach and administrator in the sport of Shooting, and came to Australia for the Shooting test event in March 2000. As Don indicated, his skills were not fully utilised, but he certainly enjoyed his time in Australia, and could see the Games-time event would be a success. Thanks for your contribution Don.

Ean Lapshinoff came all the way from Canada to be part of the Olympic experience as a Spectator Services Host. A special moment he witnessed on his very first day was when Mohammed Ali came through his access passage and embraced one of the ladies in attendance. Ean recalls, 'As he moved away, her emotion was obvious, and I quietly said to her, *He still stings like a bee!*'

'I live in the United States, and was looking forward to serving as a Village Volunteer in Sydney. Although I had already served as a volunteer at the 1996 Atlanta Olympic Games, nothing could have prepared me for what was ahead of me. From the moment my host and friend and fellow Village Volunteer, **Richard Keegan**, picked me up at the airport, it was just one amazing experience!

'I returned to the United States the day following the parade, feeling as if I had both left a piece of me in Australia, and also brought back a piece of Oz with me. Thank you all!' ... **Jean-Pierre Caravan**

'I live in Brisbane, and this was my first time in Sydney – Wow! Being part of the 2000 Sydney Olympic Games was just unbelievable. However, being allocated to Information Technology in the Athletes Village, in close contact with athletes when they required support, made me feel that I had contributed in a very special way.' ... **Michael Smith**

Family Impact!

Alisha Crook's Olympic Volunteer involvement had a major impact on her family, as her mother Kathy recalls: 'Alisha's excitement was infectious, for family, neighbours and friends – but by the time she had packed and unpacked her bag hundreds of times in the final six weeks, we were nearly glad to see her go!

'The experience was obviously life changing, and to this day we still enjoy hearing about it, and hearing from fellow volunteers who still communicate with her by email. Living in Perth, we obviously

IBN HELP INFO VOLUNTEER – PAULA FISCHER FROM GERMANY

KERRY HANSEN – COUNTRY FIRE AUTHORITY VOLUNTEER TO TECHNICAL SPECIALIST VOLUNTEER AT THE OLYMPIC STADIUM

UNA GRANTHAM AND DAUGHTER JENNY BLANCH FROM MANILLA (CENTRAL NORTHERN NSW)

spectator services volunteer Johanna Mullen (from vienna, austria) with japanese supporters

the sign says it!

(l to r) Joan Schloss from queensland with sydney colleagues – Wendy, Florence and Leah

(l to r) Chris Morris, Donna Stanford, Dave Smart, Col Burnes, Sharne Kershaw, Steve Campbells, Sharon Newell, John Hickey, Coral Lorimer, Susie Darrant, John Lennan, Carmen McDonald and Paul Mathews – a team of volunteers from tamworth and gunnedah who were support crew for photographers

dual olympic hockey gold medallist – Renita Garard – celebrates with north queensland olympic volunteers in townsville photo by Stewart McLean felt a little isolated from events, but the parade was a fantastic experience for the families of the Perth volunteers, as I am sure it was for the families in other states. It gave us a chance to be part of what our loved ones had participated in. I know I was bursting with pride when Alisha paraded with her fellow volunteers and the Olympians.'

'Coming from Darwin in the Northern Territory, it was a bit of a shock to be getting up at five o'clock on a cold Sydney morning! It is interesting how passion and excitement can change habits. I was pleasantly surprised to find that my supervisor at the Aquatic Centre one day was a fellow Territorian from Darwin, called Tricia, who lives close to me in Darwin.

'Credit must go to my sister Olive and her family, with whom I stayed in Summer Hill, Sydney. Without their help, I might not have been able to attend the Games.' ... Dez Wilde (Spectator Services Host)

'My father had defended this country, so my peacetime contribution was as a testimony of appreciation for his sacrifice. My initiation to the Olympic Games was in Ballarat in 1956, where the rowing events were held. The seed had been planted, and after my disappointment of Melbourne not succeeding in its bid for the 1996 Games, I was determined to be part of Sydney's Games.' ...
Bill Kirk (Spectator Services Host)

Years of volunteering at the Wandin Park Horse Trials in Victoria provided Andrea Banbury and Bob Adam the expertise and opportunity to be volunteers at the Olympic Equestrian events – Thanks for the contribution.

'My parents, Ralph and Joan Stilgoe, had been working as SOCOG Pioneer Volunteers for some time and were full of praise for the whole program. Consequently, I was elated when offered to be part of the hockey test event, which has now resulted in me being a volunteer at the Olympic Hockey events. It has been wonderful to share this experience as a family.' ... Lynda Peters

Robert Pearce carried the Olympic Torch as a 16-year-old in 1956, and is now being touched by the Olympics for the second time. Robert has taken time off from his practice as a plastic surgeon in Perth, Western Australia, to do medical support at the World Swimming Championships in Perth in 1991 and 1998, the Olympic Swimming Selection Trials in Sydney and the Olympic Games. Satisfaction that far outweighs the sacrifice.

Four residents of Wangaratta in central Victoria were part of the Olympic Doping Control Team. They were Ric and Jenny Chivers, Noel Boyd and Jayne Anderson. All enjoyed the one-on-one contact with athletes, as they escorted them to press conferences, medal ceremonies and finally for drug testing. Noel said, 'I think the IOC is going to get right behind doping control and will put lots more funding into it, because there are still a lot of drugs which are undetectable.'

'I have had the best 17 days of my life, at the Sydney Olympic Games. I am from Charters Towers, a small town in Far North Queensland. Our volunteer parade was a day to remember. The people were wonderful, thanking us for our services, but I could never thank them enough for allowing me to be part of the Games.' ... **Jennifer Oss**

'I was a volunteer at the airport in logistics. And we felt the spirit of the Games from the first moment that Olympic Family members began to arrive. To be involved in this absolutely well organised event is the best experience I could ever get. I have taken this unforgettable experience and the unbelievable Olympic Spirit back with me to my friends and family in Germany.' ... **Oliver Spellmann**

Coral Evely has worked with swimmers for over 30 years, and the announcement that Sydney would host the 2000 Olympic Games stirred her interest. 'One of the most exciting moments for me was when I received my letter advising I'd been accepted at the Aquatic Centre venue as a Print Distribution System Operator. I was really going! Not just watching on television!

'Having worked at the test event, it was easy to slot in with a great team of people who worked well together. On top of being so close to the action, this just contributed to a wonderful experience.' ... **Coral**

'At 19 years of age it was a huge commitment to come from Perth, Western Australia, to Sydney for the Olympic Games. As a result I am very grateful to my Uncle and Aunt for providing a home.

'To be rostered for the Opening Ceremony was unbelievable, but I was ecstatic when I was sent to look after the first 50 rows in the southern stand directly opposite the Cauldron. The Opening Ceremony was magical – for the very first time in my life I felt immense pride during our national anthem. It was then that I realised I was part of something huge. I thought about how 60 years ago, young people my age would have swelled with pride at the anthem as they left for war to defend this nation. It dawned on me that instead of feeling pride in war, I was experiencing pride in peace.' ... **Kylie Marmion (Spectator Services Host)**

SOUTH COAST NSW VOLUNTEERS PREPARE FOR STREET PARADE IN NOWRA

SPECTATOR SERVICES HOST ALBERT NHEU-LEONG WITH JOSE RAMOS HORTA. ALBERT IS FROM EAST TIMOR, AND NOW LIVES IN WESTERN AUSTRALIA

'I am a university student studying Physical Education at RHIT in Melbourne. I could not think of a better way to spend my holidays than as I did as a Spectator Services volunteer in the Main Press Centre at the Sydney Olympic Games.' ... **Sam Ditty**

'Coming from Bundaberg in Queensland, this was really a trip into the unknown, but sport is a major part of my life, both as sports editor of Bundaberg's daily newspaper and as a player and administrator in a number of sports. After having had the honour of carrying the Olympic Torch in my home town on its 100-day journey around Australia, working as a volunteer in Sydney gave me a special affinity with the whole event.

'Working at the Equestrian Centre as an Olympic News Service reporter was mostly hard work, but we were looked after well. Having to provide my own transport from Queensland, and find accommodation, was a small price to pay for being part of a great celebration of sport and humanity.' ... **Vince Habermann**

'I worked at the Uniform Distribution and Accreditation Centre (UDAC) at Redfern, then for variety went to Archery Park – memories of which are life-long. However, it was all in jeopardy, because as soon as I arrived in Sydney from my home in Rockhampton in Queensland, I came down with the dreaded flu, and unaware that I had become allergic to Penicillin, I came out in a bright red rash all over my body.

'Fortunately, with medical help and determination I went on to enjoy the volunteer experience. The spirit was still very much alive on my return to Rockhampton, with the visit of Olympians and Paralympians, plus award functions.' ... **Janice Keys**

Bill Kirtley travelled from Geelong in Victoria to volunteer as a Venue Staffing Assistant at the Baseball Stadium at Sydney Olympic Park. Bill recalls: 'The movement of people was phenomenal. There were many highlights, but the main highlight was the atmosphere – the organisational triumphs and the enjoyment achieved by all the volunteers. The motto of our staffing group was "We are here to serve and look after you". This I believe was carried out by everyone who was fortunate to be a volunteer.'

At 2 am the volunteers are tired, but closing ceremony tickets are the prize!

Lesley Lincoln from Wingham (Mid North Coast NSW)

Ian MacRae from Parkes (Central Western NSW)

'The atmosphere was amazing – almost unexplainable. All the emotions were mixed up. I didn't know what I was feeling – sadness (because it was all over); the realisation that this was the Closing Ceremony of the OLYMPICS – the big thing that all our lives stop for every four years; joy because I was there and I'd been part of it, pride, honour, proud to be Australian – all mixed up inside of me, leaving me not knowing which emotion was making me cry!' ... **Sally Summers**

Macedonian volunteer – **Peter Vrtkovski** from Newcastle – was kindly assisted by Accredited National Interpreting and Translating Services in expressing his thoughts: 'It was extremely exhilarating and rewarding to be among people and athletes of the world. Along with the whole world I waited every day with impatience and much happiness. They were days that will be remembered forever, which people will talk about for the rest of their lives. There were days that would allow me to personally convey to others certain moments, but more significantly to tell my family about very important days and moments for my children to know and remember. For them they were images that cannot be erased, dates and figures deeply entrenched with inspiration as well as pride in our hearts. The experiences of this period will always be a very diverse topic for discussion. The contents are endless, as for their historical worth, this is sealed in the world print.'

'This was a huge adventure from Perth, so after uniform collection on my first full day in Sydney, I ventured excitedly to Olympic Park for the first time. All I had seen of it were pictures in the media. I remember so well my first sight of the Olympic Rings as you leave the train station, and the feeling of awe and amazement. Soaking it in, I walked all the way around to the entrance at Gate K and was initially surprised that I was permitted entry into the Stadium. However, it quickly dawned on me that I actually did belong here. For a second time in minutes the feeling of awe and excitement overcame me as I got my first glimpse through Aisle 131 into the Stadium – what a moment to remember! From then on I knew I was in for a treat!' ... **Shaun D'Monte (Winthrop, Western Australia)**

(L to R) Josette Bennett (Sydney), Julie Fergerson (Sydney), Andrea Penny (York, WA) and Karin Lawrence (Newcastle)

The two-hour trip each way from Newcastle!

Nessie McGuire from Maryborough Queensland – 'You can arrest me any time!'

(L to R) Giulana Sigala, Akiko Gregory and Gloria Lee – volunteers at the technical officials village

Mark Elsley from Muswellbrook

Spectator services host Beryl Wagner with local hero Justin Norris in Stockton, NSW

'They were memories of a lifetime – enriching experiences with people who helped overcome the difficulties sometimes encountered. I will not miss the 2.30 am rise to catch a train from Newcastle, nor the severe attack of influenza. However, it was worth it all to be part of a momentous occasion in Australian history.' ... **Mary Power (Spectator Services Host)**

'There were just so many special moments about my Olympic experience that they blend into one. However, something which stands out for me is the people – from those at the bed and breakfast where I stayed to my fellow volunteers. If I met you while I was in Sydney, thank you for enriching my life, and I do sincerely mean every person I met.

'I managed to get one of the $1300 tickets to the Closing Ceremony, but I was returning to Perth that evening and couldn't go. Instead I gave it to someone I had met only days earlier who had come from Canada to be at the Games. So many people have since told me that I was mad to give it away, but to me that is not what the Olympics are all about. It was just my way of hopefully making someone else as happy as being a volunteer had made me.' ... **Michelle Gavranich**

'One moment that will always remain with me was on the night that Don Elgin won his medal. A young girl and boy sitting in the stands were yelling to Don as he came back from the track through the "mixed zone". Don couldn't come across the zone to them, and our job was to ensure that nobody got from the stands to the athletes. Don obviously knew these kids and on the spur of the moment my colleague and I broke the rules and helped these two kids over the fence so that they could get to speak with Don. A National Technical Official stormed towards us ready to go ballistic over the breach of security. He pulled up short when he saw both kids take off their legs to have Don sign them. Neither of us volunteers knew that both kids were amputees till that moment, and the NTO with tears in his eyes thanked us for doing what we had done, trying to say that this is what the Games are all about.' ... **Neil Hinton (from South Tacoma, NSW)**

We started before the sun came up,
To work in the sunny heat.
But being a volunteer at the Games
It really can't be beat.

Just open up this volunteer book
Whenever you're feeling sad.
And you will smile once again,
Knowing it was the best time you ever had....

Geraldine McKinnis (from West Brunswick, Victoria) Spectator Services Host

W. Carrol Reynolds is a 74-year-old former member of the Australian Men's Hockey Team, and came from Glenelg, South Australia, to be an ORTA volunteer. Carrol recalls: 'There was so much good about my stay in Sydney, from the patience of the volunteers, to the friendliness of the spectators, and the athletic achievement. However, after associating with the Paralympians, and seeing what they overcome in everyday life, I will never ever complain about anything again!'

'There has been much said about the sacrifices that volunteers had to make – time away from family back in Perth was the only sacrifice I really had to think about, though it was my wife Sharon and children Jessica (eight) and Mitchell (five) that encouraged me to go. It would be a month away from them – a couple of days was probably the most we'd been apart before – but they were prepared to make their own sacrifices to allow me to have an experience of a lifetime. I was a little worried though, when after I had been gone for three days Mitchell packed himself a backpack, including food, and announced that he was off to Sydney to see me! There were others who made sacrifices too – Graham and Melissa Hynson, my brother and sister-in-law, took me in to their home with their two young children. I lived in their lounge room for three-and-a-half weeks and I can't thank them enough for the sacrifice they made.' ...
Mark Hardy

'I am a keen equestrian and hope to breed my champion dressage horse this season. That's why when the opportunity arose to become involved in the Olympics as a volunteer, I never hesitated. I was fortunate enough to have been placed in the Equestrian Centre as a Team Leader Spectator Services for the Olympics, and I couldn't be prouder. To have the world's best here at home is an occasion not to be missed.' ... **Michelle Zielazo (from Coffs Harbour)**

'I was 12 years old when Sydney won the right to host the Olympic Games. Now I am at university, and a Games Technology Volunteer at Darling Harbour. There were just so many good things about being involved in this wonderful event, I had an absolute ball! As George Gershwin would say: "Who could ask for anything more?"' ... **Joshua McKay (Gosford, NSW)**

South sector spectator services hosts on closing ceremony night. Sylvie Beaudoin (front) is from Otterburne, Manitoba, Canada

Spectator services host Sally Summers (from Blackburn, Victoria)

(L to R) Phillip Friend (team leader), Bronwyn Stanborough (from Lake Macquarie) and Noel Butler (from Lake Macquarie)

Husband and wife team Peter and Heather Moore from Forbes in central western NSW. Although working at different venues, they have fond memories to share from their time at Sydney Olympic Park

My home during the trials in August – with five trips to Sydney, accommodation became the issue – John Kneen (Cheltenham, Victoria)

(L to R) David Clarke (from Mount Gambier), Bob Powles and George Northend (from Melbourne) – volunteers at the Equestrian Centre who had one fantastic adventure at the opening ceremony!

(L to R) Martin and Christine Gregory share the paralympic experience with son and daughter-in-law, Neil and Lynette Gregory

'My time as a volunteer was a most rewarding experience, it was demanding yet challenging and showed just how the human spirit can rise above often difficult personal circumstances and soar!' ... **Rosslyn Hamilton (Clarinda, Victoria)**

Out of Town Comments

'In the volunteers group I worked with, there were many countries represented: Greece, Philippines, Hong Kong, China, Indonesia, Cambodia, Ghana, Australia and France. If the Olympic Games did not exist, we would never have met. To share our own experiences, our cultures, was really worthy and rewarding.' ... **Yves Mayanobe (France)**

Frith and Heath Hatfield are sister and brother who travelled from Aitkenvale in Far North Queensland to be Spectator Services Hosts at Sydney Olympic Park. Heath recalls: 'We stayed in a motel at Gosford on the Central Coast, and travelled in by train each day. The greatest part about being volunteers at the Sydney Olympics was being able to meet and work with so many different people. It was a great thrill to be able to exchange contact details and have photos taken with some of our volunteer teammates. Receiving an invitation to a barbecue lunch at the home of one of our fellow volunteers was also very special. We now have friends in many places we previously did not.'

'My volunteer experience was a magical one. What an honour to serve at the Olympic Village, to meet athletes from all over the world, and not only to experience the Olympics, but Australia!' ... **Susan Thomas (Montana, USA)**

'As a Spectator Services Host in the Common Domain at Sydney Olympic Park during the Games I was amazed and thrilled at the number of people who came up to me at the end of my eight-hour shift and thanked me.' ... Chris Gore (Queensland)

'The best part about it was the atmosphere everywhere in Sydney and the way in which we, as volunteers, all contributed to that buzz! For many of us, this Parade represented the only time in our lives that we would be recognised in this way, and it was very, very special.' ... Daughter and Father – Michelle and Ian Hansen (Melbourne)

'I don't consider working as a volunteer at the Olympics and Paralympics as a job, but as an achievement of a lifelong dream.' ... Yvette Chapman (Collie, Western Australia)

'I came from Queensland to be a part of the Games and it was all worth every penny I spent because I had fulfilled a dream for my late mother who was able to see me prepared to do it but did not get to see me actually go.' ... Stephen Hughes

'I was privileged to work at the Main entry to the Village, greeting guests of the IOC and athletes. I spoke with representatives of most countries, all enjoying the high we all felt for those two magical weeks in September.' ... Betty Charge (Melbourne)

'After having a wonderful time in Sydney for the Olympics and Paralympics, I returned to Melbourne only to have a drama-filled arrival. When I proceeded to get my suitcase off the airport bus at Franklin Street, it was not there. Apparently off-loaded at the previous stop! The driver took me back, but there was no sign of it. He asked what was in it, and when I said – clothing, Olympic volunteer uniform, souvenirs, camera and mobile phone – he immediately called my number on his mobile phone. Much to my surprise, we received an answer – it was a policeman! The irony of the story was that the lady who took it to the police station was a volunteer at the football at the MCG.' ... Grant Smith

That will look good on your CV Gran! '... so said my 20-year-old grandson when told I was to be a volunteer at the Paralympics. Well I had an absolutely marvellous time at the Shooting Centre. Thank God for good health and the co-operation of my family – my thanks to all, and to coin a phrase – I wouldn't have missed it for anything. And NO, I won't worry about compiling a CV!' ...
Mary Cunningham (Lithgow, NSW)

'I am British born, and live with my German husband south of Munich. Once I completed the required procedure for becoming a volunteer, we did a house swap with friends in the Sydney suburb of Mosman.

'What a wonderful experience, and to cap it all off with that awesome Volunteers Parade! Our local newspaper has been doing articles on my experiences, and the German people are very impressed with what Sydney achieved.' ... Paula Fischer

Briefs from passionate people

'Special thanks must go to those within the NSW softball community who billeted volunteers like myself. Their willingness to open up their homes was greatly appreciated and made the whole volunteer experience much more enjoyable as the booking and cost of accommodation was one thing that I and others did not have to concern ourselves about.' ... Sandra Drummond (Isabella Plains, ACT)

'In 1956 we were engaged at the Ballarat Rowing Olympic Venue, and went to events daily in Melbourne. Now 44 years later we attended daily in Sydney – as volunteers.' ... Alan and Davia Smith (Renmark, South Australia)

'I was born in Argentina and have lived in Australia for 36 years. I volunteered to offer my ability to speak Spanish. I am glad I was able to do so, as I had a most wonderful experience at the Tennis Centre.' ... Marilen Gibson (Maroochydore, Queensland)

'My scepticism was soon erased. As soon as we landed in Sydney there was a completely different atmosphere. Although I don't know how to put it into words, I know that everyone who volunteered in Sydney will know what I mean when I speak of the amazing atmosphere in Sydney.' ... Adele Vosper (Melbourne)

'Because most of our work happened late at night and into the wee small hours, we were fortunate to be rostered on at around 10 am and be able to watch from our accredited seating most of the competition before we had to start work around 5.30 or 6 pm usually finishing anywhere from 11 pm to 2 am, then with two hours of travelling to reach the places most of us were billeted in.' ... Diana Woodward (Kempsey, NSW)

'My Olympic Friends may come and go, and nobody knows wherever. But my Memories of the Olympic Games will stay with me forever.' ... Gert Riley (Inala, Queensland)

'Success breeds success. Positive and electric energy from all men, women and children at Homebush generated an energy field that transferred from one to another, then across Sydney, the State and maybe even the Nation.' ... Jill Street (Rockhampton, Queensland)

'I became a volunteer through my employer BHP Minerals. I work at the Cannington Mine in north west Queensland, where we mined the silver donated for the Olympic and Paralympic medals.' ... Cherie Dolan

'My companion Wink Morand and I were Spectator Services Hosts at the Equestrian Centre, and enjoyed the experience and hospitality so much, until Wink became ill, and we had to return home abruptly – our apologies to those we did not say goodbye to.' ... Marjory Vanghel (Florida, USA)

'I had a wonderful time, but by the time the Olympics and Paralympics were over I was glad, due to the long hours and missing my family for two months. But guess what! I have just put my name down for the Goodwill Games in 2001.' ... Roberta Lawson (Queensland)

(L TO R) DANIELLA RIZZATO, ADELE MASCORD, MAUREEN CASTLE (FROM MACLEAN, NSW), SONIA O'SULLIVAN (MARATHON SILVER MEDALLIST FROM IRELAND), JAN FONTANA AND CHRISTINE AGOPIOU (SITTING)

PARALYMPIANS AND VOLUNTEERS AT CIVIC RECEPTION IN ROCKHAMPTON, QUEENSLAND

'I had never volunteered for anything in my life. I've always been too selfish and full of excuses ... by volunteering at the Sydney Olympic Games, I had made a difference and it will continue to make a difference in me.' ... **Graeme Smith (Wagga Wagga, NSW)**

Brother and sister – **David and Kellie Saundes** – live in north-western NSW. Being eight hours by car from Sydney they had to plan well for their pre-games training, especially as David was in his Higher School Certificate year, and Kellie had many weekends in Sydney for National Olympic Committee Assistant training. However, no matter what the commitment, David and Kellie felt they were part of something special.

Leigh Reis came from Brisbane to volunteer as a Venue Staffing Assistant at the Main Press Centre. Her local newspaper printed an article regarding her proposed trip, and before she knew it, another volunteer, Jenny, who was travelling from Brisbane suggested she could stay with her mother **Pat**, who was also a volunteer. Another case of volunteers supporting one another.

Leigh recalls: 'The amazing thing about being in Sydney was that for three weeks I was surrounded by happy enthusiastic people. We gained free entry to a nightclub because we were "vollies". When there was a language barrier, smiles seem to take care of all those words that weren't understood. Our job was to make sure everyone was having fun, we were the "fun" police.'

'I travelled from Dapto south of Sydney to Homebush every day – approximately three hours each way. Because of my interest in Tennis, I was glad to be working as a Swiss Timing Assistant at the Tennis Centre, and being court-side meant seeing the action first hand. The dedication of volunteers, and the appreciation shown to them, was part of the unity established by all people.' ... **Sharad Kotwal**

'I applied to be a volunteer in medical, but was advised that all positions were filled. Then came the offer to be a Spectator Services Host. Well, I couldn't believe what a wonderful experience this turned out to be – the great attitude of the people, camaraderie and appreciation. I think I have had a little insight to what our creator wished us to be.' ... **Margaret Stephen (Bathurst, NSW)**

'I had both my knees replaced 18 months ago, and with my multiple sclerosis I never dreamed I could get up at 2 am to catch a train for an early start at Sydney Olympic Park. Every morning I would go and stand under the Cauldron and look up at the Flame, it was still dark and not very many people around, and I would think – I can't believe I am looking at the Olympic Flame in Australia!' ... **Rita Potten (Tuggerah, Central Coast, NSW)**

John Hughes, from Christies Beach in South Australia, enjoyed two special Olympic experiences. First, he carried the Olympic Torch into Adelaide, having been nominated for his work with Life Line and other organisations in Australia, plus volunteer work in the Pacific Islands, Papua New Guinea, India, Nepal and the Philippines with children in poverty. John then brought his caravan to Sydney to be a Transport Operations volunteer.

Kevin Baker (NOC/NPC Driver) and **Kathy Rein** (Spectator Services Host) jumped at the opportunity to volunteer for the Olympics and Paralympics, even though it meant travelling from Nowra on the south coast of NSW. Kathy recalls: 'I will probably volunteer for other things later on, at the moment I am trying to recover. It is called the Green and Gold Malaria!'

'I was an interstate volunteer from a small Queensland town called Gin Gin. I put my job on the line and came away with just the best memories. Something I never thought I would experience was people cheering and congratulating volunteers, it was absolutely fantastic. Now I know how the athletes feel.' ... **Helen Driver**

'As the primary school students sang "G'day, G'day" at the team welcome ceremony tears began to well in my eyes. At this point I realised the true ideal of the Olympic and Paralympic Games, and I was part of it.' ... **Brian Taylor (Charlestown, NSW – Volunteer Resident Centre 18 – Athletes Village)**

(L to R) Sharon Sands, Keryn McPherson, Sharon Solomon (from Greenwell Point, South Coast NSW) and Jenny Rouland (Ceremonies Audience Leaders)

Davi Howard (Spectator Services Host) from Queensland

Belinda Tewes (from Gidgegannup, Western Australia) with fellow volunteers (L to R) Dirk Djkstra and Hugh Watson

'Working in the Athletes Village, it was amazing to see the difference in the athletes from when they arrived till they left. Initially subdued, the atmosphere gradually changed with all countries living and eating together. I like to think we Aussies with our ready smiles, friendly easy-going ways, talking to everyone and doing our PR best helped to change that.' ... Jan Bell (Adelaide)

'I have smiled a million times
Walked a million miles
Taken a million photos
Shared a million happy stories
Best of all received a million praises
What a privilege to have been part of it all
Thank you SOCOG it has been an honour...'

Carolanne Odgaard (Dysart, Queensland) Spectator Services Host – Common Domain – SOP

'I reside on the north coast of NSW in the town of South Grafton, and have had a long association with sport. However, nothing could have prepared me for the wonderful two months I spent in the Athletes Village as Info Help Officer (Technology). Having to service equipment throughout the Village gave me a special appreciation of the world's athletes living in peace together.' ... Stephen Manning

'When my husband of 40 years passed away in January 1999, running our property of mixed grain and sheep was beyond me, and thankfully my son Stewart and his wife Gayle came home to run it. I guess the opportunity to become involved in the Olympic and Paralympic Games was the tonic I needed to give me a focus.

'I worked in Spectator Services at Sydney Olympic Park sharing the excitement of passionate supporters – then for the Paralympics it was off to the Shooting Centre, and the inspiration of these athletes left me vowing never to complain again.' ... Judy Day (Ardlethan, NSW)

'For a long time the thought of being accepted as a volunteer at the Olympic and Paralympic Games seemed surreal to me because I live approximately 1500 kms north of Sydney in a town called Maryborough, Queensland. I can still remember the day I received my letter of invitation – what a day! I believe my life changed direction that very moment.

'There were some hurdles to overcome – like accommodation and travel expenses – but wonderful friends and family helped with car washes to raise funds. This experience raised many firsts for me, like the 21-hour bus trip to Sydney – never having been outside Queensland before – plus my maiden voyage on a plane when I came home.

'My most memorable moments included the camaraderie and friendships among volunteers, encouraged by our wonderful managers, Kathryn Bendall and David Woods.' ... Noreen Wroe

(L TO R) BEV MUSCAT, JANE ROOKES AND KATE CLEMENT (TAMWORTH, NSW)
WHO IS HOPING TO BE AN EQUESTRIAN PARALYMPIAN IN 2004

MAJELLA SMITH SPECTATOR SERVICES HOST FROM THE CENTRAL COAST, NSW

'It started with carrying the Olympic Torch on 23 August 2000. Then I was a Resident Centre Assistant at the Technical Officials Village at Macquarie University, where it was pleasant to meet colleagues from my years as a Tennis Umpire. Finally the Resident Centre position in the Paralympic Village reinforced the generous "can do" attitude and great appreciation for others.' ... **Wayne Binch (West Tweed Heads, NSW)**

Uplifting Moment!

'On my first day as a volunteer I made a dash to the porta loos near the P1 Car Park, only to make a hurried exit when I heard a tractor motor nearby. Luckily I did, otherwise I would have been relocated to another part of the Regatta Centre on the front of a forklift!' ... **Jan Flint (Cobar, NSW)**

'Before I left Melbourne, people were saying, "Why are you doing this for NO pay?" giving me strange looks as if I had gone completely MAD. When I said that I would resign if leave was not approved there were further looks of shock. Now I am back home, they all wish they had been part of this wonderful experience.' ... **Sue Poyner (Lilydale, Victoria)**

'We experienced so much in such a short time, and no one else could possibly fathom what it was like. After attending five training sessions in Sydney (I am from Torquay, Victoria), I was assigned as Protocol Assistant to the IOC Member for the Philippines. He and his wife were the loveliest people and we shared many a laugh. This experience has changed me forever and given me much more confidence in myself.' ... **Jane Cox**

'The Games may have come and gone, but the memories will be with us for a lifetime. We came from far and wide as strangers and left as friends.' ... **Carol Tygielski (Guyra, NSW)**

Denise Dunstan and her husband **David Locklee** live in Tamworth, NSW. While their volunteer roles were in different venues and different capacities (Denise – Olympic Volunteers in Policing, and David – Spectator Services), they both came away sharing similar great experiences and new friendships to share. 'We've placed our names down as volunteers for the Winter Olympics at Salt Lake City in 2002. Here's hoping!'

Rebecca Bosworth was an 18-year-old school student in Nowra on the NSW south coast, when accepted as a Guest Pass Assistant in the Athletes Village. Before she even took up this position, she was also offered the position of Placard Bearer for the Central African country of Belize in the Opening and Closing Ceremonies. 'I have loved every minute while performing these two very exciting roles, and it is a wonderful way to begin my after school career in the travel industry.'

'Coming from Victoria, a lot of people were sceptical about the fact that I had to pay to get there, they just didn't understand. I was going to be part of something huge! The company I had only been working with for four months was so understanding of my passion and excitement, and gave me the five weeks off to go to Sydney. To make things even better, a colleague in our Sydney office offered me a spare room for the whole period. Could it get any better? YES!!! IT COULD!!!

'I drove to Sydney on adrenalin! When I got my uniform it totally transformed me! It changed my personality, I couldn't stop smiling in it, I couldn't help asking people if they needed help, chatting to strangers offering directions!

Mandy Chapple (from Warialda, NSW) with tennis player Mark Woodforde

(Second from left) Audrey McDonald (from Wamberal, NSW) joins fellow volunteers in the volunteers parade

Jenny Bottrell, of Wagga Wagga, NSW, shares the excitement with Brazilian bronze medallist at beach volleyball

Lesley Hopley works in the not so positive environment of the South Australian prison system, so jumped at the opportunity to volunteer with this positive group of people

'All I can think of is "What if I hadn't done it? Look what I would have missed out on!" ... **Tara Dimond (Spectator Services Host – Tennis Centre)**

'After the announcement of Sydney's successful bid, my wife Jeannie said, "Gee wiz, won't this be a great celebration, I wonder if we will live to see the Games?" It was only the next year that Jeannie began her fight with cancer, which she lost on 4 April 1996.

'After pulling my life into gear, I made up my mind to become involved as a volunteer as we had discussed back in 1993. I was to become a Spectator Services Host at the Millennium Marquee at Sydney Olympic Park. There were many exciting moments for me, from the happy faces of our patrons to the lighting of the Cauldron by Cathy Freeman.

'One special moment for me was while standing beside the Baseball Stadium during the Closing Ceremony, looking at the Flame and the stars above. Suddenly BOOM as if it came out of the Baseball Stadium, the plane flew directly above my head, and looking up I saw the Flame had been extinguished – GONE! It was as if at this precise time all my wife's aspirations of 1993 were achieved, for with tears flowing down my face I knew my late wife had not missed the Games.' ... **Ian Murray (Budgewoi, NSW)**

'Both my brother **Steven** and I were volunteers – he was in the Athletes Village and I was in the Media Village. As young people, we not only enjoyed the atmosphere and experience gained through performing our duties, but we couldn't get enough of the excitement and party atmosphere of Sydney. It was a privilege to participate in such a magnificent event, but I did not want it to end!' ... **Jonathan Lindsay (Newcastle, NSW)**

'I live with my family in Brisbane, and my father lives in Kiama, south of Sydney. After considerable discussion we all decided to become volunteers – Father, **Neville Burnett** (Driver), Husband, **Quentin Brown** (Driver), Son, **Nathaniel Brown** (IBM Help Officer), Son, **Samuel Brown** (Events Results Runner) and myself (Spectator Services Host).

'A man my husband met when in Sydney for training offered all the family accommodation, within walking distance of Sydney Olympic Park. This was obviously of great benefit to us all, and while as a family there can be the normal difficulties trying to fit the pieces of the jigsaw together with all our different rosters, it was wonderful as a family to be making this all happen. Three generations shared this special experience.

After celebrating his 70th birthday on 15 November 2000, Neville Burnett was rushed to hospital – he died on 7 December 2000. He was proud to be a Volunteer.' ... **Pamela Brown.**

'I live in the old homestead on a 4500 acre Poll Hereford Stud Cattle property at the foot of the Snowy Mountains. The thought of nearly half a million people in what we would regard as the creek paddock, horrified me!

'Well scepticism aside, I became a volunteer for both the Olympics and Paralympics, and it was one special experience! I must admit that being given a megaphone to direct people instead of cattle was different, and I am sure it weighed 220 kg by the end of the shift!' ... **Greg Davies**

'I was a volunteer with the fast-paced and highly productive media machine covering Softball and Baseball at Blacktown Olympic Centre. My title was Flash Quote Reporter, and I was interviewing athletes and coaches as they walked past the Mixed Zone after a game. This was an opportunity for a university student to get firsthand experience for a journalism assignment!

'I was to be working with media from around the world, face to face with the world's best athletes. On the first day of volunteering I walked along a dirt path, winding its way to a white tent filled with people I didn't know, from all corners of the world. I was scared – no petrified. Reflecting on the final day, I didn't want to leave, loving the atmosphere and the people I had worked with for two weeks.' ... **Kara Nicholson (Lismore, NSW)**

'I was successful in gaining a volunteer position as a Medical Records Clerk at SOCOG Headquarters, and I can't explain the pride I felt. Since I applied, I have had a baby daughter who is now over eight months old, so there were some adjustments to be made.

VOLUNTEERS (MOSTLY FROM VICTORIA) AT EQUESTRIAN CENTRE

KATHERINE BEDFORD WITH HER FATHER, NOEL (PRESIDENT, YAMBA ROTARY) AFTER GIVING A PRESENTATION ABOUT HER OLYMPIC VOLUNTEERING EXPERIENCES

PHOTO BY BELINDA MELCHERS, *LOWER CLARENCE REVIEW*

GORDON AND GWENYTH WILKS TRAVELLED EACH DAY FROM KOONAWARRA (SOUTH OF WOLLONGONG)

(l to r) Val Raffanelli, Jean Smith and Antonette Mezzino – all from port pirie, south australia

Carole Barford and Paul Apter (ulladulla, south coast nsw)

resident centre volunteer Pamela Pybus (from rosny, tasmania) with canadian paralympian and performers

Leonie Barron (food and beverage assistant – athletes village) from maryborough, queensland. in a family contribution, Leonie's son Marcus was a volunteer at the olympic football in brisbane, and her daughter naomi worked with the british olympic team at their pre-games training on the queensland gold coast

mother and daughter – Barbara and Kimberley Martin from gatton, south east queensland – 'we have no public transport, just one taxi, so sydney was different!' Barbara's brother, Phillip Clucas and her father, John Clucas (both from sydney) were also volunteers, making it a three-generation contribution

Chris Brotherston (centre) from the thriving metropolis of merrygoen, nsw (population about 47)

'My main duty was data entry of medical incident forms, and it certainly was an eye opener as to what goes on behind the scenes. I think the funniest forms I came across were of a sprinter who sought medical attention for shortness of breath, and a pole vaulter who got vertigo during his event!' ... **Natalie Clark (Georgetown, South Australia)**

'I volunteered at the Sydney Olympic Games because while living in Melbourne in 1956, we had two Korean boxing officials staying with us. I attended events with my father, and became aware that the Olympics were something special.

'Working at the Uniform Distribution and Accreditation Centre was a rewarding experience, but I did also get to attend some events, including seeing my cousin, Jane Saville, come close to winning the Women's 20 km Walk.

'On Sunday, 10 September 2000, I held a "Champagne Breakfast" in my frontyard for 80 of my friends to greet the Olympic Torch as it came through Ulladulla on the south coast of NSW. This was a great build-up only 5 days out from the Opening Ceremony.' ... **Heather Baker**

'My daughter **Fiona** and I were passionate to volunteer at the Olympic Games, so my husband and I had to organise our beef farm a year ahead – the bulls had to go with the cows earlier so that the majority of calving was over before September. Fiona and I then went off to experience a wonderful three weeks in Sydney.

'Among so many special and exciting moments, one which stays with me was the day I met the Paulucci Family. Wendy Paulucci was the graphic designer with Bonds who designed our uniforms, so now whenever I was asked who designed our uniforms, I could not only say who, but that I had met Wendy.' ... **Ruth Holmes (Dorrigo, north coast, NSW)**

'We have a uniform. Strangers talk to uniforms. There's a feeling of security in that. Passengers on public transport, shoppers and neighbours are confident they will get answers to their questions. And the amazing thing is, if you wear a uniform you DO have knowledge. Not necessarily what you need to know, and not always what the person wants, but you can look confident. I have a theory: the more different coloured sleeves you speak to the more you find out!' ... **Janice Mason (Bunbury, Western Australia)**

Three members of the **Breen Family** from Casino on the north coast of NSW were volunteers for the Olympic Games – sisters **Lucinda** and **Katrina** were performers in the Opening Ceremony, while brother **Chris** was involved with the Road Cycling and Marathon events. Chris said: 'Although I am a keen cyclist, I also enjoyed seeing the world's best marathoners at close range.'

'My daughter **Samantha (Sam) Langford** was a volunteer at the Beach Volleyball at the Sydney Olympic Games. Through having worked at tournaments in Toronto, Canada, and being referred by visiting

New Zealand delegates she worked as an administrative assistant in the office of Dr Ruben Acosta Hernandez, President of the FIVB. Of course Mum and Dad had to cough up the cash for her ticket, but that's what we do for our kids, isn't it?' ... **John Langford (Proud Father in Canada)**

Out of Towners to be also recognised are: **Kevin McIntosh (Mollymook, NSW), Lesley Senior (Yass, NSW), Fred Husken (Port Macquarie, NSW), Julie Bingham (Adelaide), Debbie O'Carroll (Brisbane), Michele Vogt (Bathurst, NSW), Jane Wilson (Brisbane), Sherelle Graham (Brisbane), Steven Stefanopoulos (Prahran, Victoria), Sandra Smith (Arundel, Queensland), Stan Jenkins (Coraki, NSW), Trish Robins (Rockhampton, Queensland), David Isaacson (Perth), Wendy Holtom (Perth), Justin LeFebvre (Northern Territory), Leigh Halprin (Northern Territory), Florence Ramsay (Burpengary, Queensland), Joan Jarman (Korora Bay, NSW) and Peter Dawson (Wentworth Falls, NSW).**

Out of Town snippets

'What a blast! I thought there would be only a handful of volunteers turning up for the Parade!' ... **Eileen McKeogh (Perth)**

'It was an experience that is very hard to put into words when explaining it to others who were not part of it. I will never forget the bus queues at South Gate on Opening Ceremony night, or the small child who gave me a pin from his hat because he had two, but I especially will not forget the thousands of people who stopped to talk or to have their photo taken. It was an experience that went beyond my wildest expectations. I had an absolute ball, met some great people and enjoyed helping Sydney put on the best games ever.' ... **Kirsten Aldrich (Melbourne)**

'The cost of many trips to Sydney for training was always questioned by my friends, but once I was in the Olympic Village working with the wonderful team from Cayman Islands, I knew that I was experiencing something that they could never appreciate.' ... **Phillip Snedden (Currumbin Beach, Queensland)**

'We convinced a lady driving a mini bus to take us to the city – well the combination of her being from country NSW and us from Adelaide – the more we got lost the more we laughed.' ... **Jenny English (Adelaide)**

'You will only get out of life what you put into it – I am justly proud of the efforts of all those involved in the XXVII Olympic Games.' ... **Debbie Gibson (Perth)**

'It was a fantastic job – not only did I get to be in Sydney, but I also got to meet some fantastic people.' ... **Fiona Ryan (Adelaide)**

'I met Margaret and John overseas two years ago, and now I was having the best experience of my life, as staying with them allowed my dream to come true.' ... **Ruth Hallett (Tyabb, Victoria)**

'It was really great to see people from all over the world put aside their differences and come together for this wonderful sporting event.' ... **Janette (Jenny) Ballangarry (Nambucca Heads, NSW)**

'I travelled daily by train after driving 50 kms to Wyong Station arriving home most times at 2 am with a daily start of 3 pm.' ... **John O'Donnell (Central Coast, NSW)**

'My ten work days were great – the happiness, crowds, size of Olympic Park, the Venues, the glorious array of green and gold hats, wigs, clothes, flags, faces, etc.' ... **Dawn Trethewey (Redcliffe, Queensland)**

'In preparing for my first roster at the Hockey Centre, I compared myself to a cat on a hot tin roof! I just couldn't wait to get started. From the opening game I believed that I was not only a SOCOG volunteer, but an ambassador for my country.' ... **Mark Grant (Brisbane)**

'I cannot compare it with anything I have ever done, it was just amazing.' ... **Marilyn Sutter (Morphett Vale, South Australia)**

'The crowds were starting to get impatient, then to our surprise the Gold Medallist from Egypt came out, thanked us for what we were doing, then proceeded to talk to the waiting people and showing them his gold medal.' ... **Brendan Lambourne (Tivoli, Queensland).**

'If it wasn't for the support of the supervisors in Spectator Services I would not have enjoyed myself as much as I did. They made me feel at ease and gave me the confidence I needed to fulfil my dream.' ... **Danny Dalton (Tamworth, NSW)**

(L to R) Volunteers Julie Davis (from Austinmer, NSW), David Aust, Lanna Barrett and George Tarjan, with members of the Costa Rican delegation

Jean, Ian and Jacinta Blencowe from Melbourne, used school holidays, long service leave and leave without pay to make sure they would be available for the Olympic Games

'What started as a very boring day, turned out to be the best day ever – sharing the joy of the Cameroon Football players in winning their country's first ever Gold Medal.' ... **Marg Dawson (Castlemaine, Victoria)**

'I work as an Underground Mine Geologist on a two-week on, one-week off, fly-in-and-out roster on a remote Gold Mine some 800 km north of Kalgoorlie, Western Australia. My first ever visit to Sydney was as a Spectator Services Host for the Olympic Games! Amazing feelings, Amazing memories. Thanks Sydney!' ... **Tracey Edmonds (Dog Swamp, Western Australia)**

'I was only accepted as a volunteer in April 2000, after thinking I wasn't successful, to be told by my then boyfriend, "no you are not going". The relationship ended and I WAS going! Through countless emails through friends of friends, I found a couple named David and Kim, who were offering a room. There were many wonderful experiences and adventures during my stay in Sydney, but the highlight was my host family, without them I would not have had such a memorable time.' ... **Penelope Schulz (Barossa Valley, South Australia)**

'In all, 12 hours travel for less than two hours orientation! Was it worth it? Probably not! I told myself I wouldn't do it again! But I did!' ... **Bev Wilkinson (Nowra, NSW)**.

'I was in awe when I looked across to the Stadium to see the Flame burning so brightly against the dark sky. It was amazing. It was such a feeling that a tear of joy came to my eye. This was the Olympics!' ... **Fiona Lemmon (Morisset, NSW)**

'When my accommodation arrangements fell through at the last minute I was fortunate to be put up by the Potts Family. I cannot thank my "Olympic Family" enough for their generosity. **Kerry** and **Georgie Potts** and their daughter **Kylie**, who I had met at the Australian Swimming Selection Trials, treated me like family. Kerry was NOC Driver for Poland and Kylie worked with me at the Aquatic Centre – we had so much fun. Georgie was our TOTAL support.' ... **Rhiannon Avery (Kaleen, ACT)**

'The smile was sufficient remuneration, especially when shared with another nation.' ... **Maureen Greenhalgh (Bribie Island, Queensland)**

'In the area of personal development, I was able to take on several roles unfamiliar to me, and succeeded well beyond my expectations.' ... **Martyn Kibel (Melbourne)**

'The reason I became a volunteer was for the experience of being around so many people. I thought to myself, it's one way to overcome fear of crowds! I worked at Uniform Distribution, and day by day I increased in confidence meeting people from different cultures and nationalities – it was great.' ... **Mary Griffiths (Wagga Wagga, NSW)**

'In reflection, I worked as a Spectator Services Host Volunteer at two elite events with elite athletes (I had to keep reminding myself that these were the world's best, and I was there) and with people from all walks of life. Isn't it funny how dozens of people came up to me and thanked *me* for the greatest Games, as if they were *my* Games. Thank you to all of the people who made it happen and for allowing me to be part of it.' ... Ian Cook (Melbourne)

More to Recognise:
Graeme Bryce (Gympie, Queensland), Junene Stephens (Ulverstone, Tasmania), Kylie Kemp (Camberwell, Victoria), Pat Cooper (Ocean Shores, NSW), James Barlow (Orange, NSW), Marjorie Johnson (Kingsley, WA), Stephen Virgona (Geelong, Victoria), Michael Swift (Lithgow, NSW), Debbie Gibson (Hamilton Hill, Western Australia), Cynthia Jones (Clayton, South Australia), Sarah Boersen (Brisbane), Steve and Beryl McDonald (Sandy Beach, NSW), Emma Kelly (Townsville, Queensland), Toni Harris (Essendon, Victoria), Peter Evans (Northcote, Victoria), Lyn Williams (Coffs Harbour, NSW), Kate Howell (Clapham, South Australia), Debbie Bell (Waikerie, South Australia), Diana Edmonds (Singleton, NSW), Christine Ashley-Coe (Gowrie, ACT), Stefanie Krupp (Germany) and Mike Nicholson (Brisbane)

Out of Town quotes

'Although a Physiotherapist, I decided to be part of Spectator Services.' ...
Libby Loneragan (Bathurst, NSW)

'My volunteer experience towards the Olympic Games started when I was 18, and worked as a team Liaison Officer at the World Junior Athletics Championships in Sydney.' ...Jenny Birtles (Brisbane)

'One of the greatest things I will remember is how friendly all the people in Sydney were and their hospitality. People would talk to you on the train, in shopping centers, crossing the street, etc., simply because they wanted to know what it was like to be working at the Games.' ... Juanita St John (Townsville, Queensland)

'What a glorious experience – four days at the Sailing with a view to die for, and five days at Beach Volleyball.' ... Inge Vezer (Dandenong, Victoria).

'Some days I get butterflies in the stomach thinking about working at the Olympics and all that it requires, and other days I am so excited that I am just jumping from one thing to the next and organising everything in my head.' ... Linda Bilney (Kojonup, south of Perth)

'I got interested in the volunteer program by sheer curiosity and I haven't looked back.' ...
Kris McBride (ACT)

'As Olympic and Paralympic volunteer, and Paralympic Torch Bearer, this is the best experience of my life.' ... Linda Kezovska

'I was a volunteer in the Paralympic Village, and besides it being just a wonderful atmosphere, I loved the just do it attitude of the volunteers and athletes. By the time we had our closing of the Village party, I realised that this had been the greatest adventure of my life.' ... David Pollard (Rockhampton, Queensland)

(L TO R) LODIE WEBSTER AND SHIRLEY DUNCAN (SPECTATOR SERVICES HOSTS – ARCHERY PARK)

BOB AND LINDA KEZOVSKI FROM BLACKBUTT SOUTH OF SYDNEY, TAKE TIME OUT TO ENJOY THE ATHLETICS

'Working as a volunteer at the Olympic Games brought an unexpected reward for me. The spirit of the Olympic Games should never be underestimated in its ability to bond people from all over our wonderful diverse world' ... **Nada Richards (Warranwood, Victoria)**

'I had a great time at the Olympic Games as a volunteer, and am so proud to have been part of it all.' ... **Melissa Copland (Tuggerawong, NSW)**

'I became a volunteer because I love meeting and helping people.' ... **Jean Freeman (Chinderah, NSW)**

'Overall the greatest memorable part was the small band of volunteers that I worked with on a daily basis.' ... **Helen Inglis (Cohuna, Victoria)**

'When the opportunity arose to volunteer at the Olympic Games I would have done anything just to be part of it all.' ... **Gary Maher (Deception Bay, Queensland)**

'I was in Australia studying when I decided to volunteer for the Olympic Games – an experience for which I will always love Australia.' ... **Sofia Berntsson (Sweden)**

'We will never forget the great experience we had – thank you Sydney.' ... **Kevin and Clare Doyle (Cheltenham, Victoria)**

'What a thrill it was to be a photographic supervisor at such an event.' ... **Luis Ordonez (Brisbane)**

A total of 17 volunteers were provided by the School of Environmental and Recreation Management at the University of South Australia for Volleyball events, they were:

Olympics – **Kelly Jackson, Melissa Costanzo, Sally Kidd, Jenna Harrison, Rebecca Pearce.**

Paralympics – **Darren Adamson, Rebecca Hansen, Susan Parobiec, Carly Galpin, Ivan Saavedra, Jon Herd, Ali Jacka, Amanda Matusch, Louisa Meyer, Emma Campbell, Ceitlin Walker, Eleanor Taylor.**

The students were able to learn from a great team of administrators at Volleyball and now have an amazing insight into the running of international events.

Karin Blondell is an Australian who married a Swede and moved to Sweden in 1975. By accident, she and her daughter Josefin (19) and son James (15) became volunteers at the Sydney Olympic Games, through surfing the Internet in July 2000. Some very hurried airline bookings, and the opportunity to stay with her mother, Margaret Persson, who still lives in Sydney, enabled them to grasp this experience.

Karin recalls: 'Our family involvement with Handball enabled the children to be Field of Play Marshals, and for me to help the match speaker with facts and figures on the teams. James is a good Handball player, and was given the opportunity to play in a training match with volunteers from all over the world in a game against the Australian Team – unbelievable! Josefin met a coach of the Norwegian women's team who came from the same town we live in. The whole experience was wonderful – not a harsh word, lots of laughs, long hours, yet a feeling of being part of one big family despite coming from all parts of the world.'

'There were some difficulties but they all seem funny now that it is all over – things like having to move three times in order to miss Olympic Rates Accommodation. My $60 a night room I was staying in went up to $360 a night in 24 hours, which meant it was time to move again. The worst thing was losing my luggage on the first day – I got off to a bad start – but things did get better. Actually, they got lots better, and there are so many wonderful stories to tell. It was sad to be going home in the end, but I did need some sleep!' ... **Sue Flett (Perth)**

BADMINTON VENUE TEAM – ROBIN METSON (THIRD FROM RIGHT AT BACK) IS FROM COLCHESTER, ENGLAND

(L TO R) GENEVIEVE BOURGEOIS AND MAJORIE LAUZON FROM QUEBEC, CANADA, WITH FRENCH CYCLIST FLORIENT ROUSSEAU

RIVERINA AREA VOLUNTEERS GATHER AT THE WAGGA WAGGA LEAGUES CLUB

Venue accreditation help office staff – State Sport and Hockey Centres

(L to R) Lesley Gillis (ACT), David Cavanagh South Australia), Marita Brady (Victoria) and Kylie Crossfield (NSW) – timing stewards at the Equestrian Centre

(L to R) Karen Newburger (USA), Samantha Halliday (Sydney) and Natasha Fyles (Darwin) with swimmer Ian Thorpe

Firearms armoury volunteers at the Shooting Centre

Carolyn Docking (second from right – from Tasmania) with colleagues (L to R) Robyn, Mick and Fiona

PROTOCOL

As with any visiting dignitaries to our shores, adopting the correct protocol will always provide a better communication and rapport, resulting in better understanding and more positive relationships. The success of our Olympic and Paralympic Protocol Program was most certainly evident in the worldwide commendation of the events of Sydney 2000.

Our Protocol volunteers were dignified in their smart jacketed uniforms, and formed good working relationships both with their clients, and other volunteers as their work situations overlapped.

'My excitement had been building gradually since 1993, but from 1999 onwards, it was just one huge crescendo!

'My member arrived in Sydney on 10 September 2000, but to my distress, I did not hear from him till the 16th, and then to be informed that I was not required! I had been rejected, not wanted, not required, after a build-up of seven years. I contacted SOCOG, only to find out that three other volunteers were in the same situation! I was devastated, but agreed to leave it with them.

'The following night I received a call from SOCOG to attend an interview at 10 am the next day – more interviews, I couldn't believe it! However, I was desperate, so agreed, and went along with a colleague **Liz Rummery**. We were to report to Wharf 8, where the majestic *Seabourn Sun* was moored, chartered by American NBC. We were interviewed by five people, and apparently answered all their questions satisfactorily, as we were asked to commence immediately!

'We had to begin with the most difficult task of all – Accreditation! The next six days just flew by, as we packed so much in. It was demanding and tiring, but very stimulating and satisfying, especially to farewell our guests, although a little exhausted themselves, but very happy.' ...
Maggie Staines (IOC Relations and Protocol Volunteer)

'As a university student coming to Sydney from Melbourne, it was not only the excitement of a new city, and the atmosphere of an Olympic Games to deal with, but getting up at 4 am was a culture shock! However, the stimulation of my role as a protocol attendant at the airport gave me all the satisfaction required to keep me coming back.' ... **Justin Zammit**

Martyn Kibel came from Box Hill North in Victoria, to volunteer as a Protocol Assistant for Olympic family members from the British Virgin Islands. Martyn recalls: 'Not all went well during my three-and-a-half-week stay, like the lack of sleep and having my car stolen. However, the memorable and exciting moments made it the experience of a lifetime.

(L TO R) JO LUDEMANN AND INGRID COHEN (PROTOCOL ATTENDANTS) CHECKING THE SIGN AT BEACH VOLLEYBALL!

RELAXATION TIME AT THE AIRPORT!

SOMEBODY GET THAT PHONE! – PROTOCOL ATTENDANTS RELAXING IN THE TENNIS CENTRE LOUNGE

MY UNIFORM – THEN I KNEW IT WAS FOR REAL! – NORM GENT (PROTOCOL ASSISTANT FOR LIBERIA)

(L TO R) PROTOCOL ASSISTANTS MAUREEN PARIS AND IRENE TURNER

'It was wonderful to attend both the Opening and Closing Ceremonies, meet athletes, meet Mr Samaranch, visit the Athletes Village and attend events. However, the most memorable aspect is the friendships developed with my guests, fellow Protocol and NOC Assistant volunteers, and the quality time I had with my God-daughter and her family who were my fantastic hosts.'

'Thank you for the friendships and congratulations to all volunteers for a job well done and also to SOCOG for giving us the opportunity to volunteer in this most amazing event of Australia's history.' ... **Grazyna (Grace) Wojcik (Protocol Assistant)**

'My hopes for a perfect Games were fulfilled in every aspect, but away from the fun and euphoria there was a quiet and sombre ceremony at the Moriah College in Randwick. It was the Memorial Ceremony and Dedication Service for the 11 Israeli athletes killed by terrorists at the 1972 Munich Olympics. I was privileged to be there, accompanying the German IOC Member, Professor Walther Troeger, who had been the Mayor of the Olympic Village in Munich and was involved in negotiations with the terrorists. This was an emotional ceremony.' ...
Arno Koenig (Protocol Assistant)

'Arno, I was not able to attend that service, but my thoughts are with you, as I attended the emotional ceremony in the Munich Olympic Stadium the day after the massacre.' ...
Laurie Smith (Author and Volunteer)

'I have friends who tell me – "I feel so envious of you. I wish I had been a volunteer! How did you get the job?" – I feel sorry for the people who were not volunteers, they will never know what we shared. For me it was such a special relationship shared with my Italian guests and a wonderful ex-cop named **Ron**, as our driver. He listened, he smiled, he was resourceful, punctual, worked hard and is a skilled and masterful driver.

Arno Koenig – protocol assistant

The monument on an 11-sided polygon base, bearing the names of the 11 athletes killed in Munich in 1972

Ron Alexander and Sandra Groom share the torch relay enthusiasm

'In contrast though, it was interesting to sit in the staff break area, and listen to the gossip, and observe some jockeying for "power" and "position" and "pecking order". Even we volunteers have a structure. It is amusing to see, and sometimes irritating: I remind myself that people who have low self-esteem need to prop themselves up ... And given a uniform, it doubles their power! This is a minor irritation however, and as always, I am blown away by the kindness and generosity of these people, my colleagues and who they are in their lives.

'What Ron and I shared with our lovely Italian guests can only be appreciated by those who have experienced it. When it was time to say goodbye, Ron decided not to come to the airport, saying he would be "a basket case". Well he was just about like that when he did bid them farewell – my eyes filled with tears as a small Italian man and a big Australian man embraced, bound by the Olympics. The airport departure for me was just as emotional, but we vowed to reunite.' ... **Sandra Groom (IOC Relations and Protocol Assistant)**

'As one of the Protocol Attendants in the Olympic Family Lounge at the Convention and Exhibition Centre, Darling Harbour, I was privileged to be part of a workforce which did Australia proud. Of course, in a group this size, we also observed the usual spectrum of human behaviour – volunteers who were not prepared to share the good and not so good posts! Fortunately, these situations were eventually resolved, and as I actually experienced, sometimes the best situations happened at the least likely locations – like having extended time to chat with Muhammad Ali, when accreditations had to be replaced at a carpark entrance!' ... **Rosemary Russell**

'As a Protocol Attendant at the Olympic Stadium, I had a wonderful exposure to the world's dignitaries as well as both ceremonies and some wonderful athletics. I was even given a ticket to the

Closing Ceremony by an IOC Delegate, which I was able to give to my husband Ken. We as a family also hosted the father and brother of a Mexican swimmer, and it was great to see the Games through the eyes of a competitor and family. All round, a very fulfilling experience.' ... Pat Watson

'When my husband Noel and I arrived at the International Airport for our first shift as Protocol Attendants, we wondered why so many of our colleagues were making comment about having seen me in Pier C! Our supervisor eventually put me straight, telling me that there was a huge photo of me on the wall in Pier C. When I eventually got to see it, I was amazed. Sydney photographer, Peter Elliston, had won a competition with photographs he had taken the previous year! It was quite strange presenting myself in smart Protocol uniform, only to see myself in a bikini.' ... Eileen Slarke

'I live at Lake Macquarie, two hours north of Sydney, so I stayed with friends in Sydney for the duration of my volunteer experience. I was part of the IOC Relations and Protocol team initially at the Triathlons, and then at the Darling Harbour Convention and Exhibition Centre. I count myself very privileged to have been part of such a monumental event. As an Australian by choice (I was born in America) it was a special chance for me to give something back to my adopted country. As if that weren't enough, on 15 October 2000, I had the very great honour of carrying the Paralympic Torch.' ... Terri Nowak

'I enjoyed the most wonderful Olympic experience as Protocol Attendant in the VIP Lounge at the Superdome, under the direction of our great leader Greg Tighe. However, all this would not have been possible if my wonderful mother had not come all the way from Nundle in northern NSW to live in our house at Ulladulla on the NSW south coast, to look after my four daughters. Thanks to the volunteers behind the volunteers!' ... Janelle Collins

'I was inspired by a meeting in Newcastle in 1998, about Olympic volunteering, so sent in my application, already excited about the prospect.

THE SIGN SAYS IT ALL!

(L TO R) BARRY STEVENSON, LORRAINE BULMER, JANET EDWARDS, LOUISE PARSONS AND LEWIS KLIPIN (IPC RELATIONS AND PROTOCOL STAFF AT STATE SPORTS CENTRE AND STATE HOCKEY CENTRE)

Eileen Slarke (VIP protocol attendant) posing beside a larger-than-life photo of herself on Pier C at the International Airport

Protocol Attendants meet the Prime Minister of Australia – John Howard – in the Superdome Olympic Family Lounge

'Meanwhile in January, 1999 I was diagnosed with Breast Cancer. It turned out to be Stage III Cancer and was in my lymph nodes as well. I had two operations and then started on Chemotherapy. I had to stop work and spent most of my days on the bed. During this time my partner and lovely daughters and friends were my support and comfort, without them I know I would not have been able to keep my spirits up and keep the positive attitude that is so important for cancer patients.

'One day towards the end of June 1999, a letter came from SOCOG – they had accepted my application and would I come down for an interview in July. Would I? Well, I did not have a hair on my body, was quite weak and hadn't been any further than the hospital in weeks. But I had a wig and a friend, Pat Hogan, who was at the time 78, and very willing to go with me. She was so excited to be going to SOCOG.

'I never for a minute thought that I would get a position, but within a few weeks I had a letter to say that I would be a Protocol Attendant at the Games!! What excitement, but would I be well enough? I still had a six-week Radiation therapy course to get through and had to recover from the tiredness that this causes as well. My doctor kept reassuring me that all would be well in time and so I set out on the road to recovery. My hair grew back, very grey and very curly, which has changed now thanks to a good hairdresser, and I also have eyelashes and eyebrows as well.

'The training had started for the Olympics and I could see myself doing the job at last. Of course by this time I had discovered what a Protocol Attendant was and while being very proud I still found it hard to believe that this had happened to me. We were told that we were going to be doing the Welcoming Ceremonies for all the athletes and also showing visiting dignitaries and Heads of State and NOC and IOC members around the Village.

'Unfortunately the doctors struck again!!! I was having further trouble with the medication. I started taking every vitamin that I thought would help, drank vegetable juice each morning and prayed a lot.

'My Doctor said I would make it, and I have!!

'I sat next to a lovely young woman, **Marianne**. We soon discovered we both came from the Central Coast and she lived ten minutes away from me. Can you believe that! We liked one another on sight and made arrangements to travel together if we could get the same shifts. This we have done, after speaking to Vanessa, our supervisor, our shifts have been almost the same. I have told Marianne my story and she has been so caring and kind to me that I don't think I could have managed without her. We both feel that we will be friends for life.' ... **Bev Tucker (Protocol Assistant)**

'I first saw volunteers at the athletics when I attended the Los Angeles Olympics in 1984. I thought it would be an interesting role! When the opportunity came up to be involved in the Sydney Olympic Games, I immediately applied.

'My role as a Protocol Attendant at the International Airport was not only a wonderful experience in the training I received and the friends I made, but it has given me valuable insight to becoming a volunteer member of the Golden Ambassador Team at the International Airport when I retire.' ... **Allan Cameron**

The time of my life

'After two years of anticipation, five trips to Sydney from Brisbane for training (by semi-trailer because of my limited budget), the time had come!

'The anticipation and excitement was immense. Both within myself, and in the air as I arrived for the big event in beautiful Sydney-town. The city was alive and showing her best as I embarked on the adventure of my life.

'My Olympic adventure is now over – in my heart, mind and being it will live long and loudly. Memories of people, events, friendships immersed in the files of my mind will gladden my heart forever.

'Looking back at the time I spent as a volunteer Protocol Assistant at Sydney 2000 is like immersing myself in a fairytale!' ... **Robyne Sandison**

PROTOCOL ATTENDANTS CELEBRATE AFTER THE VOLUNTEERS PARADE – (L TO R) CATHY LEE, DEBBIE LOW, DEBORAH GRECH, SUZANNE HYATT, SANTINA FERELLA, PAM CALLAGHAN, STEVEN KENWORTHY, ROB CALLAGHAN, FIONA HENDERSON, MARY STANLEY AND GARY LEE

PROTOCOL ATTENDANTS – SYDNEY INTERNATIONAL AIRPORT

We are Airport Protocol, we will show you where to go,
Off the plane to accreditation, Athletes from most every Nation,
Through to customs collect your bags, hope you don't get Jet lag,
Catch ORTA bus to accommodation, Party on in moderation,
Good luck in your respective races, Gold, Silver, Bronze are the places,
Eleven days of competition, will see your dreams come to fruition,
Spectators will cheer you on. GO FOR GOLD EVERYONE. ...
Sonja Lloyd (IPC Relations and Protocol)

'During the latter part of my volunteer experience, I had my most disarming enquiry – and there had been a few odd ones! While the NOC delegate was at meetings, his wife came for advice about places to go, shopping, etc. After talking with her for about ten minutes and supplying her with information and maps and booklets, her reserved daughter, who I estimate to have been about ten years old, could maintain her reserve (or was it embarrassment) no longer, and reluctantly asked me where she could have her hair dyed in the colours and pattern of her national flag! As a mere male I was floored, and replied that that was one enquiry that I would just have to hand to my female colleague. But even she struggled with it, although she was able to make suggestions of possible hairdressers; later she commented to me that she really was not of the right age group to know about such fashions.' ... Dr Peter Rickwood (Protocol Attendant – Regent Hotel)

'Two of the most special days for me were being present at Rushcutters Bay when Australia won two Gold Medals in Sailing, and later at the medal presentations. Then being asked to be Protocol Attendant for HRH Princess Anne, when she spent a day on one of the motor launches to watch the racing. This could only happen by volunteering!' ... Beverley Stewart (Protocol Attendant)

'When I presented myself for my first shift as Protocol Supervisor at the Convention and Exhibition Centre, Darling Harbour, I found myself in a situation where part of me wanted to run away! We'd had great training, but how do I identify two dignitaries in a crowded competition venue, who I had to escort to medal ceremonies?

'If only I had some idea what they looked like!

'Through a process of elimination and some good advice from my manager, the exercise was resolved, and in fact I was to share a little time with a lovely gentleman, Mr Anton Geesink, who was an Olympic Gold Medallist in Judo from Tokyo, 1964.

'It did not take him long to realise I was not familiar with Judo, and to my surprise he took a book out of his pocket, signed it and gave it to me. He had written the book on Judo, and politely said, "You read my book, and you learn about Judo!" Thank you Mr Geesink, you've kept me coming back!' ...
Robert Parovel

Ruby Coon (protocol attendant – Darling Harbour) with granddaughter Lucy

Christina Kazan (protocol assistant – Former Yugoslav Republic of Macedonia)

Brian Walsh (protocol attendant – tennis centre)

Smaranda Kafka (protocol attendant – international airport)

Bob and Veronica Barclay made several trips from their home in Melbourne to participate as protocol attendants at the international airport

Sophie Barclay worked with her parents as protocol attendants; Adrian Buncle was spectator services host at the Sydney Cricket Ground

(L TO R) ROSEMARY MULA, ADHEMAR FERREIRA DA SILVA, TANIA MARA SIVIERO AND WILFRED MULA

GRAHAM DONNELLY (PROTOCOL ATTENDANT – INTERNATIONAL AIRPORT)

It began in 1956

As a schoolgirl, **Rosemary Mula** attended the Melbourne Olympic Games in 1956. She and her friends were right on the fence for the final of the Triplejump, and with no Australian to support, they decided to support the defending Olympic Champion – Adhemar Ferreira da Silva from Brazil. Adhemar went on to win an unprecedented second Olympic Gold Medal, and to this day is the only Brazilian to have done so.

A friendship developed between Rosemary and Adhemar, which has endured to the point that Rosemary and her husband Wilf hosted Adhemar in their home during the Sydney 2000 Olympic Games. They live in the suburb of Newington (north of the Olympic Village), so Rosemary was able to continue her role as Protocol Attendant for Team Welcome Ceremonies in the Village.

Soon after the Olympic Games, Rosemary and Wilf were invited to Brazil for the launch of Adhemar Ferreira da Silva's book (see photo). This was a very exciting and emotional time for Rosemary and Wilf, as Adhemar is a National Hero.

Only a matter of weeks after their return to Australia, Rosemary and Wilf received the devastating news that Adhemar Ferreira da Silva died on 12 January 2001. Rosemary's parting words: 'You have enriched my life beyond measure and I will miss you greatly.'

'If I never experience such euphoria and elation again, I'll still be smiling – Forever!' ... **Anne-Maree Thurecht (Protocol Attendant)**

'I am a successful woman living with Cerebral Palsy, and that has not prevented me from enjoying a wonderful experience during the Paralympics as Protocol Supervisor with IPC Relations and Protocol.' ... **Lisa Murray**

There were those of few words who expressed appreciation at being involved: **Jeanette Manson (Protocol Attendant), Dushan Djukic (Protocol Attendant), Kristine Kilburn (Protocol Assistant – Brazil), Cheryl Haywood (Protocol Assistant – Egypt) and Alex Kats (Protocol Attendant).**

(L TO R) SIMONE PETERS, JUDITH TEULON AND BARBARA NICOL – IOC RELATIONS AND PROTOCOL ATTENDANTS – OLYMPIC FAMILY HOTELS

Volunteers Parade...

NAVIGATOR

OLYMPIC VOLUNTEERS IN POLICING (OVIP)

The NSW Police Service assumed overall responsibility for all security personnel involved in the Olympic and Paralympic Games, including training.

State Emergency Service personnel were the largest contingent of volunteers to assist police in the road events, while if you thought you could gain entry to any venue without 'passing the time of day' with Rural Fire Service volunteers at 'Mag and Bag', then you had another thing coming! There were also contract security companies and government staff on re-deployment involved.

SES and RFS volunteers have many stories of experiences, and relationships with one another and the paid officers. However, they did also play a significant part in the success of the two Torch Relays.

JENNIFER FALCONER, DANCING WITH KANGAROO
DRESSED BY NETHERLANDS SUPPORTERS!

Tony and Helen Styan live at Lake Munmorah on the Central Coast north of Sydney. Both were thrilled when Australia was going to host the Olympic and Paralympic Games, but having two small children presented some challenges in becoming volunteers.

Helen was fortunate to be a community-nominated Torch Bearer, for her work in the disability field and six years with the Lake Munmorah Rural Fire Service, with which Tony was also involved. However, when it came to Olympic volunteer training, they shared alternate weekends, and when it came to Games time, Tony worked the Olympics and Helen the Paralympics. Helen's parents were the support behind the volunteers, providing the Sydney-based accommodation at Turramurra.

'We had some wonderful experiences, and some challenges! On one shift, I left my hat on a hook in the toilets. I realised ten minutes later and went back – it was gone. I got rather upset – mainly because I had my RFS badge and Olympic Launch badge on it. The volunteer staff at the desk were great, they calmed me down and gave me another hat. Then a young high school girl handed in my hat. In gratitude I gave her my spare one.

'During one shift, I was stationed where people in wheelchairs and with strollers came through. The Police Officer with us was a real character. He "valet parked" the strollers and entertained the kids as only police can do, while we inspected the parents' bags and got them to empty their pockets for the magnetometer.' ... **Helen Styan**

'As a member of the Captains Flat Branch of the NSW Rural Fire Service, I worked as an Olympic Volunteer in Policing (OVIP) together with hundreds of my RFS colleagues from all around New South Wales. We were attached to the Olympic Security Command Centre (OSCC) managed by the NSW Police Service. My involvement in Sydney from 12 September until 2 October was mainly in security at the Olympic Stadium in the areas used by VIPs, entertainers, the Olympic family and the media. I also assisted in the security of athletes at the Sydney International Athletics Centre (SIAC) adjacent to the main Stadium, and came into contact with many of the track and field athletes who used this arena to warm-up before their events in the main stadium.

'I stayed at The King's School at North Parramatta, where SOCOG provided accommodation, meals and transport for 450 Rural Fire Service personnel and 150 Police officers. Living in a dormitory of 24 grown men (23 of whom snored), and with varying shift commitments, meant very little sleep during the three weeks. But the excitement of being a part of the "best Olympics ever" kept us all going. We worked long hours, but had a ball.' ... **Wayne Seymour**

Brian Bennett was an Olympic volunteer from the Richmond Valley Rural Fire Service, and his Olympic adventure began in the northern NSW town of Casino: 'On arrival at the railway station one could have been forgiven for assuming that the train due in was to be a troop train. Not since my army days had I seen such a unified group! The trip to Sydney was quiet, with most members making use of their first chance to relax and rest up – having had to fight fires almost continuously for the previous two months.

'As the train snaked its way towards the "big smoke", more volunteers joined it. I recall one volunteer who began her journey south of Coffs Harbour. She had just managed to make the train – still in her

Paul Maindonald – security volunteer

SES – OVIP's (L to R) Trevor Kidson, Helen Boddy, Shaunagh Buckley and Wayne Tsipouras

Paralympic gold medallist Gabriel Shelly, with Arthur Birch (OVIP)

"yellows" and covered in ash – that's dedication! The train trip was over when we arrived at Hornsby. We were met at the station by members of Baulkham Hills RFS, and bussed out to The King's School – our accommodation and base whilst carrying out our tasks as Olympic volunteers.

'The different personalities and experiences of the volunteers made for some humorous yarns and events – far too numerous to relate here. But one I recall was about a chap who – rostered on the early shift – had trouble sleeping. He eventually got up, got ready, put all his gear back in his locker, and headed for breakfast and the bus. Trouble was, he forgot to turn his alarm clock off!!! To the distain of the afternoon shift, it just kept ringing and ringing! Not being able to get into the locker to turn it off, a few fellows just grabbed hold of the locker, and carted it outside and left it. You can imagine the look on the owner's face when he returned!

'It would be remiss of me to ignore the many RFS volunteers who for a host of reasons were at all times in the background, but always there for us – especially those of us from the various country regions. **Chris Anderson** and his Team, plus members of NSW Police who formed the Administration Team at The Kings School – Thank You!

'Finally, with the Games over, the only thing left was goodbyes to a lot of new friends, the trip home and a lot of reminiscing. 1 October 2000 – 6.35 pm – the Gold Coast XPT arrived at Casino and it was time for myself and a few friends to alight the train – a quick photo and head home, thus ending an excursion, and the memory shall forever remain.'

Gordon Heckendorf, a RFS volunteer from Narromine in north western NSW, believes that the ten days in Sydney added years to his life! He is disappointed that some of his colleagues pulled out of the opportunity because of the negative media – they now wish they had been part of it!

Arthur Birch attended the Opening Ceremony of the 1976 Montreal Olympic Games, and certainly wasn't going to miss being part of the action when the Olympic Games returned to Australia. His first 'warm-up' event was the 1996 World Junior Athletic Championships, where he formed lasting friendships with athletes and volunteers.

While Arthur enjoyed many great experiences and made plenty of friends during the Olympic and Paralympic Games, a special contact was that with Irish Boccia competitor Gabriel Shelly. First they swapped pins, and then Gabriel went on to become the first person from Ireland to win a gold medal in Boccia, then they swapped shirts. 'I was inspired by this athlete, and moved by his courage and determination,' said Arthur.

RFS volunteer, **Naree Norton**, from Lake Munmorah, says: 'The Olympics may have been thrilling, but the Paralympics were inspiring and humbling!'

'We live with our children in Kyogle, a picturesque rural town in northern NSW, not far from the Border Ranges National Park. Our Olympic volunteering came as an extension of our involvement with the Rural Fire Service. Yes we were the "Mag and Bag" mob – those lime-green sleeves who met and greeted you with the request, "could you please open your bag – thank you, have a nice time." The ever obliging populus would offer their proficiently packed, purposefully planned, packs, purses, ports, camera bags, trolleys, film bags, bags of all kinds, parcels, boxes, flags, flowers, footwear, watches, wallets, coins, mobiles, old tissues, lolly papers, pins, pens, keys, the occasional Gold, Silver or Bronze Medal, the kitchen sink, not to mention the Hills Hoist!!!

'Although spectators, athletes, volunteers, officials and VIPs generally moved through our area fairly quickly, on occasions we had the opportunity to share a little conversation, as was the case one day with a team doctor, who was also a volunteer fire fighter in his home country, France.

'We have the memories that are priceless, saw the most spectacular show on this earth and in our lifetime. We loved it, lived it and now miss it.' ... **Ray Honey and Robyn Murphy**

'The days were sometimes long and everyone became tired towards the end, but the more tired we became, the more ridiculous the humour! I think the visitors enjoyed it! Overall a wonderful experience! I wouldn't have missed it (even the 4.00 am get-ups)!' ... **Susan Buxton**

David Gray (SES – Mount Druitt Unit) was involved in security at several venues, but it was a family contribution with wife Beverley at the Blacktown Softball Stadium, and daughter Rebecca at the Main Press Centre.

Yarralumla/Queanbeyan RFS volunteers – (L to R) Darryl Parker, Murray Pearce, Ronnie Mifsud and Graham Parkins

'I don't care if your name is Elvis ... open the bag' cartoon by John Bowie

(L to R) RFS volunteers – Brett Aitchison (Westleigh Brigade), Michael Mina (Brooklyn Brigade) and Bobby Tamayo (Canonlands Brigade)

(L to R) Chris Copp, Dave Appleby and Jack Price – dome and pavilion, security

Alan Neville and Raeley Best (both with sunglasses) enjoy athletics before commencing afternoon shift of 'mag and bag'

Kathleen Eyers has been a State Emergency Service volunteer with the Ryde unit since 1994. The Olympic and Paralympic experience gave Kathleen a great insight into the security aspect of policing, in addition to the enjoyment of participating in such an exciting event.

'My decision to make myself available as a volunteer for the OVIP program was based on my reaching 25 years of service with the Rural Fire Service in March 2000, and that attendance in an official volunteer capacity in September 2000 would cap off my career with the organisation prior to retirement.

'What a finale it was having that Thank You parade, the same experience felt in the 1994 bushfire fighters' parade was evident during this parade. A large lump in the throat and swelling tears in the eyes, and a strong sense of wellbeing coupled with an extremely huge pride of being Australian and doing the Australian thing – volunteering. In one word: Unforgettable!

'During the parade I received a call on my mobile phone asking if I was available for duties at a large fire in the Armidale area. The answer of course was a clear YES!' ... **Michael Mina**

OVIP **Rod Kammel** enjoyed the mix of Police Service, RFS and SES volunteers in providing an efficient security service. 'I found it an exhilarating experience, and I don't think anything will come close to boosting Australia's image to the world like the Olympic and Paralympic Games,' said Rod.

Lesley Howell is a 19-year-old completing an Office Administration course at Cowra TAFE, although she lives in the small mid-western town of Grenfell. Lesley's mother had signed her up in the Rural Fire Service because she was bored, but besides providing a host of new skills and friendships, it led to the 'once-in-a-lifetime' opportunity to be involved in the Olympic and Paralympic Games. What may it lead to in the future?

Blacktown Security Check.

Lets join the parade!

Security volunteer Pauline Ripley – 'My grand-daughter's first question was – "Will they give you a gun?" – thank goodness they didn't!'

AN OVIP'S LAMENT

My toes are sore, my poor feet ache
I think my back's about to break
I've searched to see what I can find
I've looked in bags until I'm blind
I haven't found a single gun
As for bombs, not even one
No animals, guide dogs excepted
No bowie knives, blades unprotected
Nothing banned has by me passed
Not even bottles made of glass
I've said thank you and I've said please
But nothing have I had to seize
Now I'm not saying it's made me sad
But I thought I'd find just one thing bad.

Anon

SECURITY SERENADE

We greet you and we check your bag
With a pleasant smile and a friendly gag
We take your knives and glass bottles too
And hope machines don't beep as we pass you through.

SECURITY – that's what we do
So venues are safe for me and you
SECURITY – we're the first you meet
As you get off the bus and rush down the street.

We come from various walks of life
And help you out when you're in strife
We're Police & Fireys & SES
Defence, Security and Volunteer VIPs.

SECURITY – we see your faces
But don't get to see any games or races
SECURITY – we're always visible
And the hours we work are quite incredible.

So raise your glass and give a cheer
You must be pleased that we're always here.
We're what is known as the Green Sleeves mob
And like all volunteers – we enjoy our job!!

Nerida White

MEDICAL

While the St John Ambulance volunteers were a very obvious face of medical support at all competition and non-competition venues, a little less obvious were the qualified practitioners who could accommodate everything from a toothache to an athlete's massage. Some of these volunteers were retired, and felt they still had plenty to offer of their lifelong skills. However, the majority gave up many hours, days and weeks from busy practices, to provide much needed and appreciated services to athletes, staff and visitors.

These were the Red Sleeve Brigade, and while plenty were seen around Olympic and Paralympic venues, they provided an enormous back-of-house service, including the operation of the Polyclinic at the Athletes Village. The following stories of passion, drama and frivolity will help us all appreciate another very important aspect of *how it was achieved!*

'There had been some severe dehydration of spectators during the morning at the Beach Volleyball, including one requiring intravenous fluids. I went for a brief stroll in the stadium to have a look at the crowd for the afternoon session. It was obvious that many were unprepared for the hot weather. There was a distinct lack of hats and sunscreen.

'Deciding prevention was better than cure, it was decided that we should make some form of public announcement warning of the usual dangers of the heat and sun. Dave the Lifeguard, who was the MC and responsible for leading the spectators in dancing, Mexican waves and general good fun, grabbed the spectators' attention between points in the volleyball game by getting them all to stand up and sing the Slip, Slop, Slap song. At the end of which everyone having joined in the fun did as they were asked, and put on their sunscreen and hats.

'Chelsea Clinton was a spectator for the afternoon with an entourage of three others, she did not have a hat.

'Play resumed, and when the ball next went out of play, two male spectators stood up. They wore gold T-shirts with AUS on one and TRALIA on the other. They started chanting "CHELSEA, CHELSEA, PUT ON YOUR HAT!" Chelsea was laughing and the rest of the spectators joined in the laughter and chanting. One problem – she did not have a hat! A quick-thinking volunteer found four white volunteer hats and to cheers gave them to Chelsea and her friends.' ... **Dr Brian Wiseman**

'As a Medical Volunteer, in a non-competition venue the HAAC (Homebush Arrival & Accreditation Centre), the clinic was staffed by a roster of a doctor, a nurse and two ambulance officers. The medical clinic was extremely well equipped, with a very satisfactory range of supplies and equipment, far better than one would see in many a doctor's surgery. It included a portable defibrillator, but fortunately this was not required. The parade of athletes, the staff and volunteers at 15 Carter Street, were a healthy, robust lot.' ... **Dr Tom Kail**

OH!! THE MEDICAL OFFICER? – THAT'S THE ONE ON THE LEFT – DR BRIAN WISEMAN

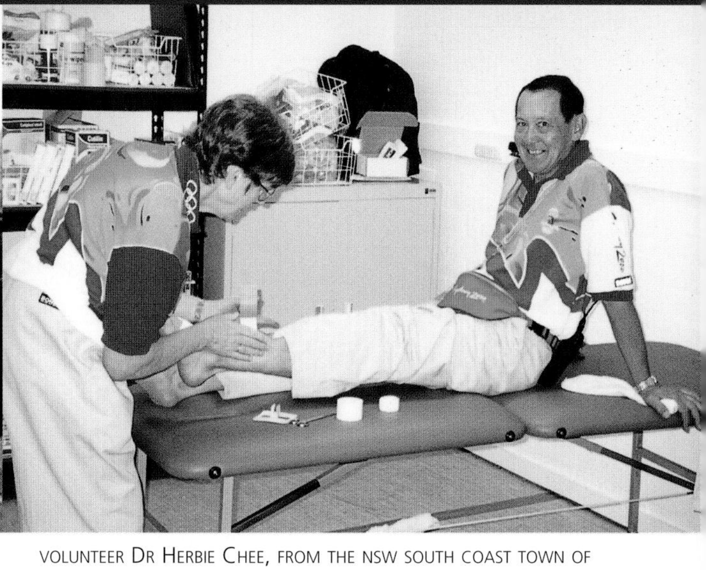

VOLUNTEER DR HERBIE CHEE, FROM THE NSW SOUTH COAST TOWN OF MOLLYMOOK, TESTING THE SERVICES OF PHYSIO, AILEEN CLARE

Part of the Athletes Village Polyclinic Medical Staff

Pharmacist John Rourke (filling condom bowl)

PHARMACY AT THE OLYMPICS

The thrill of just being there was the reaction of the three Victorian Olympic volunteer pharmacists. **Bill Davy, Kate Tognarini** and **Bill Horsfall** all 'had a ball' being in the pharmacy, working in the Olympic Village and being part of the now famous volunteer work force.

'It was amusing to observe, giant basketballers, wide weightlifters, beautifully-built sprinters, diminutive marathon runners and portly officials walking into the pharmacy, heading straight for the condom bowl. Male and female, embarrassed and brazen, giggling and animated, it was all good fun to see them loading themselves up with supplies. How many were used during the two weeks and how many were for later use is anyone's guess.

'The whole experience was great fun, and an honour to be involved. Just fascinating to be a pharmacist in the Polyclinic surrounded by interesting people from all corners of the globe.' ... **Bill Horsfall**

John Rourke has been volunteering most of his life, basically for the satisfaction of helping others. When he first applied to become involved with the Olympic and Paralympic Games, John sought involvement in the areas of sailing and swimming, which were his sports of expertise. He was not sure how he would combine this with his profession as a pharmacist, but he would cross that bridge when he came to it!

John did not receive any response in these areas, but a chance meeting with another volunteer, Gill Gorrick, turned his focus to the position of pharmacist in the Athletes Village Polyclinic. After some persistent follow-up, John was accepted to one of the 42 pharmacists' positions. In the lead-up to the Olympics, John decided to retire from the workforce, and took on additional volunteering with the Samsung Athletes Family Host Program.

MEDICAL VOLUNTEERS – OLYMPIC STADIUM

MEDICAL VOLUNTEERS WITH MEDICAB

MEDICAL IMAGING VOLUNTEERS – POLYCLINIC (ATHLETES VILLAGE)

The Athletes Village was a memorable place for John, and he recalls a special meeting with a Paralympian: 'An Israeli athlete came into the pharmacy and as many of them were, she was in a wheelchair. What made her a bit different was she only had legs from the knee up. She also had no arms, and her hands were attached to what were virtually her shoulders. Whenever time permitted I tried to learn a little about these athletes. She was a particularly cheerful girl. When I approached her about her disability she replied, "I was in an armoured personnel carrier which was blown up." It was a very sobering experience for me!'

'I have a lot of pleasure and pride in being able to say I was a volunteer for the Sydney 2000 Olympic Games. I did a lot of doctoring at various venues, but I was amazed at the number of people who came up to me and asked things like, "Which street is George Street?" or "Where's my bus?" or "Do you know where my seat is?" We were all part of a team.' ... **Dr John Frith**

'For an athlete to suffer any form of injury, mild or serious, at this time can be a total disaster with years of hard work instantly lost. To be able to treat just one athlete, with the result that they can perform to their full potential, is the greatest feeling in the world because it means that I also have performed at my full potential.' ... **Diana Ellem (Volunteer Physiotherapist – Regatta Centre)**

'The opportunity for me to volunteer came almost four years ago. I was still at university as a student nurse when I applied. I was already involved in other volunteer organizations such as St John Ambulance and SES. I *really* wanted to be a nurse volunteer at the Olympic Games, but unfortunately lucked out and was offered a position as Medical Clerk at the Stadium. I didn't mind one bit, I just wanted to be there. I would often not get home to my Central Coast home (NSW) until 3 or 4 the next morning. Some days I would also have to be up at 6 am to work my regular job!! To all my colleagues and patients out there who had to put up with my tiredness and grumpiness, I salute you!

'When the Olympics were over, I reluctantly dragged myself out of bed to work. Life for a while there had been exciting, and different, and I met some terrific people who worked with amazing dedication, stamina, and cohesion when they initially did not know each other at all. I also witnessed the rare (and priceless) interactions of doctors and nurses working side by side with mutual respect and concern for their patients AND each other.' ... Sandra Thorne

Cameron Richards chose to leave his Brisbane practice in the capable hands of another therapist while he spent two months in Sydney as a Massage Therapist for the Olympic and Paralympic Games. Cameron was located for a short period at Archery Park, but for the majority of his stay he was located in the Athletes Village.

Highlights for Cameron: 'A Danish sailor I treated chose not to put his shirt back on after treatment, but instead signed it and gave it to me. I treated many Iranian athletes during the Paralympics. One wheelchair athlete told me he would be competing in the javelin the next day, so in some time off, I went over to the Stadium, just in time to see him presented with his Gold Medal!'

'Being a volunteer at the 2000 Olympic Games for me was, and always will be, one of the greatest achievements in my career as a Massage Therapist. Most of my shifts were at the Unilever located in the Athletes Village, but I also had various shifts at the Aquatic Centre. I massaged athletes from a wide variety of sports, many who didn't regularly receive a massage as part of their training regime. What left a lasting impression on me was how excited and composed most athletes were – win or lose, they had achieved their dream of representing their country.

'I also remember the night Lorraine Graham from Jamaica came into the Unilever after she had qualified for the 400 metres final. The smile on her face said it all, she was so proud just to have qualified for the final. The following day she went one step further by winning Silver behind Cathy Freeman in the 400 metres final. It was moments like these that I will always remember.' ... Belinda Serafin

'Okay, so I admit it – I'm from Melbourne, and I was jealous when Sydney got the Games. However, that wasn't going to stop me being involved!

'I'm a doctor – in fact, almost a paediatrician – so when I volunteered it was with all my fingers and toes crossed that they'd actually think I could be of some use amongst big crowds of people. Someone must have been on my side, because I was lucky enough not only to be selected, but also assigned to the Aquatic Centre. Could it possibly get any better than this?

'The short answer is yes – when I applied as a volunteer it was driven by my love of sport and my desperate desire to be part of the Olympics in any way possible. What I hadn't considered were what turned out to be the highlights – the amazing, spine-tingling surge of pride I rediscovered in being Australian, in showing my home (okay, okay, not quite my home, but I figured near-enough for two weeks) to the world, in singing my national anthem with 100,000 others while the tears coursed down my face and I thought my heart was going to burst.' ... Dr Nikki Fowler

In the 24 August 2000 edition of *The Farmersville Times* (Texas, USA), reporter Sheryl Hamilton disclosed the adventure local 'trauma nurse' **Jeannette Vaughan** was about to embark upon as one, of only two, international nurses recruited for the Sydney 2000 Olympic Games.

Jeannette works for the Neuro-sciences/Trauma Unit at Baylor University Medical Centre in Dallas, Texas. 'They [the Olympic Organisers] made it clear from the beginning that I would be going strictly in the spirit of volunteerism and would be responsible for my own expenses,' Jeannette explained. Fortunately, her employer, Baylor Healthcare, has an active global community service program and agreed to sponsor her trip through a grant.

Jeannette spent two weeks training for the event in Australia, and believed that stricter laws for gun control and for drinking and driving, combined with lower speed limits and an effective mass transit system, eliminated many types of trauma seen on a daily basis at Baylor.

Jeannette was based at the Main Press Centre, and since returning home, has expressed a desire to become involved in any future Olympic Games hosted by the United States, following her involvement in the 'best Games ever'!

'As a massage therapist, and natural therapist, to care for people is a way of life ...

'But to place myself in a position where I have the sporting cream of the world literally in my hands, is a concept beyond contemplation ...

'At the peak of the Olympics, our team of Sports Massage Therapists, located at the Massage Centre within the Olympic and Paralympic Village, did no less than 400 massages per day. That's a lot of athletes!

'Athletes were always complimentary about the volunteer support, but one comment that will always stay in my mind is that of a German wheelchair rugby player, who asked me as soon as I met him, "Are you paid by the massage or by the hour?"

Marianne Reimann (medical secretary) – passionate Victorian who was not going to let hundreds of kilometres get in the way of an Olympic experince!

Jeannette Vaughan shows off her Olympic uniform to son Harrison
photo by Chad Engbrock

Janis Palamara (polyclinic dental assistant) met Olympics minister, Michael Knight in the Olympic village

'When I explained that we were all volunteers, and that he had nothing to worry about, as we were all professionals, all attached to clinics and professional premises, his face visibly softened. "You mean to tell me that you are doing this all for nothing?" Then it was my turn to visibly soften. "No, we are not all doing this for nothing. It is our honour to be serving and assisting you through these Games." I have never seen this man cry. I do not know if he does, but he was visibly moved by my words. And then he muttered, "I cannot believe you Australians – you give everything of yourselves." It is great to know we are appreciated.' ... **Lyn Gough**

'We were the only vessels, along with the Sydney Harbour Ferries, accredited to remain on the water after the events. In the spirit of surf club adventurers, and unsure if we were breaking any harbour boating regulations, we undertook the challenge of chasing Sydney Harbour Ferries on their trip from Circular Quay to Manly. The size of the white wash created by the ferries was comparable to a mild surf at Maroubra. As "clubbies", these were our conditions. We surfed the white wash created by the ferries in our surf rescue boats designed for that purpose. We could not resist! The waves were great, but the backdrop of the bridge beat even the best days at Maroubra Beach. Of course the ferries were packed with tourists who responded to our calls of Aussie, Aussie, Aussie brilliantly.' ... **Mark Schembri**

Sally Gibbs is a Registered Nurse who was based at the Sarah Durack Clinic (Sydney Olympic Park). Sally relates the following story: 'One of my patients/visitors was an older English lady who knocked her leg on a garbage disposal unit. Her wound needed a daily dressing, so I told her that if she were visiting Homebush, to pop in and the staff would attend the dressing and observe for infection.

'On one such occasion, she brought her daughter along with her, whom she hadn't told about her injury, as she didn't want to worry her. The daughter had beautiful strawberry blonde hair, but very red English skin. I asked her what had she been doing to get so red? "Just running around" she replied. I told her to put some block-out on, and to go and buy a hat. She replied that she didn't have time. "Don't be ridiculous (in my matronly manner) make the time! What do you do that you can't spare the time to buy a simple hat?" "Oh, I play hockey for Great Britain, and I've just come off the field."'

MEDICAL RESCUE TEAM FOR THE SAILING EVENTS ON SYDNEY HARBOUR

(L TO R) MARNIE JONES (PHYSIOTHERAPIST), SAMANTHA BAIRD (NURSE), EDMUND GRAHAME (DOCTOR) AND GEOFF CUTTER (DOCTOR) AT RUSHCUTTERS BAY MARINA

CORAL SHARROCK (MEDICAL VOLUNTEER) FROM VICTORIA

(L TO R) FRAN POWER AND KAAREN SUTTON – MEDICAL VOLUNTEERS AT SOCOG HEADQUARTERS

JAMIE WHITMAN CAME FROM CANADA TO WIN BRONZE IN THE SONAR CLASS SAILING, WHILE BRONWYN SUTTON (MASSAGE THERAPIST) CAME FROM MACLEAN ON THE NSW NORTH COAST, TO ASSIST ATHLETES IN THE VILLAGE

'I was part of the medical team from room 702 of the Main Press Centre. With over 10,000 members of the media to care for our task seemed enormous. A team of one volunteer doctor, one volunteer nurse and two ambulance officers per shift kept the main press centre in shipshape condition. At times we didn't think the stream of patients was going to end, yet when it did a sense of satisfaction filled the room.

'The spirit is what this small team of 21 staff had. We called upon the language services to translate for us and the logistics team to transport us in the golf carts; I guess you can say our team was 47,000 strong.

'We came together from Sydney, Perth, Brisbane, Melbourne and Texas, all with an aim to share the experience, and an experience is what I got. With thanks to **Dr Kim Short** and **Jeannette Vaughan** my time spent in the MPC was one of enrichment and friendship which will burn forever.' …
Kim Vernon (Volunteer Nurse)

'I worked in the Medical Records Department in the Polyclinic within the Athletes Village, and at the Co-ordinating Medical Centre at Sydney 2000 Games Headquarters.

'Being a little behind the scenes, one of the most memorable moments for me was when an inquisitive Australian Men's Basketballer showed interest in what my role involved. After I gave a brief outline, he gave the most wonderful compliment. He told me I was doing an important and unrecognised job. This athlete made my night!

'To my fellow volunteers, supervisors, athletes and coaches, it has been a pleasure knowing and working with you. To my family and friends, thank you for your support.' … **Sophia Cassimatis (Health Information Administrator)**

'I was proud to be part of a group of 127 medical imaging professionals who were responsible for a large part of the medical diagnostic area of the Olympic Games.

'One significant feature of the Medical Imaging Department was the use of Computer Radiography. This is the production of X-ray images that are displayed on computer monitors rather than on X-ray film. This technology is still relatively new to radiography so it was a great advantage to have it for the Olympics. One major benefit (of many) with this technology is that it joins with all other forms of medical imaging examinations (CT, MRI, Ultrasound, etc.) in providing images in a digital form. This allowed the department to operate in a "filmless" environment. That is, X-ray films did not have to be produced as diagnosis was made by viewing the images on special diagnostic display monitors.

'To say it was a once-in-a-life time experience would be a very conservative comment. To have the opportunity to work with and associate with the elite athletes of the world was one prospect very few will ever have the opportunity to embrace. I am sure that I speak for all the Medical Imaging Volunteers when I say that it was an experience we will hold in a very special part of our memory.' ... **Luke Barclay**

Lorraine Emerton, Liz Hoad, Alvin Pun, Paul Mulhearn and podiatrist **Jayne Arlett** are medical volunteers who expressed a feeling of great significance in being able to contribute to the success of the Olympic and Paralympic Games.

There were hundreds of medical volunteers we have not been able to mention in these pages – however, their efforts are no less significant, and obviously remain in the debit of those they directly assisted. Thank you for sharing your skills in the caring and selfless manner of which you can all be so proud.

Ann Fenwick (spectator nurse – paralympics) with lizzie

YOUTH PROGRAMS

The Youth of the World may have been looked upon in many people's eyes as the competing athletes, but youth played a substantial role in much more varied situations, from performing in Ceremonies to the Ryde – Canada School 2000 Program. However, two major programs involving youth were the Olympic Youth Camp and the Youth Ambassador Program.

The Olympic Youth Camp (OYC) was instigated in 1912, and young people have since then been involved in every Olympic Games through camps or other related programs. There have been two youth camps at Winter Olympics as well – Lillehammer (1994) and Nagano (1998).

Campers were chosen based on either their academic or sporting achievements, and for the Sydney 2000 OYC, the 388 campers came from 173 of the competing Olympic nations. Nine management staff and 95 volunteers hosted the campers at St Joseph's College (Joeys) at Hunters Hill (Sydney's north) for 15 days. There were also three days where campers were on an Aussie Family Visit, and four days in Cairns, North Queensland.

The OYC presented to campers the three Pillars of Olympism – Sport, Culture and Environment aiming to educate youths through sport, promoting cultural exchange and sharing the Olympic Spirit.

The Youth Ambassador Program through the Department of Education and Training, in conjunction with SOCOG, the Australian Olympic Committee, Sydney Paralympic Organising Committee and the Olympic Co-ordination Authority, provided opportunities for students to be involved in activities leading up to the Sydney Olympic and Paralympic Games.

Youth Ambassadors were involved in a variety of activities including – assisting event management, interpreting, site escorting, hospitality, peer support and youth advisory roles. Countless events benefited through their involvement, including – Pan Pacific Swimming, Venue Opening Celebrations, World Environment Day and the Pacific School Games.

WE ARE INDEED INDEBTED TO OUR YOUTH

OLYMPIC YOUTH CAMP STAFF AND VOLUNTEERS

THE NINE AUSTRALIAN OYC PARTICIPANTS FROM ATLANTA 1996, WHO BECAME OYC VOLUNTEERS FOR SYDNEY 2000

THEY COULDN'T TAKE THE SMILES OFF THEIR FACES!

Olympic Youth Camp

'It is hard to put into words just what sort of impact this Youth Camp experience has had, and will continue to have, on me. Having been a youth camper at a previous Olympics, I was very committed to ensuring these young people had the best time of their lives; knowing that they would return home with a new understanding of themselves, a new outlook on the world within which they live, and a sense of mutual camaraderie with friends from all over the world. My work was not hard, but it was exhausting. I averaged five hours sleep a night, but that was a small price to pay for the privilege I was afforded in working with these young people. I would like to think that I have had a positive, enriching and lasting impact on each of the lives with which I came into contact.' ... **Claire Geary (OYC Volunteer)**

Yvonne (Von) Wong was a passionate OYC Volunteer who says: 'Imagine this – an environment full of respect, appreciation, encouragement and support. A continuous circle of friendship, where everyone amalgamates to share with each other their life, its lessons and its heartaches with mutual understanding, enthusiasm in knowing the thoughts of one another, their love of life – a will.

'Thank you to all you volunteers for spreading your heart to the world, in support of our Olympic Youth Camp motto – *Together we are one.*'

'My volunteer work – although I very rarely refer to it as such, because I regarded it more of a desire lived out, a passion fulfilled – at the Sydney 2000 Olympic Games constituted being involved in what I consider the best-kept secret – The Olympic Youth Camp. A phenomenal, inspirational experience that has been running in conjunction with all but one Summer Olympic Games since 1912 in Stockholm.

OYC PARTICIPANTS AND STAFF IN DRAMA ELECTIVE!

'I was not a camper at OYC 2000. However, I knew exactly the emotions the campers were experiencing. The awe in their eyes, I could easily relate to, and the continuous smiles on their faces allowed me to remember the time I had experienced at the 1996 OYC in Atlanta at Berry College. I had been chosen, along with nine other Australian Youth to represent my country at the Olympic Games. They were the proudest days of my adolescent years, and I vowed to be at the next OYC.

'Never again will I literally have hundreds of campers individually hug me goodbye, tears streaming down their faces, telling me – a mere volunteer – that I helped create for them, one of the most amazing experiences of their lives (when really, they had neglected to see they had done exactly the same for me).' ... **Cassidy Jackson-Carroll**

'Two years ago I had never heard of the Olympic Youth Camp. I could never have imagined the tremendous impact it would have upon my life and the inspiration it has given me and everyone involved to follow their dreams. Some people might think that the highlight of the three weeks was watching the Opening Ceremony or being at a particular event, but although these were amazing experiences, the memories I will treasure most are the friendships I have formed. Although saying goodbye to my new friends was one of the saddest experiences of my life, I know that it was far better to have met them and had to leave them, than never to have met them at all.' ... **Heidi Tugwell (OYC Volunteer)**

'The participants were a very elite group of young people from every corner of the globe. Many many times I stood back and thought, this is utopia! People from all different nationalities, languages, religions, cultures, customs, beliefs and lifestyles – living, working, eating and playing together. Every morning I met someone from a different country at breakfast, or sat on the bus next to someone who's country I knew absolutely nothing about. Now I can probably tell you where they are, what language they speak, and what are their national sports. A truly educational experience.' ... **Dahni Barron (OYC Volunteer)**

'When I was called out from assembly, I was unsure of the reason, but to my surprise and delight, I had been chosen to be part of something special – The Youth Ambassador Program.

'Unbelievable opportunities came our way, as Dianne Fielding and everyone involved spent weekends organising our dreams and how to make them come true. When I was finally given the opportunity to be a tribune runner at the Olympic Shooting I had no idea of the adventures ahead of me.

'These experiences have changed me for the better, and the best lesson learned is that having belief and making sacrifices leads to achievement.' ... **Vicky Wong**

'The Youth Ambassador Program, plus support from my German teacher, Mrs Watson, and my school, Jannali High, provided the ultimate volunteer opportunity – working in the Athletes Village for the Paralympics. I was located in Resident Centre 12, working with the Technical Officials. I may have struggled with missed schooling, but I learned so much from this opportunity that it has been well worth the sacrifices.' ... **Katherine Allan**

'The privilege of volunteering at the Olympic Games as a print distribution runner was not in my wildest dreams when I first became part of the Youth Ambassador Program. Just being able to help people and know that you have made their day just a little better was my motivation. Now I know that volunteering is such a worthwhile experience, and I would recommend it to anyone.' ... **Samantha Van**

OYC volunteer Cassidy Jackson-Carroll with Benni from Switzerland

Youth ambassador Vicky Wong with Annemarie Forder – Olympic shooting bronze medallist

OYC volunteers Heidi Tugwell (front) and Claire Geary with participants from Rwanda and Uganda

SAMSUNG ATHLETES' FAMILY HOSTS

As part of Australia's bid for the 2000 Olympic and Paralympic Games, the Rotary Club of Sydney initiated an outstanding community program whereby host families in the Host City would share their homes with relatives of athletes competing at the Olympic Games. The idea was tested in Atlanta in 1996, with considerable success. So when it became Sydney's turn, the call was put out for host families, and as with the tradition of volunteering in this country, the response more than accommodated the visiting families. In fact, maybe due to the cost of travel to Australia, there was not the demand for host families as initially anticipated, so several host families did not get allocated visitors. This was naturally very disappointing, and a sincere thank you is extended to those families who went through the orientation training only to be left without visitors come Games-time.

Olympic swimming gold medallist – Kevin Berry, shares his Olympic passion with Host Services staff, and prospective host families from the Broken Bay Catholic Community

Brian Mooney and his team comprising **Lynn Robinson, Graeme Hodge, Genevieve Tutaan** and **Catherine Kelman**, were supported by a group of dedicated volunteers, both at SOCOG Headquarters and in the field as co-ordinators within the ranks of host families. If this team had not performed so well, there would probably not have been so many disappointed families!

Hospitality, Opportunity, Sharing, Tiring, Inspiring, Never forget it, Great fun

Leanne Wicks, her partner **Robert** and daughters **Kaitlin** and **Mikaela** were duel hosts. First hosting Risto and Vanka Bosevska from Macedonia during the Olympic Games, then Kristy Carkner and Dorothy McLean from Canada during the Paralympics. Risto and Vanka are parents of Mirjana who swam three personal best times and three national records. Kristy and Dorothy are sister and grandmother of Tara Carkner, a Paralympic swimmer.

Leanne reflects: 'The ideals of Olympism and Paralympism were priceless lessons to have children see and learn. To have strangers become part of our family is the closest way to lead by example for world peace that I can think of. My family's perception of the world and humanity has deepened from our experience, but I feel that Sydney has changed also. This very special form of volunteering has enabled my family to share our spirit, and their pictures are engraved in our hearts.'

Robert's reflection of the experience comes to the heart of Olympism – 'If everyone hosted a family, there would be no war!'

Judy and Graham Field hosted brothers Estanislao and Eugenio Paulon, who's brother Ezequiel was a member of the Argentinean Hockey Team. 'We spoke no Spanish, they spoke only broken English, but with hand gestures and patience we were able to communicate quite well. A warm and friendly smile speaks all languages though.

'The boys were a pleasure to have stay, and their fascination with such items as an eggtimer, orange peeler, our budgie, Vegemite (which they hated) and seeing a kangaroo and koala for the first time was fun to watch.

'The confidence and experience we have gained was invaluable, but the best of all was a short note we have just received. It was from their mother in Argentina, thanking us for the care and love we showed her sons, and expressing how much they enjoyed their stay with us, and how much they love Australia.' ... **Judy Field**

For the **Bond Family** of Glen Alpine the duel experiences of hosting relatives of a Swedish Olympian and being part of the Olympic/Paralympic volunteer force made for a very emotional September and October. To cap it all off, Pia Hansen, the wife and daughter of their guests, Rudolf and Karl-Axel, won an Olympic Gold Medal in Shooting. 'It was so exciting sitting next to Pia's father at the event when she won the Gold Medal, he had tears in his eyes and his heart was pounding. A few nights later, after taking Pia to a wildlife park, she came back to our house for dinner. She brought her Gold Medal, so we had neighbours and other host families come to meet her. She left about 9 pm to return to the Athletes Village, she was so happy to have shared with us all.' ... **Judith Bond**

'Our Olympic hosting experience began with frustration, as we were advised that we would be hosting the parents of a female judo competitor from the USA. On calling them, we were advised that they had made other accommodation arrangements. We were then advised that we would host the brother and trainer of a French boxer Brahim Asloum. On telephoning France we were advised that the brother could not come to Sydney, and that the trainer would stay in a hotel, as he spoke no English.

Host Leanne Wicks wears the Australian flag in her cap so as children from Gladesville Primary School can see her more easily

Hosts Kerry and son Michael Powell, with their guest Brahim Ouajif (Papou) and the boxer he coached to Olympic gold – Brahim Asloum

'We were of course now very disappointed. However, third time lucky, we were then allocated a lady from the Dominican Republic named Adelaida Hernandez, who had a cousin on the men's judo team. Adelaida was a lovely lady, and we enjoyed attending events together, but unfortunately she had to return home after only one week.

'On the Sunday night (24 September), we were about to go out to dinner when we received an unexpected telephone call from the Samsung Athletes' Family Host Program, informing us that our guest from France had arrived! A sudden change of plans, and we were at Redfern to collect our guest who was the boxer's trainer Papou.

'While driving home, Kerry rang a friend named Judex Jasmin who she remembered spoke French. Judex to our eternal gratitude packed his family into the car and came over and interpreted for a couple of hours so as we could get to know our guest. Papou was a lovely fellow, and the next week became a very happy and emotional time. Papou supplied tickets to Brahim's fights, and it was very exciting to see him go on to win an Olympic Gold Medal. Brahim also showed his kind nature by giving my son Michael his France Tracksuit.

'Probably the most enjoyable part of the whole experience was having Papou stay with us, and become a loved and important part of our family, through his kind, gracious and generous nature.' ... Rick Powel

'We learned that our guests were the Mum and Dad and a friend of a French athlete, competing in the Modern Pentathlon. I went to the library and took out some books on France to familiarise myself with where they come from. Monsieur and Madame Clergeau and Mademoiselle Huin arrived on 27 September and were to stay for five days. Their son Oliver was competing on 29 September, and they arranged some tickets for us to attend his event.

'Our time with them was most enjoyable, and we even loaned them our car to go to the Blue Mountains for three days. When it was all over there were a few tears shed at the airport, and a promise to meet again. They have gone home to learn English, and I have started a French course. Our 17-year-old son said it had been a great experience and had broadened his outlook on life. I would recommend hosting to anyone.' ... Leah Mooney

'As a family new to Sydney, we decided to offer something so volunteered to host an athlete's family. We were all disappointed when we were not assigned a family. So to enhance our Olympic experience, we decided to see if there was another way to host someone in need.

'As luck would have it, Tsui, a volunteer from Adelaide, was in need of accommodation so that she too could volunteer her services at the Olympic Village. Tsui was welcomed into our home for her stay in Sydney. Our eight-year-old daughter Christina said: "We liked having Tsui stay with us because she was fun to talk to, played my games, and was very kind to be with."

'We also hosted Matthew for the Paralympics. Matt, also from Adelaide, volunteered in the Paralympic Village and brought home many interesting stories about life there. Our 11-year-old son

ATTENDEES AT THE LAUNCH OF THE SAMSUNG ATHLETES' FAMILY HOST PROGRAM

VOLUNTEERS READY TO HAND OUT THE 'GOODIES'

Nicholas said: "It was good to have Matt stay with us to hear the funny stories about what happened and about what he did in the Paralympic Village."

'It was a worthwhile experience.' ... **Keith and Dianne McPhee**

'We hosted the parents of Javier Conte who represented Argentina in the 470's class men's sailing. This was a very rich experience! Jorge and Maria Conte were an excellent match for us. They come from Buenos Aires in Argentina. We found we had many things in common including a love of travel and animals, which helped develop a very warm friendship. The highlight of the visit was when their son won Bronze in the 470 class.

'Our volunteer experience was very satisfying because we felt we had contributed to their success. We plan to visit Argentina, which we would probably not have done if we had not met the Contes. Jorge suggested we charter a boat together for the Athens Olympics. His son wants to go for gold – sounds great to me.' ... **Robyn Coleman**

'We were delighted to be involved in the Samsung Athletes' Family Host Program, and enjoyed a great few days with the Langford Family, who's daughter was a member of the Canadian Kayak Team.' ... **Gabriella Pusner**

David Johnson's link with the Olympic Games was that his niece Emma Johnson had represented Australia at the Atlanta Olympic Games. So when David decided to become involved in the Sydney Olympic and Paralympic Games he did it in a big way.

First, David was appointed as a National Olympic Committee (NOC) driver for the Egyptian Team based in the Athletes Village, plus he was allocated the position of T3 driver for the Paralympics. Just to make sure things weren't too quiet at home, David became involved in the Samsung Athletes' Family Host Program, through which he hosted the parents of New Zealand swimmer, Vivien Rignal.

When David was not driving for the Egyptians, he enjoyed showing Sydney off to his guests, including taking them to the Blue Mountains.

Another dedicated volunteer who now has to find other ways to overload his life!

A special thanks is extended to the many families who registered, became excited, and then missed out on being allocated a guest. Many of these families still made the most of their involvement with the Program, particularly prospective hosts like **Nita Byrne**, who enjoyed the Samsung function, the lead-up meetings, and the opportunity to attend the Opening Ceremony Dress Rehearsal. Thank you Nita.

'We had signed up as hosts with the Samsung Athletes' Family Host Program, and then had the anxious wait. Our first contact was a phone call from Canada early one morning about a month before the Games to tell us they were our guests. On the other end of the phone was Tania, who was the sister of the Canadian National Archery Champion. She, her husband and baby would be staying with us, and her parents had been allocated to a family down the street from us. What followed was a rush of emails back and forward as we asked questions, answered questions and got to know each other.

'When they finally arrived on 13 September 2000, for their allocated eight days, we felt like we were already old friends, and what proceeded was one of the most fun times of our lives. Our home became like "Canada House", with visitors from down the street, and even team members visiting between events.

'When it was time for them to leave, they did not want to go and nor did we want them to leave. So with a lot of pleading with QANTAS we managed to change flights – almost impossible during the Olympics – and the eight days became 15!!. To add to this, a coach came to spend some time with us after the Games, so eight days really extended to seven weeks. We loved every minute of it, and now think how lucky we were to be a part of the Olympic experience.' ... **Margaret Farrand**

The **Jerapetritis Family** enjoyed a fulfilling involvement, not only in hosting Steve and Carol Heyns from South Africa, but also by becoming involved in the promotional support of the Samsung Athletes'

(L to R) – Host Family John, Susie, Sally and Sophie Jerapetritis, with 1996 dual Olympic Gold Medallist, Penny Heyns, and her father Steve Heyns and his wife Carol

Bronze Medallist Javier Conte with mother Maria (hiding), and Host Family Anthony, Robyn, Karen and David Coleman

Family Host Program pre-games. Sally's mother, **Betty Robertson**, also hosted visitors, and they were the mother and sister of Australian athlete Kyle Vander-Kuyp. To cap it all off, eldest daughter, Susie, sang in the Opening Ceremony of the Paralympics. Sally Jerapetritis confides: 'We did not want to be just onlookers, and while we enjoyed showing our guests some of Sydney, in hindsight, I may even have volunteered in my profession as a nurse. However, it was a great experience, and we do still keep in touch with our guests.'

Disappointment!

Mention has been made of the prospective hosts who unfortunately missed out on being allocated guests, and this in no way reflected their unsuitability. **Doug and Dot Hamilton** attended all the orientation and became excited about the prospect of having overseas guests, but they were unfortunately part of the unlucky group. However, they decided to persist. Doug recalls: 'Through contacts, we were able to get in touch with the Swedish Paralympic Team, and were introduced by email to a Swedish lady whose son was competing. We exchanged emails with her and got on really well. She was very excited about coming and we got excited about meeting her in person. We gave her our web address so she could see photos of us and our home and country, and she got excited about the dog she saw. When we emailed back and told her we no longer had a dog, but had two cats, she replied that she was heartbroken, but wouldn't be able to stay with us, as she was violently allergic to cats!

'Finally, we arranged to host the sister of an athlete, for the last week of the Paralympics, but she discovered she had a friend with a relative who lived closer to the games venues. So, no one! – However, we did love the Games, especially the Paralympics.'

Our phantom guest

'As part of the Samsung Athletes' Family Host Program, our family hosted an Eastern European guest. He was his brother's coach, and was expected to stay more than a week.

'On the day he arrived with an interpreter and Attaché, it was arranged that I would accompany him to Lidcombe the following morning, where he would be driven to the Village to meet his brother. After a quick breakfast we set off, and on the train I thought "How is he going to find his way back to us at night, with no knowledge of English at all?" He did not return!

'Our volunteer daughter saw him occasionally in the beginning. But when the days went by we started to make telephone calls. His belongings were still in our room. Panic! Nobody knew anything. We vaguely knew his date of departure, and at 1 am on that day we received a telephone call from his brother, *'could he collect his possessions?'* This was promptly done at 8 am!

'A lovely man. Such a pity that we could not get to know him better, although we have been invited to visit his home.' ... **Jean Hudson**

THE GENERAL CONSENSUS

WAS IT A DREAM?

'When I awoke this morning (2 October 2000) my soul seemed separated from my body. I felt I had awakened from a dream.

'Fresh in my thoughts was the greatest experience of my life. This day I feel so proud to be Australian.

'Over the 26 working days, feeling my way at the Guest Pass MPC, I have experienced the pressure from journalists desperate for access to a story, the uniting of Nations as I worked with Volunteers from around the world, the thrill of gold regardless of the nationality, the heartbreak of not reaching the finishing line, being blown away by wind and baked by sun, being congratulated often by the man on the street, and the tears as hands touched in farewell.

'I had the time of my life! Thank you.' … Rhonda Gibson

'For those who have had the experience of being involved in a major event, no explanation is necessary. For those who have not, none is possible.' ... **John Withell (Results Print Systems Operator – Aquatic Centre)**

'Anyone who has been associated with any project, whether saving the world or a lamington drive, knows that there are six phases. Put them up on your wall now, as a reminder of the next seven years:

Euphoria

Disenchantment

Search for the guilty

Persecution of the innocent

Successful completion – and finally

Glorification of the uninvolved.' ... **John Huxley** *(Sydney Morning Herald) – 1993.*

Doping Control

'I was a doping control officer at several venues, and really enjoyed the experience. However, even before the Games commenced we had one of our funniest incidents at our accommodation at Potts Point. After a late night out, a certain doping control volunteer found himself locked out with no sign of the guards, so decided that the only way to get to bed was to jump the fence! Well, as he hit the ground three flashlights shone on him, and he was greeted by a snarling dog. CAUGHT!! Having explained himself to the guards, and using some volunteer charm, he managed to remain inside and get to bed. The next morning we were greeted by a directive on the notice board reminding doping control volunteers about security procedures.' ... **Stu Baker (Palmerston North, New Zealand)**

PITTWATER HOUSE SCHOOL ON THE NORTHERN BEACHES OF SYDNEY HAD MANY CONTRIBUTORS TO THE OLYMPIC AND PARALYMPIC GAMES – AS CAN BE SEEN BY THE VARIOUS UNIFORMS

VOLUNTEERS WHO MAINTAINED EFFICIENT SERVICES IN BOTH ATHLETICS WARM-UP LOCATIONS – SIAC 1 AND SIAC 2

'It took me three days to come down off a high. You may ask, "What is a high?" I can only describe it as an extremely elated feeling, one experienced after a certain event. No, I was not taking a banned substance, I had not won an event and I had not qualified for Olympic Selection. In fact, I really can't explain why I happened to feel this way, but I do know that the excitement felt by my athlete, whom I was escorting to Doping Control, also rubbed onto me – she had just won a place on the Australian Olympic Team!' ... **Linda Broschofsky (Doping Control Escort)**

'After a stimulating experience in Doping Control at the Olympic Games, I took on a Protocol role at the Athletes Village for the Paralympics. One morning after one of the Team Welcome Ceremonies I was walking near the Amphitheatre when I tripped and fell, landing flat on my face. For a split second as I lay there I thought "Oh no, I've broken my glasses, nose and teeth!" As I had managed this performance in front of a rather large crowd, many people came to my help.

'I sat on the ground in agony, bleeding from a cut lip, and saw a lady coming to offer me some tissues. I couldn't believe my eyes when she tripped on the same gutter and fell beside me. Despite the pain and embarrassment, we sat there laughing. She said she had gone out in sympathy with me. It wasn't till five days later that I found out I had fractured three bones in my hand.' ... **Denise Tugwell**

I'm just a volunteer

I'm just a volunteer mate, trying to do my share
Of getting this here sporting show away without a care
I've given up my day job, taken leave without my pay
I'm just a volunteer mate, what more is there to say.

I'm just a volunteer mate, just helping where I can
Just pitching in with others, be they woman, youth or man
They've come out of retirement, put their work life to one side
We're just volunteers mate, glad to do our bit with pride.

I'm just a volunteer mate, I've done it all my life
Whether Meals on Wheels or Red Cross and always with my wife
It just comes second nature, the Australian thing to do
I'm just a volunteer mate, along with you and you and you.

I'm just a volunteer mate but now I'm trained by TAFE
To better do my job and keep the public safe
And in my Bonds uniform I'm full of Chesty pride
A happy volunteer mate, that I just can't hide.

I'm just a volunteer mate working with the team
I just go and get the job done while there's a head of steam
And it matters very little what the task may be
I'm just a volunteer mate, I'm not doing this for me.

I'm just a volunteer mate and now the job is done
And we've had our march up George Street and a little bit of fun
And in my happy musings a thought comes to the fore
I wonder if there is a spot for me, in Athens, in '04.

Graeme Turnbull (Doping Control Volunteer)

Technical Officials

Unlike most Olympic sports, virtually all the officials for Athletics are appointed by the host country's national federation. Athletics Australia has, however, included six New Zealanders and two Pacific Island officials in the group, in recognition of the importance of the Games in the development of officiating in the Oceania region.

The complement of appointed officials represents a very full picture of the demographic spread of the Australian population. Each state and territory is well represented, as are both sexes, all age groups and a wide range of professions. The last time the Olympics were held in Australia, in Melbourne in 1956, just three women officiated in athletics – for Sydney 2000, 74 women are included.

Proving age is no barrier, three officials under 25 years have been appointed. They are: **Simon Ware** (Melbourne), **George Proimos** (Melbourne) and **Natalia King** (Brisbane). Meanwhile, five 70-something officials have also been appointed: **Fred O'Connor** (Sydney), **Fred Napier** (Western Australia), **George Tempest** (Western Australia), **Geoff Grant** (Victoria) and **Noel Ruddock** (Hobart) who has the unique distinction of having been appointed to the Melbourne and Sydney Olympic Games.

Pamela Smith and Carol Flint are Technical Volunteers from Victoria, who are very appreciative of the hospitality extended to them by **Margarette D'Arcy (Peggy)**, who made her home theirs during the Olympic Games. Pam and Carol recall: 'Peggy lived her Olympic experience through our eyes. Every morning we would have a debrief of what we had done and seen the day before, it was a great way of recapping and remembering all that happened on those 16 magical days.'

BASKETBALL STATISTICS CREW FOR THE OLYMPIC GAMES (BACK ROW L TO R) BELINDA MITCHELL (VICTORIA), MARK QUINN (VICTORIA), BRENDA WILLIAMS (NSW), MALCOLM HALL (TASMANIA), VICKI CROUCHER (NSW), GARRY GILLAM (WA), LEANNE ROBERTS (VICTORIA), COLIN LUCAS (TASMANIA), LAURETTA CLAUS (NSW) (MIDDLE ROW) JENNY-LEE COLLINS (ACT), LYN HARROWER (VICTORIA), BARBARA DUNN (SA), COLIN NEUCOM (QUEENSLAND), MELISSA HIRD (NSW), SUE BUTLER (TASMANIA), JASON CROSBIE (VICTORIA), TRISH NICHOLS (NSW), LAURA HOWLETT (NSW), MELISSA LETHAM (NSW), WARWICK LINDSAY (NSW) (FRONT ROW) MAUREEN ELPHINSTON (NSW), KAREN MARSHALL (NSW), DEAN GRAY (WA), TRACEY QUINN (VICTORIA), ASHLEY MCCALLUM (VICTORIA), JAN GIBSON (NSW), JAMIE SCHULZ (VICTORIA), MICHELLE AUSTIN (NSW), RICHARD NOBLE (ACT), JENNY MARSHALL (NSW), NORMA BACIC (NSW)

Technical Quotes

'It would have to be the pinnacle of my officiating career.' ... Kim Owens (Sydney)

'I didn't see the final or the presentation of the event as I was busy with my duties. When they came back to get their rifles, the Silver Medal winner gave me his flowers to thank me.' ... Leonie Zutenis (Technical Officer – Shooting)

'So many Paralympians shook my hand after their events that I thought my hand would fall off. I officiated at 11 Shot Put, nine Discus, four Javelin and one Club events and witnessed the establishment of no fewer than seven World Records – Wow!' ... Carol Hall (Sydney)

'As Technical Officials, there is a great deal of camaraderie, as we have not come together for the first time for this event. Most of us have a long history in Athletics, and many still compete. The Olympic and Paralympic Games are a highlight in any capacity as a Technical Official.' ... Rob Blackadder (Sydney)

As Bachelor of Business students at UTS, Sydney, Marissa Daras and Kate Hacking were first involved in 1999 through a practium subject offered jointly by UTS and SOCOG. It involved the outsourced interviewing of prospective volunteers. Kate recalls: 'The best part was seeing the enthusiasm, selflessness and commitment displayed by those we interviewed. It was simply inspirational.

'There was such an array of incredible stories and experiences that shone through right from the initial interview stage. From those with a lifetime of experience to contribute, to others using the opportunity to test out new fields of interest, the energy and motivation was just incredible.

'The recruitment experience provided by our elective subject prompted Marissa to volunteer as a Venue Staffing Assistant and gain further HR experience, while I pursued the opportunity to work at the Main Press Centre and gain some experience in Public Relations and Journalism in conjunction with my own studies.'

'Where I was situated, in the Venue Communications Centre of the Olympic Stadium, we had a great group of managers and volunteers and this made a big difference to our workdays. Everything from transport to meal times worked perfectly for us and I cannot remember one bad moment that I experienced.' ... Kerry Wallace

On Sunday, 26 March 2000, volunteer Annette McCrae of Oatley helped organise a 'Fun Olympics' to raise money for Cystic Fibrosis. In keeping with the theme, there was an opening and closing ceremony, uniforms, medals, Aussie tucker, approximately 15 events, a band and guest appearance from a Queen. Annette opened her heart and home to about 200 people. Well done Annette!

TECHNICAL OFFICIALS (L TO R) MICHAEL HUNTER AND PETER HANNAN

(L TO R) SISTERS VICKI AND MONA KASSOUF (VELODROME AND CEREMONIES VOLUNTEERS RESPECTIVELY)

VOLUNTEERS AT BLACKTOWN POOL TRAINING VENUE (L TO R) PETER, PHIL, YVETTE CHAPMAN, CAROL AND LISA

(L TO R) JOHN BURGESS, ALISON LOANE AND KEVIN MCDONALD AT THE HOMEBUSH ARRIVALS AND ACCREDITATION CENTRE (HAAC)

ACCREDITATION VOLUNTEERS AT THE HOMEBUSH ARRIVALS AND ACCREDITATION CENTRE (HAAC)

PASSING ON THE BATON – LAURIE AND BARBARA SMITH WITH JA HAWKINS. JA HAD BEEN LINKED WITH LAURIE AND BARBARA THROUGH THE AUNTIES AND UNCLES PROGRAM FOR OVER SIX YEARS, AND BECAME AN OLYMPIC VOLUNTEER

Volunteer Lyn Williams with Hockeyroo Nikki Hudson

Volunteers of Maltese descent – proudly Australian

(L to R) Noreen Fielding and Seta Dikranian at the Homebush Arrivals and Accreditation Centre (HAAC)

Patrick Wedes – photo manager – cycling

(L to R) Gary Beer and Clive Simpson – baseball diamond preparation – Blacktown

Volunteers at the baseball test event

Reg and Shirley Chirgwin were a T3 Driver at Jones Street, and VCC Operator in the radio control room at the Tennis Centre, respectively. Their Olympic experience commenced as road marshals for the Host City Marathon in April 2000, and that set the tone for a rewarding volunteer contribution. Reg recalls: 'People have asked "why did you do it?" and my answer is – because I saw a need and wanted to participate, and couldn't have lived with the regrets of later saying to myself – if only!!

'This wonderful, unique experience will never be repeated in my lifetime, and my wife and I did not for one moment regret our involvement. One overseas visitor asked where all the volunteers came from, as we are a relatively small nation. All I could say was – it's the Australian way!'

Those also recognised for their contribution are:

David Frede, Narelle Stoll, Catherine Hector, Therese Baldwin, Maureen O'Hara, Elio Zadro, Tricia Fullerton, Michael Swift, Gail Page, Lauren Quick, Maureen Bell, Helen Garvey, Margaret Randall, Chemene Sinson, Libby Thomas, Darryl Wilson, Rosslyn Hamilton, Kirsty Last, Adrian Gilderdale, Celia Grace, Douglas Cairns, Rachael Sy, Eliza Jacobs, Margaret Knight, Carol Lynch, Cheryl D'Alrena, Stefan Hofmann, Patrick Haynes, Yvonne Harris, Majorie Causer, Adrian Wyatt, Colin Leung, John Elliott, Rhonda Gibson, Sonya Lloyd, Caroline Nemes, Paul Whelan, Katie Gleeson, Michael Brock, John Murray, Barbara Carter, Warren O'Neill, Eric Ha, Leonarda Tannous.

A volunteer got talking with bus driver **Arthur Agius**, who came from a small town north-west of Ipswich, Queensland. Arthur was saying how much he had enjoyed working at the Games, but was really looking forward to getting home. Apparently he and his second wife were expecting their first child on 5 October 2000, but their baby daughter, Jessica, had arrived on 15 September 2000 instead. When asked why he was still in Sydney he said, 'I said I'd do it and I'll do it – but I've seen a picture!' At this stage little Jessica was 13 days old. How's that for Olympic Spirit?

Equestrian Centre Volunteers:

Giselle McKenzie (Victoria), Kate Hesse (Western Australia), Chas Stephens (Tumut, NSW), Kate Wilson (Windsor, NSW), Kathleen Vanhoff (St Marys, NSW), Arianne Lowe (Camden, NSW), Ellen Lee (Chatswood, NSW), Kim Austen (Mt Colah, NSW), Fiona Drummond (Glenhaven, NSW), Vibeke Fuglbjerg (Denmark), Graham Tippett (New Zealand), Bree Howard (Western Australia), Amanda Edwards (Batemans Bay, NSW), Cheryl Klimko (Glenwood, NSW), Caroline Scott (Great Britain), Kate Ireland (Kenthurst, NSW), Rebecca Jenner (Cremorne, NSW), Glen Stedman (Londonderry, NSW), Maree and David Pollock (Alstonville, NSW), Kelly Hattersley (Mona Vale, NSW), Ellen Knudsen (Norway), Simon Bain (Murrumbateman, NSW), Cassi and Shannon Tonkin – identical twins (Ebenezer, NSW)

'I had lots of memorable experiences during my time at the Regatta Centre – the lunches shared with other volunteers and our IBM staff, or whoever else needed a table at the time – the early morning walk over the bridge to the island where the IBM tent was situated – to be able to mingle with the athletes and appreciate their dedication to excellence – the sense of cooperation, support, appreciation for individual talents, their tolerance and respect among volunteers was a positive and uplifting experience.' ... **Beth Connor**

'My overall experiences have been ones of new and valuable friendships, an understanding of the work behind the scenes, of mixing with elite athletes, media and spectators, and the absolute feeling of elation at a job well done. Seeing sports performed at the very top level has been another benefit. I would never have met Fran, Michelle, Marion, Ventry, Dorothy, Marlene, Janelle, Donna, Beth and Yvonne – just to name a few of my fellow volunteers – and the confidence I have gained from all of this is a huge plus.' ... Carol Beattie (IBM CIS Support Officer – Aquatic Centre)

'I had not wanted to be a volunteer, and it was only my father explaining his missed opportunity in Melbourne in 1956, that motivated me to sign up. Even when I commenced my shifts at the Entertainment Centre I knew nobody and was not confident about the work – something kept me going. As the Games drew to a close, how different I felt when I left the building for the last time, from when I arrived that very first day. These people had become my friends, and we had all become part of something bigger than ourselves – it's an awesome feeling.' ... Jennie Spencer (IBM Technology Help Desk)

'Working in the Venue Communications Centre at Darling Harbour, I received a request for assistance from cleaners at the Boxing Hall male toilets. A spectator had dropped his mobile phone down the toilet and requested assistance with its retrieval. Happy end of story is that his mobile phone was eventually recovered, state unknown, nor what kind of apparatus was used!' ... Harry Goerl

'I come from Malaysia, though now living in Melbourne – but I would have come from the Moon if required – for nothing on earth was going to stop me from being at that Velodrome. It was a privilege to be allowed to serve our country, it was a pleasure to be with our fellow volunteers. And whether baking in the sun checking passes, or forgotten for five hours in the Radio Room, every minute was alive with excitement and the laughter of doing what comes but seldom in a person's life – the chance to repay in full measure and settle one's debt – and hearing utter strangers say, "You've done a great job, Ma'am!"

'I got back much much more than I gave of my time, my money or my exceedingly exhilarated, utterly exhausted self.' ... Shirin Mistry

'I made many friends both Australian and from overseas, but a highlight for me was meeting an old school friend, Michael Callan. We attended school together in Middlesex, England, from 1976 to 1978. We competed successfully in Judo, and now here he is as coach of the Great Britain Women's Judo Team. I was proud to show our visitors my new country.' ... Kaizer Austin (Results/Print Distribution) and Paralympic Torch Bearer

'My sister, Sue Cole, was in Spectator Services, my sons, Damian and Ben Gregson, son-in-law, Brendan Leamy, and niece, Jennifer Oppy, performed in the Opening Ceremony, my brother, Geoff Oppy and his wife Kathy, registered as a host family and my grand-daughter, Kaitlyn Leamy, danced

(L to R) Sally Coughlin, Peter Charles and Debbie Wedes –
photo volunteers – Aquatics Centre

at the Blacktown Olympic Centre. As for me, throughout the Olympics I revelled in the camaraderie, excitement and enthusiasm that was these Games. It was a time that drew people together from all nationalities and walks of life, a time for enjoying the visitors, athletes, coaches and team members from both here and other countries. But above all, I enjoyed the way that it drew the Australian people together with excitement, for the success of the Games.' ... **Terrie Gregson (Event Management Operations – Baseball Results Team)**

'As one of a number of volunteers at the wrestling with some background in the sport, I looked forward to seeing some of the action. For me it was even more special because one of the Australian freestyle team was a former pupil, Gabriel Szerda. It was a very special occasion to be present when Gabby (as he is known) won Australia's first match at these Olympics. We exchanged "high fives" as he passed by, and I thought back to the day ten years ago when Gabby had told a local journalist, "I want to go to the Olympics". Then I had to compose myself – after all, I was on duty!' ... **Graeme Cameron**

'Volunteers worked very hard and did a great job. They stuck to the task no matter how boring or uninteresting. They were a real asset.' ... **Bill Girdwood (Torch Relay Crew)**

'We thought us paid workers could handle the demands of the Media Village ourselves. Boy, were we wrong! But these volunteers – I tell you what, they never failed us. Even when it came to undertaking the laborious and menial tasks – there they were doing it, quite happily and ever so efficiently.

'I had felt an inkling of superiority as a paid worker, but by the end of the Games, they had received such just recognition, and I regret I was not one of them.' ... **Rebecca Kent**

'I felt that these thoughts – not new, but special – epitomised our volunteer contribution:

Friends are just people we haven't met yet.

If you see anyone without a smile give them one of yours.

It is possible to work without results – but there will never be results without work.' ...

Denise Hitchcock

'We volunteer because we want to share in the Spirit of the Games, and because it is a passion concerned with the act of giving rather than receiving. The friendships gained, skills learned and experiences developed are worth far more than anything money can buy. It is priceless! As material possessions come and go, the memories of the Olympic and Paralympic Games will last an eternity.' ... **Alan Ko (IBM Technology Help Desk – IBC)**

'I will never forget arriving at Homebush at 6 am, pitch black sky, and the Flame in the Cauldron dancing and leaping in the air. I would stand in the quiet of the early morning and think of all the people who passed on the Flame, from Greece and the Pacific nations, then all over Australia and finally to Cathy. We all felt so unified and proud. My great, great, great grandfather as ADC to Governor Phillip, was at Farm Cove in 1788 when the flag was raised, so I am a "dinky-di" Aussie first fleeter, and so glad to have been part of the Sydney 2000 Olympic Games.' ... **Judith McMahon**

SONJA GOERNITZ (IBM TECHNOLOGY HELP DESK ATTENDANT – IBC) GETTING THE RUN DOWN ON HOW H.G. AND ROY PUT THEIR SHOW TOGETHER – SONJA BEING FROM GERMANY ONLY ADDED FURTHER TO THE CONFUSION!

(L TO R) ADAM, EMY EVANS, JANET VAN ARENDONK, TONY PINCOTT AND MANDY MOORE (VENUE COMMUNICATIONS CENTRE – THE DOME AND PAVILIONS)

THE DAINTER FAMILY – (L TO R) SON WARWICK AND PARENTS SUSAN AND LES

PARALYMPIC VOLUNTEER LILIAN MCBRIDE HAVING WON THE DAILY COMPETITION

PAUL COUVRET – ATHLETICS TECHNICAL ASSISTANT (SIAC) – AT 78 YEARS OF AGE HAS THE UNIQUE DISTINCTION OF VOLUNTEERING AT BOTH THE MELBOURNE AND SYDNEY OLYMPIC GAMES

'As an 82-year-old and one of the oldest volunteers at the Olympic and Paralympic Games, I can only say that it made my life absolutely wonderful and fulfilling. The spectacle of the ceremonies combined with the many friends I made, contributed to the complete package. I am even receiving mail from Japan, Brazil, Malaysia and Cuba – who would have ever thought that this would come from being a volunteer at the Games! I am sad that it is all over, but great memories live on. I now look forward to volunteering at the Federation Parade, the Youth Olympics and the Golden Ambassadors at the airport.' ... **Mavis Symonds**

'My late sister, Betty McKinnon, was an Olympian in London in 1948, and that combined with the enthusiasm and spirit that went into a young nation hosting the Melbourne Olympics in 1956, has meant that I just had to be part of the Sydney 2000 experience. Being a volunteer meant so much to me, not only in the enjoyment and satisfaction, but in continuing a family tradition.' ... **Margaret McKinnon**

Robert Hinds' memorable volunteer experience began on 15 September 2000, as he organised, through his position as chair of the Manly Council Access Committee, a group of people with disabilities in a predesignated position to view the Olympic Torch Relay. Robert says: 'Those looks of sheer excitement is something I will never forget. People with disabilities just want to be part of it all, and the Olympics and Paralympics have certainly helped us achieve a lot more recognition.'

'It certainly was special to share this volunteer experience with my daughter **Ravin** and son **Gurbal**. However, it wasn't without challenges. As a minister of religion I had responsibilities to my community, so it was arranged that during my period in Sydney, I would fly back to Melbourne at 6 pm every Saturday, and return to Sydney 6 pm every Sunday. It was the greatest occasion of my life.' ... **Santokh Singh Padda**

The Warn Family has an extensive background in Amateur Boxing and cherished the opportunity to be involved with the Sydney Olympic Games. Father **Warwick Warn** was a Field of Play Supervisor, son **Steven**, his wife **Janelle**, and her brother **Glen Kelly** were part of the Boxing Results Team. Their unanimous comment was that it was just special to contribute to this sport at the highest level.

Michael Craft resides in Parkes in central western NSW, and commenced his volunteering at the Australian Athletics Selection Trials in August 2000 – by the time he completed his Paralympic commitment, he had done many 800-km return trips to Sydney. Michael comments: 'The close contact with athletes at the training venues was a marvellous insight to the many nationalities and their dedication. I also managed to sing the praises of my home town by expounding the virtues of our Olympians and the current hit movie *The Dish* featuring Parkes.'

'I have been interested in the Olympic Games since 1948, and was in the stands for all the athletics in Melbourne in 1956. I was not sure what to expect when allocated a volunteer position at the Uniform Distribution and Accreditation Centre (UDAC). Well it turned out to be the most wonderful venue, from the efficiency and camaraderie of the volunteers, to the unbelievable number of old friends who came through the centre to collect uniforms. There were sporting friends, former work colleagues and pupils I had taught over a 25-year-period – just a wonderful period of reunions.' ... **Shirley Preedy**

'Venue Staffing! What is that? Bondi ... well I'm a bit sceptical in light of the media coverage! Will there be protesters?

'Well I need not have worried – Beach Volleyball at Bondi was just the best! We had a great venue, great volunteers, and the atmosphere was electric!

ROYAL NORTH SHORE HOSPITAL VOLUNTEERS

PRINT DISTRIBUTION VOLUNTEERS AT VELODROME WITH CYCLIST BRAD MCGEE

'There were some family adjustments to make during training and the Games, but with the support of husband Patrick, parents and in-laws, son Tom got to know the rest of the family much better.

'I look back now with many memories and feel privileged to have played a role in the XXVII Olympic Games.' ... **Virginia O'Neill**

'I volunteered because I wanted to contribute to Sydney doing a good job, so we as Australians could be proud. I began back of house at the Homebush Arrival and Accreditation Centre (HAAC), and although prior to athletes arriving we were looking for ways of stimulation, it was great to be with volunteers of the same sentiment as myself.

'Once most athletes had arrived, many of us were deployed to other venues, and then the back of house experience gave me a whole lot better appreciation of what made everything function. This whole adventure made me feel so proud of the city which I have called home for 30 years since moving from Hong Kong, we can all be proud!' ... **Dawn Goldie**

'I am quite certain that I had the best job at the Olympics. After all, each day while "working" I had the opportunity to meet athletes from around the world as we greeted them through the Homebush Arrivals and Accreditation Centre. However, I also have countless happy memories of the wonderful volunteers who made my friend, Franca Lombardo, and myself so welcome, having come from Melbourne. These were the special personal touches which made this whole experience so wonderful for so many people.' ... **Maria De Simone**

'Special thanks must go to a Sydneysider, Elaine Huggard, who on hearing of my plight for accommodation over the Games period did not hesitate to offer me a place to stay.

'Elaine, confined to a wheelchair for her own mobility, suffers from polio, but obviously this takes second place to her concern for others. Along with her daughter Karen Fitzpatrick, a Carer by profession, and grand-daughter Melissa, who had their lives interrupted by my often hectic schedule, nothing seemed to be too much trouble.' ... **Vern Curnow (Gippsland, Victoria)**

OLYMPIC TORCH BEARER JAMIE EARL FROM TRINITY BAY HIGH SCHOOL, CAIRNS. JAMIE ALSO VOLUNTEERED AT THE GOLD COAST TRAINING CAMP OF BRITISH AND OTHER ATHLETES

SALLY WONG AT THE UNIFORM DISTRIBUTION AND ACCREDITATION CENTRE

VENUE STAFFING TEAM IN DOWNES PAVILION – (L TO R) CHRIS KELLY, ALEXANDRA PANAGIOTELIS, DOROTHY BRYANT, CATRIONA BYRNE AND GREG MILLS

VENUE STAFFING TEAM AT THE CHECK-IN TENT – OLYMPIC STADIUM

VENUE STAFFING MANAGER KATHRYN BENDALL (FRONT) WITH HER VENUE STAFFING TEAM SYDNEY OLYMPIC PARK

'As an Epileptic myself, I wanted to give something back. People with disabilities are like a big family, we're all equal and we're all caring. We will encourage each other and learn from each other. I think the Paralympics was the best thing to happen to Australia for a long time. A lot of Australians have now changed their attitudes towards people with disabilities, and to what disabilities really are. It also gave our children an experience and lesson in life that many of us never had. The next generation will have an acceptance that the previous generation didn't have.'... **Michele Robertson**

'Sometimes it is worth putting our own problems aside, so when I was diagnosed with breast cancer after being accepted as a Family Host I decided to take care of it and look to the future. Six weeks of radiotherapy and chemotherapy left me little time to recover, but thankfully I did, and I could not have had better guests if I had handpicked them.' ... **Jocelyn Anderson (Collaroy, NSW)**

Snippets

'As a mother of five, I am very proud to be a volunteer, and very appreciative of relatives from Bundaberg in Queensland, coming down to help care for the children.' ... **Veronica Hoggan**

'I enjoyed myself so much I wish it had never come to an end.' ... **Jenny Medjumurac**

'I had two years of great experiences since the first Sailing test event in September 1998, through to meeting some of the characters of the media at Games-time – certainly something to cherish.' ... **Christian Kent (Technical Specialist Volunteer)**

'Seeing Olympic events as a spectator was always going to be great, actually getting involved made it even more special.' ... **Warren Grzic (IBM Info Help Officer – Ryde Aquatic Centre)**

'After my first briefing session I still had no idea what I would be doing or where exactly I would be working. Afterwards I wandered around Sydney Olympic Park familiarising myself with the location of the different venues. Met two young female volunteers on duty. I conveyed my fears to them and one of them assured me: "Don't worry, Bill; all you have to do is smile and point." I learned more in that brief encounter than during the previous two hours. The wisdom of youth! During the afternoon I heard about one fellow who had volunteered. Unfortunately he was wanted by the cops; so when his application was submitted, it was passed on to the local police who promptly arrested him. In the subsequent court case, his lawyer pleaded: "My client was the victim of his own goodwill!"' ... Bill O'Donnell (Melbourne)

'I have now learned and understand how important everyone was in the inevitable success of the Games. From the design, construction, and management and the running of events, thousands of people were involved to create the success. I am so glad I had the chance to be involved and meet people from overseas and local, we have become good friends and I love to keep in contact with them.' ... Charles Leung (Venue Technology – MPC)

'As a Spectator Services Host I got an amazing sense of pride for having done something that people really appreciated us doing. I will look back on my time as a Volunteer with fantastic memories of a time I wished never had to end.' ... Karen Higgins (Spectator Services Host – Hockey Centre)

'There were many great times, but one of the best was travelling up from Wollongong for 17 days with my fellow volunteers.' ... Phil Stacey

'It was interesting as a volunteer to overhear somebody saying that they could not understand that volunteers chose to honour an agreement for nothing more than the success of the Games.' ... Fabian Pazmino (IBM Technology Help Desk)

'My Olympic/Paralympic experiences were immense, from 12 September 2000, when I carried the Olympic Torch till the close of the Paralympics, there was always a new adventure or emotional moment. We did ourselves proud; long live the volunteers.' ... Rosie Barnes

'It was a very warm feeling to be part of the Games. If it wasn't the lively atmosphere of the venues, it was the never ending friendship you make with your fellow team members. It was certainly a unique experience.' ... Jason Reyes (IBM Technology Help Desk)

'Our team was quite a youthful one, mostly university students out to help and attain a bit of experience at the same time. It was fun, and we made plenty of friends.' ... Luis Iafigliola (IT Help Desk – IBC)

'It was the most exciting two weeks of my life, I met so many wonderful people from Australia and overseas.' ... Angelina Panetta (IBC)

'I have experienced as a volunteer and find myself very happy, satisfied and filled with memories and happiness. I give you thanks Australia for having accepted me, you greeted me with great love and did not distinguish though I am an immigrant.' ... Jose Eugenio Mendoza

'Being part of a small team in Accreditation at Triathlon, Road Cycling and Marathons, it was my privilege to work with our wonderful supervisor, Dora Rosa and a delightful group of volunteers.' ... Pat Harland

Lee McMahon (NOC assistant – Pakistan) and Natalie Aroyan (service centre assistant – MPC/MMC)

Janette Hopkins at the Superdome

(L to R) Nicole Welsh (massage therapist – beach volleyball and athletes village), Patricia Bolsover (spectator services – Superdome and velodrome) and Meagan Mathieu (food and beverage assistant – athletes village)

Jenny Mackay and Bob Lazzarini (catering volunteers – convention centre, Darling Harbour)

(L to R) Kaoru Watanabe (Saitama – Japan) and Ritsuko Muroaka (Nagano – Japan)

'Meeting new friends, helping the press and media with queries they had, seeing athletes after their press conferences, were just a few of the great experiences.' ... Helen Kalithrakas (IBM Results Distribution – MPC)

'Our job has been made immeasurably easier by the willingness and generosity of the public to be herded/guided to where they want to go.' ... Ann Westren (Spectator Services)

'All the volunteers I met or worked with were friendly, polite and happy, and sometimes tired (I wonder why?).' ... Judy Thompson

'At 62 years of age I was too old to compete, so helping make the show happen was next best.' ... Ron Laws

'When the little boy saw my uniform he came over and proclaimed that he was going to the Olympics. The joy and smile on his face was wonderful, and I thought to myself *this is what it is all about.*' ... Glenda Olesen

'Meeting people and helping with the success was my reason for being a volunteer.' ... Wayne Lombe

'After being hit by a car two years ago, this was the first time I had really pushed myself to do something. Although it took some strength and painkillers, the experience was well worth the effort.' ... Belle Browne

'The special friendships that I have made will be cherished, and it will be nice in the future to be able to reminisce over the good and bad times.' ... Helen Butler

'I have been playing Table Tennis for 40 years, and had a terrific opportunity to watch all the top players while volunteering.' ... Karl Preuss (Table Tennis Volunteer)

'Flying from state to state, endless meetings with FIFA Officials, SOCOG Officials, Media, Security, Sports Officers, Team Doctors, Team Coaches, etc. it didn't stop from day to day, meeting other teams from around the world, with different languages and cultures all of this adding to a most incredible experience. 'The most important thing with communication is to hear what isn't being said.' ... Hassan M'Souli (Liaison Officer – Moroccan Olympic Football Team)

'My father worked at the Melbourne Olympics in 1956, and I wanted to continue the family tradition. Being rostered to work at the Athletes Village led to the most wonderful experience of cultural exchange.' ... Mike Fernando

'The first week was a struggle after a 28-hour trip, and now being ten hours ahead of my body clock. However, the adrenalin kicked in, and although I had been to the major events such as Worlds, this had a different feel to it. We felt the responsibility, but it came together, and we were proud to be part of a great event. I was also fortunate to get additional tickets to see my countrymen compete in other sports, and so added to the magic of my visit.' ... Anneleen Dekker (The Netherlands)

'Maybe the seed of Olympism was sown when taken to the Olympic Demonstration Surf Lifesaving Carnival at Torquay, Victoria in 1956 at 11 months of age. Since then I was a spectator in Barcelona in 1992, a driver in Nagano in 1998, and now a Flash Quote Reporter in Sydney 2000 – it just keeps getting better.' ... Kerryn Briody

'Being Deck Controllers at the Aquatic Centre at the Olympic Games – greeting swimmers, coaches, medical personnel and officials. It was something special and we feel privileged to have been involved.' … **Laurette and Lawrie Brown**

'I was inspired by our bid win in 1993, excited in applying to be a volunteer in 1998, and have since had the most amazing experience. Speaking with many friends and workmates about our Olympic and Paralympic adventures, it is sad that it is all over, but we have the greatest memories to sustain us.' … **Thais Turner (Accreditation Officer)**

'No one could say that they did not have the opportunity to become involved in some way, and you couldn't help but grasp the enthusiasm generated.' … **Randall Roberts**

'Wearing the volunteers uniform has given me great pleasure and raised my self-esteem. Even though I am not an Olympic athlete I still felt like a participant in these Games.' … **Isabella Kotlar**

'The UDAC was such an amazing place to work, and it needed so many people to run it. They were all so great to work with, especially the supervisors, who made sure everyone had a fair go at different duties. Meeting other volunteers, contractors and officials was truly uplifting. They came from all over Australia and several parts of the world.' … **Jenny Hoffman**

'We enjoyed so much of the Olympic/Paralympic atmosphere, our work with Quest, and the ten days at the Uniform Distribution and Accreditation Centre. The one disappointment was our experience in hosting a young man through the Samsung Athletes Family Host Program – everyone else we know who was involved had a wonderful experience, but sometimes that is the way things happen. We were happy though to have been a small part of this wonderful event.' … **Margaret Murray**

'My longest day was 15 September 2000, starting with seven hours running up and down stairs as an Audience Kit Assistant, before signing on as a Load Zone Officer. The previous day had been very special as a Torch Relay Escort Runner – what a wonderful build-up to a wonderful Olympic experience!' … **Kevin Wong**

'One of the best parts was meeting members of the Australian Basketball Team, and the worst was sitting for my Higher School Certificate during the Paralympics.' … **Darren Emerson (Logistics – The Dome and Pavilions)**

Additional recognitions:

Ric Noble, Walter Lebedew, Tamara Fak, Sean Walsh, Esme Lloyd, Wayne Low, Luis Ordonez, Ange Kenos, Peter Downs, Chris Pritchard, David Curtin, Laurie Needham, Maureen Vaughan, Laurdes Arrogante, Beula Tuxford, Betsy Eardley, Dean Bushell, Tsu Shan Lee, Peter Rienits, Chris Summers and Simon Barr.

Our Lady of Mercy College Parramatta had many volunteer contributors to the Olympic Games, they were: Doping Control Escorts – **Sr Ailsa, Pat Silsby, Blanche Mikalauskas, Robert Beazley, Augustin Tan and Julie Flynn**. Driver – **Mary Farrugia**. Spectator Services – **Marianne Brett**. Ceremonies – **Lynn Revai, Ann-Marie Herd, Jane Oxley and Clare Hinchey**. Hockey – **Suzanne Palmer and Janet Stephens**. Tourist Information – **Elizabeth Irving**. Torch Escort Runners – **Celia Maunder and Tara Millgate**.

'I fled the Fiji Islands in 1987 after the first coup, and after some years in New Zealand moved to Australia in 1994. My son Mark came from New Zealand to help when my mother and husband became sick in 1996. Unfortunately my mother died in June 1996, my 35-year-old son Mark died of blood poisoning on 6 July 1996 and my husband died in October 1996 – three deaths in five months!

'Knowing there was a need for volunteers, I decided to dedicate 2000 to helping the country that has accepted me. Nothing could replace the atmosphere of working in the Common Domain of Sydney Olympic Park.' ... **Ivy Jaganath**

Jeanette Manson says: 'I may not be a sports person. I have many medical conditions limiting me in doing so. However, this does not limit me from being part of the Games.'

Lily Bux (born Hong Kong) shared her passion while working at the Synchronised Swimming test event; she considers this such a rare opportunity to welcome everybody from around the world in peace and friendship. Lily just wanted to do her part in helping awareness of one another.

I've made it to the Olympics
I always knew I would
It's taken me so many years
To really get that good.

Just think of the excitement
The yells, the claps, the cheers
Making friends from 'round the world
Memories for years and years.

I haven't done much training
I think I'll still do well
I'll give it everything I've got
Only time will tell.

I cannot win a medal
Though my heart will burst with pride I fear
As I take my place before the race
In my role as a Volunteer!

Gladys Merle Pedley-Smith (Volunteer – Entertainment Centre)

Doug and Gwen Gay of Penrith attended the first meeting for prospective volunteers held at the Penrith Council Chambers. They had the added interest in that their grandson, Aaron Bourne, is a wheelchair fencer. After working at test events, Gwen says: 'Volunteering has given thousands of eager and enthusiastic people memories that will last all their lives. They will help Australia to put on the best Olympics ever to show the world that people from all walks of Australian life are behind our SOCOG organisers, so that athletes from many countries can realise their dreams of competing in an Olympic Games. We have made friends among other volunteers that we hope will continue for many years. At the end of a day's work many of us are bone tired and footsore, but fully satisfied with the job we have done.'

Enthusiastic volunteer, **Lynn Frew**, explains A WHOLE RANGE OF EMOTIONS AS A VOLUNTEER:

- I was honoured to put my name down to be part of the bid for the Olympic Games some six years ago.
- I was overjoyed when I was accepted as a volunteer for Stadium Australia for the Games.
- I was frustrated when trying to organise 5000 school children in two hours into seats at the Australian Track and Field Championships in February at my test event.
- But I was still excited and looking forward to September 2000.

'I still wake some nights calling "1-a buses to the right, 1-b buses to the left, Concord West station turn left through Expo!" But I hope the memory never fades, as I could not have lived with myself if I had not been a part of it all. I have found throughout life, that the more you contribute, the more you get from life.' ... **Kelvin Banks (Spectator Services – South Sector)**

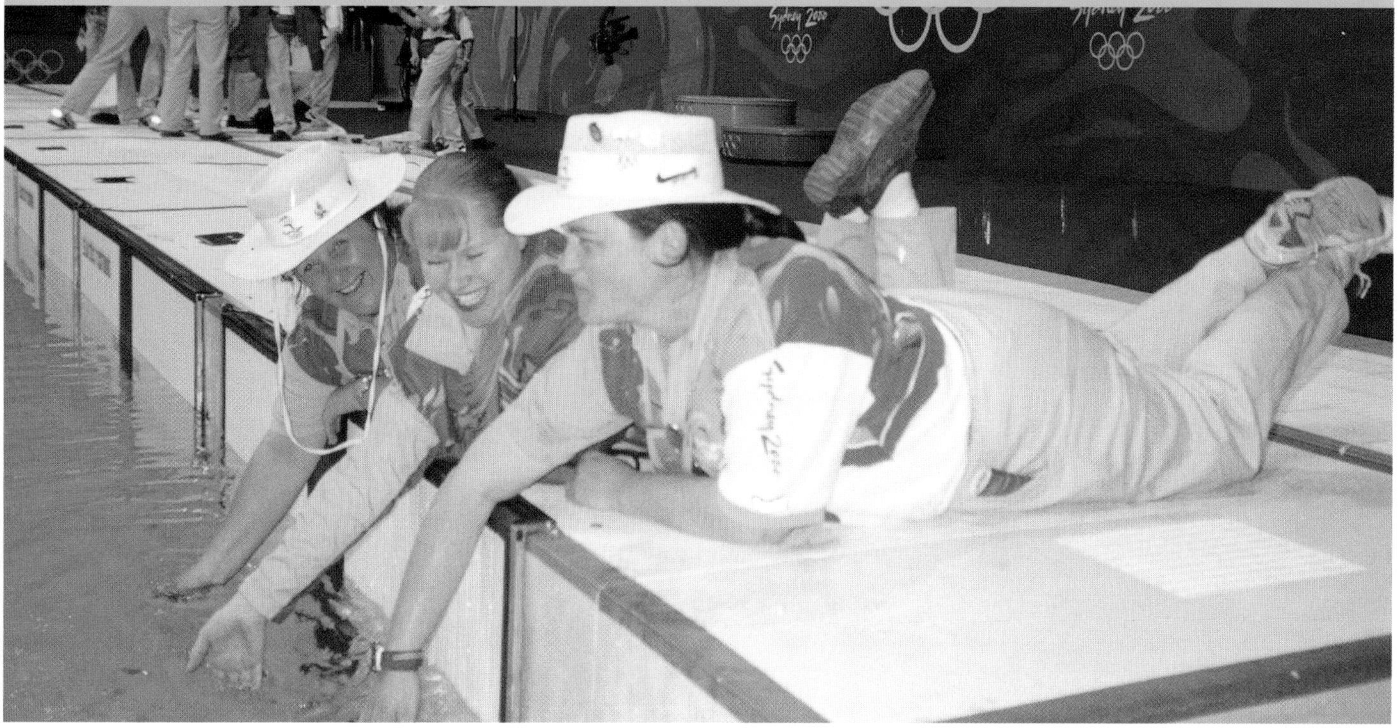

TESTING THE WATER (L TO R) ANNA ROONEY, TINA-LOUISE WIESSNER AND CAROL SMITH

The Australian Estonian community got behind the volunteer program with input from the following:

Paul Evert (NOC Assistant – Estonia), Hugo Hageri (Print Runner), Maimu Hageri (Spectator Services), Erik Holm (Estonian Paralympic Committee Attaché), Lea Holm (Language Specialist), Siiri Iismaa (Language Specialist), Tiina Iismaa (Language Specialist), Aet Joasoo-Lees (NPC Assistant – Estonia), Anni Kaasik (Spectator Services), Claire Kalamae (Resident Centre Assistant), Kalev Kakamae (Audience Kit Assistant), Richard Kalnin (Athletics Services Attendant), Belinda Kasepuu (Choir – Ceremonies), Elda Kasepuu (Driver), Ulo Kasepuu (Driver), Helju Kerema (Protocol Assistant), August Keskula (Food Services Assistant), Ingrid Koreneff (Guest Pass Assistant), Maia Lauterbach (NPC Assistant – Estonia), Juho Looveer (Volleyball Official), Marika McLachlan (Language Specialist), Tiiu Kroll-Simmul (Protocol Assistant), Olav Pihlak (Language Specialist), Vella Pihlak (Language Specialist), Robert Raska (Village Resident Relations), Arnold Tammekand (NOC Assistant – Estonia), Bruno Tohver (NPC Assistant – Turkmenistan), Robert Tohver (Estonian Olympic Committee Attaché), Mailis Wakeham (Measurer's Assistant – Sailing) and Lembit Willems (NOC Assistant – Estonia).

Jim Peng, his wife Yuen and son Harley made it a family affair in volunteering. Jim was a Sport Service volunteer at the Table Tennis, while **Yuen** was a Spectator Services Host in Sydney Olympic Park, and **Harley** was an ORTA volunteer at the University of Western Sydney. Jim says, 'We all had a wonderful time, and are so proud to have played a small role in the success of such a massive operation.'

There have been some debates over who was the oldest Olympic/Paralympic volunteer. Well **Dot De Low** celebrated her 90th birthday on 5 October 2000 (we held a parade for her!). Dot still plays competitive Table Tennis, and during her volunteer stint at the Olympic Games played an exhibition game, much to the delight of the crowd. For those who wondered if they were too old to volunteer – well don't let the facts get in the way!

'I came to Australia from England many years ago, and this country has been very good to me. The opportunity to volunteer at the Olympic Games was a chance to help project this country in its best light. I was then blessed with being given a job at the Rushcutters Bay Sailing Venue. Here I met people from all over the world, including the town of Burnham-on-Crouch where I had moved from in

Results and print distribution volunteers – Olympic Stadium – with Olympics President Michael Knight

(L to R) Paul Hanson, Alan Chang, Michael Klim and Michael Byrne

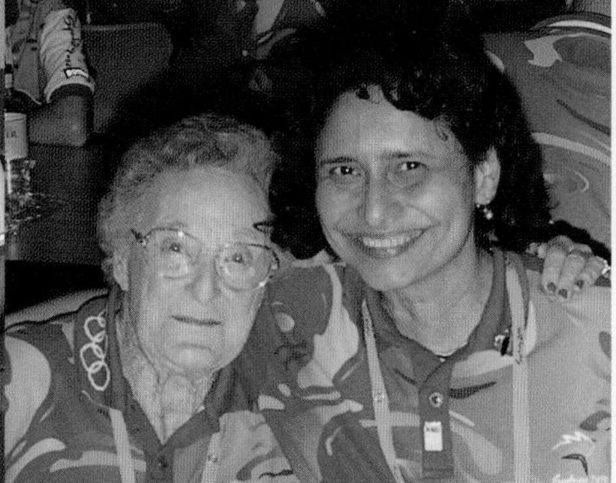

(L to R) Dot De Low and Banoo Bengali

England. This has been a priceless and very special part of history, one I am very proud to have been part of.' … **Anne-Louise O'Connor (Shoalhaven Heads, NSW)**

'I have worked at major National and International events in my radio career, so I thought I knew what I was in for. I thought it would be exciting, inspiring and professionally stimulating, indeed it was, but in fact, it was a whole lot more.' … **Doug Hogan (Flash Quote Reporter – Darling Harbour)**

'It was the greatest moment of our lives, just sheer magic for my husband and me. We have nothing but praise for our fellow volunteers and cherish the friendships we've made.' … **Elisabetta and Antonio Zappia (Accreditation – Shooting Centre)**

'Going to Sydney was always going to be an exciting adventure, and working at the Weightlifting Venue was special. However, way back on 31 July 2000, I had a wonderful group of volunteers help me with the Olympic Torch Relay celebrations at Alexandra Gardens in Melbourne, they were: **Tim Pearson, Kim Grey, Kate St Clair, David Henderson, Margaret Spier, David Brown, Catherine Yap, Judy Turner, Adam Cusworth, Adrian Stewart, Kelly-Jade Anderson, Jamie Hughes-Gage, Michael Noone, James Prideaux, Astrid Zanini, Vanda Bournadas and Marg Forbes-Biram.** Thank you all.' … **Russell McIntosh**

'My volunteer position emerged via an email invitation from our press centre manager. Jane emphasised that a volunteer was true in the *Corinthian* spirit of our sport – in other words I had to organise and pay for my travel and accommodation. Coming from the east coast of the US, the decision took all of about 30 seconds. When I was officially granted the position, it was a way of giving back to a sport I truly love.

'Each day at the Rushcutters Bay venue was unique, but the first and last image was of the Harbour Bridge – and at night with the glow of the Olympic Rings.' … **Sharon Benton**

Marathon course marshals – (L to R) Kerry Bray, Gary Shoesmith, Christine O'Brien and Christopher Breen

Barry Harris (UDAC volunteer and NOC driver)

Deborah Singerman (press assistant – MPC)

ROAD CREW AT MARTIN PLACE

JOHN WITHELL (RESULTS PRINT SYSTEMS OPERATOR – AQUATIC CENTRE)

BEACH VOLLEYBALL VOLUNTEERS ATTENDING THE OPENING CEREMONY DRESS REHEARSAL – BEST OF FRIENDS ALREADY!

MURRAY WHEATLEY (SUPERVISOR – HORSE AMBULANCE FLEET – EQUESTRIAN CENTRE). THE HORSE AMBULANCE IS A SPECIALLY MODIFIED FLOAT TO ALLOW THE EASY LOADING OF AN INJURED STANDING OR LYING HORSE

CEREMONIES PIXEL KID MATTHEW PHIPSON WITH VOLUNTEER GRANDMOTHER MARY CAGE

VOLUNTEERS AT MC MAHONS POINT FOR THE VIDEOING OF DON SPENCER SINGING 'THE VOLUNTEERS SONG'

WWW.VOLUNTEERSONG.COM

(L TO R) AMY AND JOANNA (TECHNOLOGY SUPPORT – MPC)

(L to R) Terry McGuinness, Alana Hannan and Gail Petrie from the Venue Communication Centre – Olympic Stadium

Volunteers assisting athletes wishing to vote for representatives on the IOC Athletes Commission. Aberra Aguegnehu (seated with hat) is a language specialist who has volunteered at many Olympic Games and World Cup football tournaments, and loves the camaraderie of volunteers at these events

The University of Technology, Sydney, was a substantial contributor in preparations for the Olympic and Paralympic Games – as can be seen by the uniforms, UTS volunteers also contributed in a variety of roles

IBM Technical Services volunteers – MPC

MEDAL CEREMONIES TEAM MEMBERS IN TRAINING AT THE AQUATIC CENTRE

CLOSING CEREMONY CELEBRATIONS FOR KENDY JACKSON

VOLUNTEERS AT THE WARRINGAH AQUATIC CENTRE – SYNCHRONISED SWIMMING TRAINING VENUE – MOST OF WHOM BACKED UP FOR SHIFTS AT HOMEBUSH. (BACK L TO R) ROZ HUGHES, GARY PENFOLD, BEN MOSELEY (CENTRE) GRAHAM BRUCE, CATHY GORDON, LORRAINE SMITH, JULIE LANGDON, KIM MOWBRAY, CORINNE MANN, CHRIS GOEGHAN (FRONT) ILLANA MCKINLEY

PARALYMPICS ROAD CREW – CYCLING – SECTION 7 STANDING (L TO R) DAVID FISHER, KEVIN RAINES, ARNOLD BEACHAMP, LAURIE COLEMAN, RON PERRY AND GREG MCDONALD FRONT (L TO R) JOY JACKSON, LYN SPARKS AND CHRIS BREEN. ABSENT – RICHARD LOGAN

Family contribution – (L to R) Alica Richardson (grand-daughter), Beverley Prouting (sister), Patricia Davies (myself) and Jo Ann Merrick (niece)

Volunteers at the Olympic Logistics Centre

Volunteers were very understanding of the personal grief Mr Samaranch had to deal with while in Sydney. One such volunteer who had the pleasure of meeting Mr Samaranch was Kieran Lawless

Olympians who gave of their time to be hosts in the athletes village (L to R – back) Val Lawrence (Melville) (athletics 1956), Tom Cross (fencing 1956), Ron Gray (athletics 1956) (L to R – front) Marlene Mathews (athletics 1956-60), Jenny Lamy (Frank) (athletics 1968) and Karen Moras (Stephenson) (swimming 1968)

Doping control volunteers at shooting venue

Members of the Blacktown accreditation team – (L to R) Ruth Hamer, Kim Gajda, Del Gatt, Christina Chung, Hazel Eagleton and Luke McLoughlin

Gleness Crew – one of the olympic ambassadors with tourism NSW, who manned Information kiosks in the city of sydney

Chloe Hughes (one of the many great ball attendants at the tennis) with her volunteer mother Robyn Hughes.

the community of S.C.E.G.G.S. Redlands, Cremorne, have made a huge commitment to the Olympic and Paralympic Games. The school has had volunteers in many volunteer areas, including over 60 volunteers to act as 'fitting buddies' for the uniforms of the Australian Paralympic team in the school's premises at Homebush. Above is a representation of some of the volunteers who were part of this outstanding contribution

(L to R) Rhonda Gibson (Sydney) and Sylvia Galliropoulou (Athens) – Guest Pass Office – Main Press Centre

VILLAGE VOLUNTEERS

When we hear of anything relating to VILLAGE, we tend to think of only the Athletes Village. However, there were of course also villages for the media, technical officials, and other team delegates – all of which were a wonderful mixture of nationalities. Dedicated and enthusiastic volunteers were located at each of these villages, and while they did not necessarily see much, if any, competition, they all have their special stories and experiences to share.

There was also such a contrast between the Olympic Village and the Paralympic Village, something like living in 'the land of giants', compared to playing 'wheelchair dodgems'. Again each had its own special qualities and its own challenges.

One thing is for sure, the athletes are the best judges, and they overwhelmingly endorse this Village as the best 'Home away from Home' in Olympic history.

Swedish Paralympic Chef de Mission, Hans Säfström, greeted by NPC assistants and drivers – (L to R) Lisa Slade, Barbara Smith, Joyce Moody, Christine Martin, Judy Lawler, Denise Townsend and Tina Wong

This did not happen by accident – great planning produced a genuine village atmosphere. But a competent, well-organised Village Team under the guidance of **Maurice Holland**, trained, motivated and supported the contract staff and volunteers who became the face of the Village.

We don't pretend for one minute there were no problems, but good planning for contingencies made sure that there was nothing insurmountable. Some volunteers worked so hard their tongues were hanging out, while others wondered why they were all needed. It is hoped that no matter what the situation, the sense of occasion ensured personal satisfaction.

David Reichardt is a Uniting Church minister, and considers having worked as a volunteer chaplain at the Religious Services Centre in the Olympic and Paralympic Villages as one of the best experiences of his life. David recollects: 'The Religious Services Centre, under the responsibility of the Police Chaplains, was the first in Games history in which representatives of the world's five major faiths were housed in the same complex.

'Though I don't often use clerical garb, I found that wearing a "dog-collar" under my volunteer uniform shirt was excellent "advertising", and helped start conversations. "I never thought that there would be a religious centre in the Village," some people said. The period of the Games was certainly a special time. Many people remarked with wonder that it was as though someone put a happy drug in Sydney's and Australia's water supply for the duration! I believe that the Olympic and Paralympic Games provided Sydney, and through Sydney the rest of the world, with a glimpse of how life is meant to be lived.'

Mendel Carlebach is a senior student at the Rabbinical College of Australia, and was a last-minute recruit for the Religious Centre in the Athletes Village. Mendel recalls: 'Besides having the opportunity to communicate with and assist the athletes, it was nice to spend time talking with clergy from other religions. The evening of the Paralympic Closing Ceremony was one of those very special occasions which I was able to spend with the members of the Israeli Team, sharing their joy.'

The Olympics helped me through breast cancer

'I had applied to be a volunteer, and we as a family had applied for tickets, but on 26 August 1999, I was diagnosed with malignant breast cancer. When we told the children, my 12-year-old daughter said: "Well, is it going to kill you?" The question had to be asked, and strangely I was grateful for her forthright attitude. Possibly, but the Olympics will be on, and I intend to be there.

'Two days before I went into hospital for a partial mastectomy, I received a letter asking me to go for an interview for a volunteer position in one month's time. I was excited, as it was something to aim for. During six weeks of Radiotherapy and six months of Chemotherapy, I let the negative media get at me. However, all the time there was an undertow of excitement and a feeling "it'll be right on the night!"

'Attending events and working in the Village was as I had expected, a once-in-a-lifetime experience. The excitement of the Village was stimulating for me. However, when it was all over, it was like walking through a ghost town. The Village, which I had nicknamed "Pleasantville" – was empty. At work, a quiet morning, no athletes, no support team. What's on TV? Desperate for some hype I changed channels – ironically I came upon talk about Cancer Awareness Month, stressing the importance of self-examination for women to detect early breast cancer.

'I smiled to myself – life turns full circle – *been there, done that!* I thought, and I'd hardly noticed – thanks to The Games of the XXVII Olympiad.' ... **Anita Fursland**

PERFORMERS OF ABORIGINAL DANCE (FROM SOUTH COAST NSW) AT THE TEAM WELCOME CEREMONIES, WITH MEMBERS OF THE ZAMBIAN DELEGATION

RESIDENCE CENTRE 15 STAFF

'It started with an enquiry back in November 1999, as I was interested in being involved with the Olympic Village. One thing led to another, and before I knew it I was working two days a week with the Villages Team in the SOCOG office. I enjoyed interviewing prospective volunteers, and getting an early insight as to the village operations.

'Come Games-time I worked in one of the Residence Centres in the Athletes Village, and if I thought I had met some people before – this was a real adventure. Athletes, my fellow volunteers, team officials and contract staff – and the great thing about it is that I know some of these friendships will last a lifetime.' ... **Fred Daniels**

'I never dreamed I'd be lucky enough to be working in the Athletes Village. My role was a runner/key lock-out, in the blue and red zones of the Village. This meant I often did deliveries and errands around the Village, but my main role was letting athletes and officials back into their accommodation when they locked themselves out.

'The afternoon of the Closing Ceremony was amazing. At 5 pm, when most athletes and officials were ready to leave for the Ceremony, I got called to a lock-out for a Deputy Chef de Mission who'd been out swimming. The Chef de Mission was very pleased to see me, he kept thanking me saying I'd saved their delegation. You see, the Deputy had all the tickets for the Closing Ceremony!

'I still can't believe I spent the two weeks surrounded by the world's most elite athletes.' ... **Meredith Redman (Resident Centre 15)**

'Some days it was difficult to hear due to the cheering of the residents (athletes and officials) watching the events on television. They often cheered for the Aussies! The laundry was overloaded at times, but by day's end the job was done, the residents retired knowing we were there to solve their problems.' ... **Loretta Harding (Resident Centre 15)**

'I have seen the Berlin Wall go up and come down, but nothing compares to five weeks working with the most friendly people serving the athletes of the world, crowned by the experience of being a Horse Handler at the Opening Ceremony and Field of Play Marshal at the Closing Ceremony. I am proud to be an Australian.' ... **Joseph Futymed (Resident Centre 15)**

The Allotment Team

'We worked during the Olympics and Paralympics as allotment assistants. Our job was to tag all the athletes after they were accredited, put them and their luggage onto buses and deliver them to their team offices or accommodation in the Village. We worked from the Homebush Arrival and Accreditation Centre (HAAC), and our hours spanned from 7 am through to when the last athlete was delivered safely, sometimes 2 am. Of course, we worked eight-hour shifts and our team of volunteers were amazing, but a lot of credit should go to our supervisory team.

Anne Gibson (Sports Information Assistant – Athletes Village), came from Great Britain to volunteer

(L to R) Fou Imo (Attache), Neroli Walker (NOC Assistant) and Ed Imo (Chef de Mission – American Samoa)

Mary Roche (NPC Assistant – Poland), whose brothers Greg and Paul, with their wives Angela and Jan are all volunteers

'We transported almost 20,000 athletes and officials, allotted each and every one of them a comfortable bed and hopefully made their introduction to Australia and the Olympic Village truly memorable. We came up with our own slogan for our banner in the volunteers parade – ALLOTMENT TEAM – WE BEDDED THEM ALL.' ... **Sharon McBride**

'Although I missed out on being a volunteer at the Olympics, I was fortunately selected as a volunteer for the Paralympics. I was helping out in the Italian Paralympic Office, assisting with interpreting and other duties as required. It was amazingly uplifting and motivational – it was something that needed to be experienced rather than described.' ... **Giuseppa Sarandre**

'I worked in the Village for both Olympics and Paralympics. My position was Information Station Assistant, first in the International Zone and then Main Dining.

'My favourite moment was: An English athlete, wheelchair bound with severe cerebral palsy asked "Help me." She had been around the telephone booths for some time; we wrongly assumed she was waiting for a friend. Phoneaway cards are somewhat tedious and confusing for the uninitiated and she had apparently tried numerous times without success.

'After quite a few attempts I finally understood the country code she was patiently showing me with her fingers. When the number finally connected and began to ring I handed her the phone. The voice that answered was one she knew, and when she could finally utter her extremely excited "Helllllo" we were both in tears. It was her first call home since arriving in the Village. The pure joy on her face will remain in my mind and heart forever.' ... **Sandie Grierson**

It would be hard to find a village volunteer who did not take the opportunity to witness a Team Welcome Ceremony – many attended several, and still became emotional. **Thomas and Deanna Griffiths** rated this, along with the Volunteers Parade, the most special moments of their volunteer experience. 'The climax was when the school children sang "G'day Mate!" We all had tears in our eyes because we were very proud to be Australian and we all knew we were part of something very special,' said Thomas.

'Both my daughter **Robyn Pride**, who worked in the Millennium Marquee, and I believed we worked in the best places, but words cannot express my feelings from my involvement as a Food and Beverage Assistant in the Athletes Village Main Dining Room. It all comes from within – what an honour to be part of an Olympic Games. It's hard to believe – I would do it again tomorrow.' ... **Joan Martin**

'I was confident with the training we were given in the lead-up to working with the Tunisian Team in the Olympic Village, but there is always that apprehension prior to meeting the guests. I need not have worried – the Tunisian athletes and officials were such warm friendly people, and our volunteer team of wonderful drivers and NPC Assistants – **Sandra Fisk, Nadia Batkin** and **Colin Soles** – worked so well together, it made for a period of cherished memories.

'We managed to see our athletes compete in many of their events, we took them shopping, and had them to our home for a barbecue (to meet my husband Ron, who had been having too many takeaway meals). What an experience. What new friends I have made. What fun I had. What more can I say?' ... **Leone Mather**

'It was a wonderful experience to work as a National Paralympic Committee (NPC) Assistant with the team from Belarus in the Athletes Village. Our team of volunteers enjoyed showing them the sights of Sydney, and one of our drivers organised an Aussie barbecue. However, a situation I observed on a bus touched me greatly – while two wheelchairs were being manoeuvred by their occupants, a young man from Iran, and a young lady from the US, the two wheelchairs became caught up. He surveyed the situation, reached down and lifted the other wheelchair away. Once "parked", they congratulated each other on sorting out the problem, exchanged greetings and the obligatory pin. You would see this cooperation everywhere, and it proves that we can all live and work together.' ... **Chris Cavanagh-Haimes**

RESIDENCE CENTRE 20 CREW

CONCEICAO MARIA DA COSTA SANTOS (NOC ASSISTANT – BRAZIL) GREETING THE TEAM ON ARRIVAL IN THE VILLAGE

VILLAGE VOLUNTEERS THOMAS AND DEANNA GRIFFITHS

'My reason for volunteering was to make sure people from overseas knew that Australians are good hosts. Also I have a granddaughter who is disabled and I am too. I wanted to prove to myself that I could do it.

'I live at Umina on the Central Coast, and would leave home at 6.50 am to arrive at the Village by 8.45 am after catching a bus, then a train, then a second train, then another bus. I worked at the Rate Card office in the NOC and NPC Services Centre. Other than Chefs de Mission and Assistants many people did not know that we existed for the purpose of delegations being able to secure additional equipment for their offices.

'It was nice when delegations came and thanked us for making their stay in the Village better through our service. Another thank you which is even more important is the appreciation I would like to extend to my family who put up with Mum's reduced input to the house, and the support they gave in maintaining the home, for they are the other unsung heroes.' ... Marie Burton

A special night – Go China Go!

'While relaxing in the Superdome with 120 Chinese athletes and officials, waiting to escort them into the Stadium for the Opening Ceremony of the Paralympic Games, one of the team officials came and sat next to me to practise his English. Did I still work? What work had I done? Did my children give me money now that I had no income? ... That was a new thought! I launched into a description of superannuation.

'Other members of the team came and shook my hand, gave me pins and a Red flag. I was to then share with them the experience of coming out through the tunnel into the lights and roar of 100,000 people. It was heart-stopping – the joy everywhere, the delight of the athletes and the approval of the crowd. Slowly we circumnavigated the soft track to reach our ringside seats to enjoy an evening of wonderful performances.

'The next day as I worked in the Main Dining Hall of the Paralympic Village carrying trays for disabled athletes, I met a few of my new friends. Different uniform and different location, but they recognised me. They responded: "Go China Go!" I smiled at them and they remembered the special night we had shared together.' ... Elizabeth Donnelly

'Before the Paralympics even began, I had the pleasure of chatting with a young Canadian sailer in the dining room at the Athletes Village. He related to a dream, and the fact that he had been waiting four years to compete. But it was more than competing; he was so happy and content with being in Australia with such wonderful people offering support or just a smile to say Hi Mate. If he had the chance to pick up a medal it would be a bonus.

'Then on the night before the Closing Ceremony, he once again came in during my shift. With a grin to match, he had a Bronze Medal proudly hung around his neck.

'This is what I had hoped the Games would bring to people from around the world. It is more than this, the feeling, friendliness, passion, dreams and the independence of the Paralympics.' ... Lesley Martin

'My first bonus in being a volunteer came in spring of 1999, when I had the opportunity to be at the Multidisability Championships at Sydney Olympic Park. A week there confirmed my desire to be a volunteer at the Olympics, and especially the Paralympics.

'Come Games-Time I was allocated the Athletes Village as my venue, and what a variety of experiences I had there. I was initially allocated staff check-in as things were a little hectic until everyone became accustomed to procedures. I had a short period at the Media Village checking rooms before arrival of guests, and then back to the Athletes Village where I assisted in the Transport Mall.

'Some of the days became long and tiring, and while I initially drove to Artarmon to catch the 5.40 am train, I reverted to driving to the staff shuttle bus at Lidcombe. This also enabled me to go via the Office in Balmain to do some of my regular work – however, I must admit that sometimes I actually pulled over to have a short sleep instead!

'Despite the tiredness, I think the Paralympic experience was even more moving, especially my involvement with the Ceremonies. Nothing could replace the elation of the athletes, and while there may have been times in a tired state I asked myself "why?" it was probably best crystallised for me when I was in church and we sang *The Servant King.*' ... **Richard Plaskitt**

'My employer – Franklins – became the first retailer to announce a partnership with the Paralympics, and in late 1999 they sought expressions of interest for staff who would like to become volunteers. I applied, got accepted, then set about the adventure of going to Sydney (I am from Victoria), where we were housed in the Media Village with room-mates from other states. My room-mate, **Julie Anne Lucas**, was from Brisbane, and we got on exceptionally well. Franklins set up an office in the Media Village and looked after us very well.

IT'S PARTY TIME!

'My workplace was the Athletes Village, and this location became such an inspiring place for me. My appreciation of athletes with a disability was so heightened as I observed how they went about their activities, especially in the Dining Room where I worked.' ... Julie Wilby

'While assisting the press at the Media Village, the fun and comradeship between the volunteers from Australia and overseas has been the greatest reward.' ... Geraldine Beale (Guest Relations)

Tuulikki Levin (Resident Relations) was asked by a young man if she was an athlete, she replied 'No, I am working at the Village, but next Games I will probably run the marathon' – the man looked a little surprised as Tuulikki is 68 years old!

Handover of the Athletes Village from the Olympics to the Paralympics was not a situation of which we could be proud. Organisation of housekeeping rest days was at the centre of frustration for Residence Centre Staff and National Paralympic Assistants trying to calm upset teams arriving to uncleaned accommodation with no bed linen or towels. The housekeeping staff themselves were not to blame, and they basically did a good job throughout. However, it became obvious that while they needed a rest, a different roster, or additional staff should have been rostered to make sure everything was in place as it had been for the Olympians.

As author of this book, but also as a volunteer based in the Village for the duration of the Olympics and Paralympics, I have to agree with Resident Centre 8 volunteer Phil Hogan, that the first couple of days were unorganised chaos! Phil has expressed – in some terms that can't be printed here – the frustrations experienced by all Residence Centres in the assistance of early arriving teams to the Paralympic Village. It was a shame that while the organisation and running of the Paralympic Village went so well on the whole, those first days required all the skill and patience of NPC Assistants and Residence Centre staff like Phil, to keep delegations happy.

There is a commonality about many of the expressions portrayed about life in the Village, and Kerrie Simmons (NPC Assistant) and Roger Lante (Team Driver) acknowledge that the opportunity to become friends with and assist our visiting teams was a wonderful feeling, as was the happiness and never-say-die attitude of the Paralympians. However, there was one funny but frustrating situation which confronted most team volunteers at some time or other, and some too often, that Kerrie and Roger recall: 'An official informing the driver that he was waiting to be picked up at the back of the Opera House, when he was actually on Wharf 7 at the back of the Maritime Museum.' How often were 'pick-up' directions inaccurate? And obviously, the greater the language problem, the more this situation arose! However, as far as we know, there are no Olympic or Paralympic visitors still waiting to be found by their driver!!

'Working in the Sports Information Centre of the Athletes Village was very rewarding in being able to keep teams fully informed as to training and competition needs. However, the dedication and commitment of some of my fellow volunteers was a real inspiration, especially people like **Shirley Smith**, who worked with us from 8 am till 3 pm, then went over to help out at the Table Tennis, arriving home at 11 pm, only to back up the following day. This is the type of person who helped make it the most memorable and rewarding experience of all time.' … **John O'Brien**

Cveta Lampl is a retired registered nurse who worked in the Athletes Village on the Multilingual Switchboard. Cveta recalls a most special moment for her: 'I was coming home down Coogee Bay Road, when someone patted me on the shoulder and said "thank you very much for all you are doing." They identified themself as a Sydney resident and spectator only.'

Vera Lam worked in the Gift Bag Centre in the Village Plaza. Every accredited athlete received a Gift Bag, and had to collect them personally. Vera says that the best part of her job was getting to talk to people from around the world. She has also learned new skills in communication and patience!

My wife applied as a volunteer
And then I had a little fear –
Thought I'd be missing something great
And decided to join my lifelong mate.
A wonderful time and there's been no bar
To meeting people from near and far,
From all over the world, in fact to date
And there are people now we treat as a mate.
At 6.30 am there's a sleepy band
Being met by police with a wand in their hand
But it's all very cheerful inside the gate
With everyone saying G'Day Mate!
Mardi greets us at door four
Then smiling, sends us to our chore.
We report to Andrew, Dee or Ross
All terrific to be called our Boss.
There's Lilliane, Helen, Bevan and Sue,
Suead and Sophie and Harv too.
There's others – too many to mention
But the girl with the lollies gets special attention.
We look for her coming around each day
As at the bins, or the door we stay
Checking IDs and athletes' backs
As they try to slip through with their little back packs.
We shall miss it when the Games are all over
As we 'retire' again and start to recover,
So 'thank you' to SOCOG and all concerned
For having us here and all we have learned. …

Des Joynes – Main Dining Room – Door 3

(L TO R) VAGI (EVELYN) BABONA, PASTOR ERIC WHITE AND IVAN RAVU RENEW ACQUAINTANCES

LESLEY WALKER AND GREG O'BRIEN (NPC ASSISTANTS – MONGOLIA)

'I had the privilege of serving as one of the Chaplains in the Religious Services Centre during the Olympic and Paralympic Games. One day I visited the team office for Papua New Guinea. I introduced myself to the Papua New Guinea girl in the office. I commented casually that she looked like a Tubuseria girl – she was surprised and asked how I knew. I told Evelyn that I used to teach in a school near her village in the early 1960s. I said that I had assisted the village men to build the little Seventh-day Adventist Church. Her eyes lit up! "My Uncle was the elder of the church" she said, "his name was Peruka Mea!" I know him well!

'As we talked I noticed that the Chef de Mission for the Papua New Guinea team became more attentive to our conversation. He then introduced himself. "My name is Ivan Ravu," he said, "are you Mr White from the Bautama School?" "Yes!" I said. "My father used to be your Farm Manager at the school. I haven't seen you since I was a small boy."

'It was a wonderful reunion after 37 years. It's amazing how our paths crossed again after all that time.'
Pastor Eric White

COOEE – from the Paralympic Village

A volunteer working on Bag Check at Main Dining, returned a bag to an athlete on their way out of the dining area, only to be told, 'There should be a couple of legs with that too!'

Phillip and Jenny Evenden are a couple who carried the Olympic passion since 1956, and were delighted to be accepted for positions in the Athletes Village for both the Olympics and Paralympics. Their excitement was further heightened when they were selected as Field of Play Marshals for the Olympic Opening and Closing Ceremonies.

Phillip had to overcome a personal challenge before taking up the opportunity, as he was diagnosed with cancer. He arranged for the surgery to be brought as far forward as possible in order that he would have sufficient time to recover for his first role in the Opening Ceremony. This was achieved, and the experience is history!

Phillip and Jenny experienced another pre-games special moment when Phillip's brother, Ken, carried the Olympic Torch in Rockhampton, Queensland, on day 13 of the Torch Relay, a sense of occasion after watching a family friend, Rex Bailey, do similar on the outskirts of Sydney in 1956.

Phillip recalls a personal highlight: 'While assisting with the movement of throwing equipment to the Throwing Training Area for the athletes inside the Village, I quickly struck up a friendship with Larry Hughes, an American Paralympic Gold Medallist from Atlanta, who like myself was also a Vietnam Veteran. Larry lost both his legs in Vietnam, and is a real inspiration to be around, enjoying many laughs with his new-found Aussie mates.'

Diary of a Village Vollie

'Day one as a Resident Centre Volunteer. Up before the crack of dawn. Dark. Silent. Cold. Two buses, two trains and a shuttle bus to finally enter the Village where I am pronounced "clean". Trudge to Resident Centre. I wondering "what am I doing here? I have a job, a family, bills to pay!" Greeted noisily by a choir of smiling blue birds in colourful jackets. Our first Chef de Mission arrived from a country whose name we couldn't even pronounce! Then we had to hop on our bikes and cycle around the Village. Everyone was so friendly and helpful. We were stopped by a smiling officer on a moon buggy for going up a one-way street the wrong way.

'At the end of my shift, tired but happy, I could feel the spirit of the Village and the Games. I remembered why I volunteered. I realised I was a very real part of the Olympic family. Nothing else seemed to matter.' ... **Maureen Smith**

Life changing

'This has turned me around to be a more positive and stronger person. I have learned so much from the athletes, just learning to say Hi and smiling to everybody, more positive things have come out of life since the Games. I now understand the meaning of volunteer. Now when I hear about volunteers who have finished a great job, well done, and who are now exhausted, I understand because I was also a volunteer – and loved it.' ... **June Munro (Main Dining Room volunteer)**

'Being able to offer my time was extremely rewarding in more ways than one. The fact that I was able to be of service to the media, athletes, coaching staff and officials was only one aspect. The others were being around the best and most courageous athletes in the world, and meeting and making friends with people from all over Australia.

'During the Olympic Games my role in Food and Beverage was at the Media Village, and my roster required a 3.30 am rise for a start of shift at 5.30 am. Although away from competition, this was an extremely special experience. The Paralympics on the other hand was another experience all together, as I was at the Athletes Village, and found it a humbling and magical experience to be assisting these wonderful athletes. Something never to have been missed or forgotten.' ... **Garry Blyth**

Embarrassment

'Due to none of our delegation having collected the condoms, I offered to do it, and take them to the team member at the main entrance to the Village. Once he took what were required, I proceeded back through the security check, and without thinking put the bag through the X-ray machine. The policeman on duty called his colleague and then another. They were all looking at the screen with astonishment, talking quietly and laughing. To my embarrassment one of them turned to me and asked, "Are you planning to have a wild night tonight?" ... **Jana Mader**

Horsing around!

'I enjoyed my experience driving for the Swedish delegation, based in the Athletes Village, but on one occasion, when asked to pick up nine members of the Swedish Equestrian Team at Horsley Park in the Mercedes Sprinter bus, it became a day of the unexpected. I was to deliver them to Kurrajong Trail Rides, then wait for the return trip.

'On arrival the owner of the establishment asked me to join them in the ride, and after being assured it would just be a walk I accepted. I was given a sturdy Quarter horse and a hard hat, and joined the ride in my uniform, as I had nothing else with me.

'Well, the walking lasted only a couple of minutes and then we were into a trot. When we got down to the bottom by the river flats the younger members were off into a gallop, whooping it up. We galloped and trotted for over an hour along the river flats through creeks (at one stage my horse was just about swimming), under trees, over logs, etc. With adrenalin pumping I managed to stay on the horse and actually keep up.

'Then we started going up through the bush with lovely wild flowers and birds everywhere. After a while we started bush bashing – i.e. almost no trails. My fawn trousers were starting to get black from scraping the trees trunks, which had been in a bushfire a few years earlier.

'I got them back to Horsley Park in time, and then headed back to the Olympic Village.

'You should have seen my trousers. Inside of the legs stained by the saddle and horse sweat. The outside marked black from burnt trees, green from tree leaves, water and mud-stained at the bottom.

'I suppose I have to confess the Swedish riders were the grooms, who each have been responsible for a Swedish horse for several years. However, I can still say I went riding with the Swedish Equestrian Team.' ... **Peter Benkendorff**

Electrifying!

Hard lessons can be learned when persistent outside influences are allowed to affect your judgement. In news distributed to Village staff on 24 September 2000, the following appeared: *We have a Resident Centre Runner who has defied death not once, not twice, but three times...* **David King** (Resident Centre 15). *He is now known as SPARKIE. Moral to the story ... smoke detectors are hard wired, so don't cut the red or blue wires regardless of a persistent delegation.*

Unfortunately David's misadventure resulted from smoke alarms making noise, which disturbed resting athletes. Pressure from upset officials resulted in David attempting something against his better judgement. David is fortunately still with us to share his not so pleasant experiences.

Special memories

— The unique experience of being dedicated, along with so many other volunteers, to helping – not only our team, but everybody – in the Village, on the train, in the street.

— The camaraderie of those in uniform, and the willingness of everyone to share their feelings and experiences.

— The friendships developed within our office between drivers and NOC Assistants, all working long hours and under pressure but still able to share a laugh.

— The warmth and gratitude of the Moroccans and the kind words of appreciation from the Minister of Sport, the officials and athletes.

— The surprise reaction of Sydney to the Volunteers – congratulations in the street, spontaneous applause on entering a restaurant in uniform – after so much negativity before the Games. ... **Carolyn Bethwaite and Daniele Priddle**

Thursday, 14 September 2000

'Thursday was an absolute highlight from start to finish! As a volunteer driver for the Australian Olympic Team, my first job of the day was to take the women's gymnastics team and coaches to the Superdome. I told them I was going to the gymnastics on Sunday, and they said they were competing at 10 am, so I would see them. I couldn't believe all this was becoming a reality and the Olympics were about to kick off in Sydney!!!!

'I was then off to the airport for the arrival of the entire athletics team. They were arriving on different flights, and the variety of luggage shapes and sizes had to be seen to be believed. The whole team was then taken by bus to the blazer presentation. 'Meanwhile, I was to pick up Lleyton Hewitt from the QANTAS terminal and transport him to the Homebush Arrival and Accreditation Centre (HAAC). A pleasant drive with a relaxed and chatty fellow.

'After my shift had finished I went to the city to see the Torch Relay. It was one of the most amazing nights in my life, an unbelievable atmosphere in the city. The Olympics were a day away and everyone was filled with anticipation about the next 16 days.

'After the Torch celebrations in the city, we headed to Circular Quay to soak up the atmosphere. What a day – what a night!

'Ready to be up at 5 am to do it all again!' ... **Lara Plociennik**

John Hall (NOC/NPC Driver) and **Mavis Hall** (Medical) have fond memories of the lighter side of the Games. John was a driver for the Canadian Team, and prior to the Opening Ceremony, their huge mascot Bruce the Moose went missing. A ransom note was received by the Chef de Mission, which read:

'The sky is blue, Moosey is green.
But for now, Moosey can't be seen.
You all carry Indian flags at the Opening Ceremony,
Or Moosey will be in the dining room for the world to eat.'

A reward was offered, and after the Opening Ceremony, Bruce the Moose mysteriously reappeared outside the Main Dining Hall. The sequel to this was that the Canadian Mounted Police arrested the Chief of Security for his involvement in the daring kidnap, but released him to carry out his duties till the end of the Games!

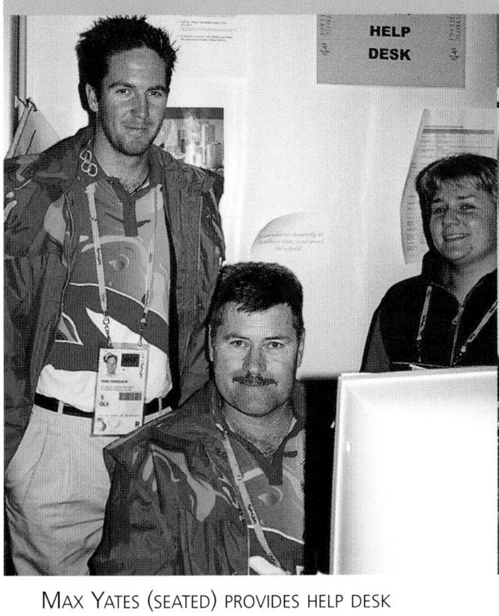

MAX YATES (SEATED) PROVIDES HELP DESK SUPPORT AT ACCESS CONTROL POINT 10

(L TO R) BARRY BATES AND ANDREAS PROESTOS IN ONE OF THE SPECIAL VEHICLES WHICH COULD BE HIRED BY DELEGATIONS WITHIN THE VILLAGE

TRANSPORT PERSONNEL IN THE TRANSPORT OFFICE AT THE NOC SERVICES CENTRE

Max and Carol Yates enjoyed the volunteer experience for both the Olympics and Paralympics. Carol was a Spectator Services Host, while Max was on Help Desk at ACP 10. For Max it was his second Olympic Games, having been a volunteer in the Security Team Program for Atlanta. To add finality to their Olympic passion, Max and Carol purchased one of the town houses in the Village, and plan a reunion with their volunteer friends once settled. Max says, 'The Kazakhstan Team stayed in our house, and we have a poster signed by the team and also one of their flags as a souvenir.'

Francis Neoh closed his restaurant and consulting service in Warrnambool, Victoria, to volunteer as a Food and Beverage Assistant in the Athletes Village. This commitment also required Francis to make a short visit to Sydney in early August 2000, for venue training. However, that was not the end of the adventure, as no sooner had he returned to Warrnambool after the Olympic Games, Francis received a call asking if he would come back for the Paralympics! The heart overruled the head, and back he came. 'It was a pleasure to be able to contribute,' says Francis.

'I was positioned as a Food and Beverages Assistant in the Catering Office of the Athletes Village. Although I initially applied as an interpreter for Greek and Bulgarian, I am very pleased with catering, because of my years of experience in the hospitality industry.

'Our team was responsible for supplying meal tickets to delegations, and meetings in the Chef de Mission Meeting Room next to our office. We also looked after the Multifunction Room in the International Zone, where teams and their VIP Guests came for refreshments and exchange of presents after their country's Welcome Ceremony.

'This was an area where my language skills were used, and we shared in the wonderful opportunity to meet so many Olympic Family members and athletes. A common thread from their comments was an appreciation of our contribution to the Olympic Games.

'My final words for those who did it – WELL DONE.

'For those who didn't – IF ONLY THEY KNEW' ... **Andreas Proestos**

'I elected to become a Language Services volunteer, as I spoke/read/wrote Ukrainian. However, I was transferred to General Services to work at the Athletes Village Main Dining Room to be a Ukrainian language provider – which came in handy for Turkmenistan, Kazakhstan, Russian, Moldavian and Polish athletes and coaches as well as the Ukrainians.

'The hours were long and exhausting, ending each day with my legs and back aching, and my feet burned until I got home and kicked off my Nikes. I do remember though a lovely Canadian official who chatted and showed genuine concern for our wellbeing. Even now as I recall our chat, I am filled with a warm glow from her genuineness.' ... **Halyna Schan**

Peter Rolls with Bruce the Moose and 'vollie rider' at the Paralympic Closing Ceremony

NPC assistants and drivers for the Swedish Paralympic Team

'I gained a lot of pleasure working with the volunteers **Bob, Ann, Fred, Katrina, Charles, Kathy** and **Peter** who formed the Villages Office Team under the direction of **Lynette Gregory**. There seemed to be no end to the variety of jobs at the SOCOG offices, but then we had the opportunity to get out in the field, which included hanging 10,000 laminated paintings, submitted by school children, in the Media and Athletes Villages. It didn't stop there, as we assisted with the inspections for structural faults, marking telephones, sorting keys for houses and units and even watering the gardens and lawns. This was all pre-Games, so we certainly knew the place inside-out once we began our Games-Time roles.' ... **Bevan Sengstock**

'I joined the volunteers because working with younger people makes you feel young. At 78 years of age, I, like most volunteers, wanted to do something worthwhile for our beautiful country, and I want my grandchildren to do the same in the future.' ... **Yeri Holobrodskyi (NPC Assistant)**

Druscilla Daly, who lives several hours drive west of Sydney, spent considerable time and financial commitment travelling to Sydney for training in her positions as NOC Assistant for Djibouti and NPC Assistant for Mali. 'The sense of satisfaction in being able to assist the two teams with their varying issues genuinely made me feel that my time and effort as a volunteer was absolutely worth the long hours and occasional angst and frustrations – particularly as they were *such* delightful people.'

Anelia Bozinovska was one of the first NOC Assistants trained in 1999, and was looking forward to September 2000 and the Olympic Games. Little did she know that after 12 years of trying to become a mother, she and her husband would be expecting a baby – in September!

Anelia considered all contingencies, and when son Adam was born on Father's Day (3 September 2000), it was only determination that had her in the Athletes Village again in less than two weeks. Devoted

(L to R) Shona Duniam, Alethea Synott and Bec Santos relax at the Christine Anu Concert in the athletes village

Druscilla Daly (NOC assistant for Djibouti)

Anelia Bozinovska (NOC assistant – Bulgaria) with son Adam

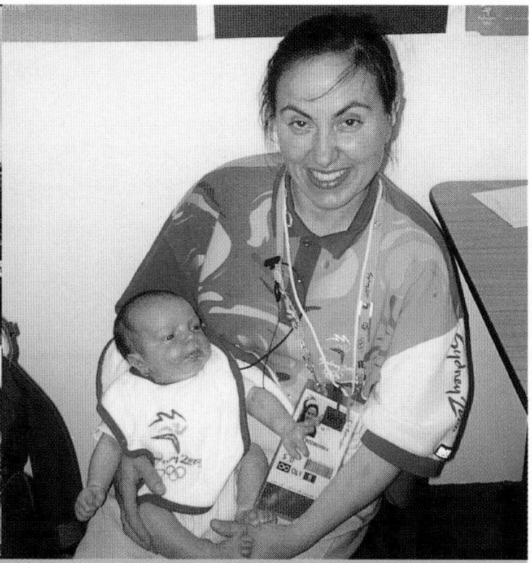

husband Michael would bring Adam to the gates of the Village to be fed on a regular basis. Anelia laments: 'No amount of training or planning can prepare you for both the Volunteer Role and the birth of a baby!'

'I was completely committed to my role as NPC Assistant for Cambodia, but nothing could have prepared me for the amazing experience I had seeing how the Australian community got behind this team who came to Australia so unprepared with competition equipment. Communities, schools, politicians, media personalities and local businesses contributed to a most wonderful cultural exchange, which embraced a very appreciative Cambodian delegation, and left one volunteer very proud of her country.' ... **Angela Valentine Flint**

Olympic High – Horse Handling at the Opening Ceremony. Best Day – Up at 4 am to take the delegation to Canberra for football, not getting to bed till 4 am the following day. Olympic Low – Nearly everyone thinking my tattoo was a transfer!' ... **Ian Bentall (NOC Assistant – Nigeria)**

'I was chosen by the Lebanese Team to be the Flag Bearer. What an honour to be carrying the flag of my country of origin, and volunteering for my new home, Australia!' ...
Minerva Saad (NPC Assistant – Lebanon)

'Life turned a full circle for me. Forty-four years ago as a sports-mad youngster I immigrated to Australia with precious Olympic tickets in my hands. In the "Friendly Games" my heroes were Betty Cuthbert and Dawn Fraser.

'By the time Sydney won the right to host the XXVII Olympiad, I had become Consul General for Malta in Sydney. I made sure that my country of birth, being a small nation of only 350,000 population, would be represented. My term of duty was to conclude in February 2000.

'I was honoured with the position of NOC Assistant for Malta, and the experience of serving my old and new countries was priceless. When I watched my hero from the 1956 Olympics, Betty Cuthbert, carrying the Olympic Torch I cried and felt enormously proud of my adopted city.

'A span of 44 years and two Australian Olympics – from one end of my life to the other! I have participated in the city of Sydney where my sporting dreams came true.' ... **Lawrence Dimech**

'I trained for months as a National Olympic Committee Assistant, and was eventually allocated the team from Bhutan. For the final three months leading up to the Games I also enjoyed assisting in the making of costumes for the ceremonies. Then just to make sure I had no idle time, I was accepted as an Athlete Escort for Bhutan, which required attending rehearsals! All this resulted in a wonderful experience, where I felt good about making a contribution to the best Olympic Games ever!' ... **Jill Tuffley**

'One afternoon from our NOC office window I saw three athletes trying to fly kites. All of a sudden four Special Operations Police arrived to check what was going on! Before we knew it, the police were running around with the athletes flying the kites. It was one of my favourite memories, because everyone was so focused on competition, security and working hard, that amongst all the seriousness, this warmed my heart' ... **Suzy Fitzgerald (NOC Assistant – St Kitts and Nevis)**

'The atmosphere inside the Village was festive and friendly throughout, despite the prevailing intense sense of competition amongst the teams. The employed staff and volunteers were extremely supportive of each other, constantly willing to assist/please, with the "nothing is impossible attitude". The perfect recipe for success!' ... **Vispi Irani (NOC Assistant – India)**

Volunteer Bill Deaves and USA Paralympian Larry Hughes 'direct' Liz Radley in drying out the throws platform after rain

(L to R) – Kevin Moon, Ramona Moon and Beven Sengstock at door 3 – main dining – Paralympic Village

CHATSWOOD PUBLIC SCHOOL STUDENTS POSE WITH MEMBERS OF THE BRAZILIAN DELEGATION AFTER SINGING AT THE TEAM WELCOME CEREMONY

'The people in the delegation were very nice, but there were some frustrations, particularly when I had to work more shifts than planned due to language difficulties. It was good to speak the language, but when other assistants did not, I was called upon more often. One of the special aspects of the volunteer experience was, wherever you were in Sydney, the uniform broke down barriers, and people wanted to talk and share their experiences' ... **Zaida Gudenus-Deuxberry (NPC Assistant – Uruguay)**

'My Olympic experience was wonderful, being assigned to the team from El Salvador. Playing the role of unofficial interpreter/translator was both challenging and rewarding, but I worked with a great team of volunteers, and at the end of a day's work you thought "yes", I actually did something to help someone today!' ... **Lissette Barahona (NOC Assistant – El Salvador)**

'Once I realised that being fluent in French did not automatically mean I would be allocated to France, I decided to put my hand up for Mali. For eight years we have sponsored a child in this poor country.

'Lost luggage and sourcing uniforms were some of the early challenges, but we overcame all, and gained much satisfaction out of helping these friendly people. Included among the many highlights of my role was inviting everyone to our home for an Aussie barbecue. As well as the Mali athletes and officials, we invited the drivers and their wives and our own extended families. The interactions were fascinating. There were children and octogenarians, many of whom had never spoken to an African before!' ... **Brenda Downes (NOC Assistant – Mali)**

'I volunteered so that I could feel I had played a part. Also, I have been a manager for around eight years – I knew my strengths and weaknesses and wanted to build on them. Through all the good and bad bits, I encountered people who would bend over backwards for you and others for whom flexibility was a novel concept. It takes all types. If the Games had been a dream run then I wouldn't have learned anything.

'It goes without saying I was heavily dependent on my co-volunteers – **Jenni, Alex** and especially **Zaida**, our Spanish-speaking saviour.' ... **Mike Smith (NPC Assistant – Uruguay)**

'Going through the highs and lows with the athletes as they competed was an interesting experience. I never realised the focus, drive as well as the heart and soul that is put in by athletes at this elite level. It was fantastic to be a part of that experience. The special bond established with athletes and fellow volunteers was the most rewarding aspect of this adventure.' ... **Lin Donevska (NOC Assistant – Macedonia)**

'Never in my wildest dreams did I anticipate the fantastic experience I would have when I put my name forward as a volunteer for the Paralympic Games. Over the past 3 weeks, helping the Tunisian team at the Village, I gained much more than I have given.

'At a stage in my life when questions arise about worthiness, I have been given a new sense of pride in myself.' ... **Leoni Mather (NPC Assistant – Tunisia)**

'My Olympic/Paralympic journey started back in 1992. My geography teacher at the time was Ms Lisel Tech, a female wheelchair basketball player for Australia (a star of the current Australian team).

'The past seven years have been like a roller-coaster ride for the entire city, and I believe I've had the pleasure of riding in the front carriage. Being able to work with other Pioneer Volunteers in at SOCOG Headquarters for the years leading up to the Games, really opened my eyes to the enormous task.

'Doing test events, then having the honour of being involved in the NOC and NPC programs has enabled me to have an experience far beyond my wildest expectations. I have met the greatest bunch of people, and I am honoured to call them my friends – I HAVE HAD THE TIME OF MY LIFE!' ... **Mark Lewis**

Slovenian gold medallist Rajmond Debevec, with NOC assistant Voni Bakija, who with her husband Dusan, enjoyed assisting their former homeland

(L to R) Amanda Stackpool, Garnet Evans and Natalie Tarance (NOC assistants – Georgia)

NPC assistants Peter Rush (left) and Ian Falconer with Polish gold medallist

NOC ASSISTANT – SAUDI ARABIA SHAUN BOYLE, WAS ALSO PLACARD BEARER FOR ALGERIA

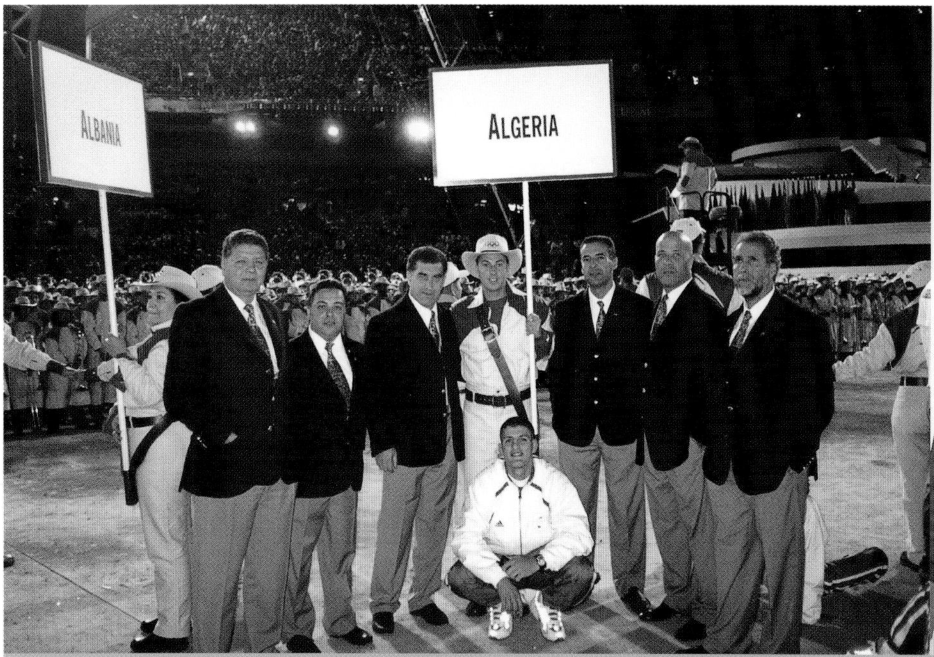

NOC ASSISTANT ANDREW TANNOS. 'AT 71, THESE WERE SOME OF THE MOST MEMORABLE DAYS OF MY LIFE'

'It was an honour to be assigned as NOC Assistant to the Oman Team, but it nearly became an embarrassment how well they treated me. There were too many highlights to mention, but being part of the Opening and Closing Ceremonies was something special. Looking after the Oman Team was extra special.' ... **Jim Couri**

Chris Cavanagh decided that his employer – Olympic Sponsor – Ansett Airlines, could do without his services during the Paralympics, so took on the role of National Paralympic Committee (NPC) Assistant for Belarus. 'It was great to come from Melbourne to be part of the Host City, and be "hands-on" with these inspirational athletes. I have gained a totally new appreciation of the magnitude of what happened in Sydney 2000,' says Chris.

'I am in my third year of an Optometry degree, and as one athlete said to me – "It is destiny that we met" – in my role as NPC Assistant for the People's Republic of China. My outlook on my future profession has been so positively enhanced, having learned so much by working closely with these visually impaired athletes. As one of the athletes said to me, "Study hard Tsu Shan and cure all the blindness in the world." Every night, I look at my little doll-sized judo suit that one of the athletes gave me. They were right; it was definitely destiny that we met!' ... **Tsu Shan Lee**

'I have had the most absolutely wonderful experience of my life working as National Olympic Committee (NOC) Assistant for Burkina Faso. They are just the most beautiful, welcoming people, and I don't think I could have been allocated a better delegation. We not only had fun in the Village, but we also had wonderful social times together. I know we will all remain friends.' ... **Lauren Malouf**

'Despite the language difficulties, we made new friends and became part of the team. Excursions to tourist locations created an additional bond, and my learning of other cultures was enhanced. My Paralympic experience extended past my own position, as I travelled between Newcastle and Sydney each day. This was a wonderful opportunity to share the whole volunteer experience with fellow commuters. I've always wanted to travel the world, but now I can say that I only travelled two hours and the world came to me!' ... **Penny Tozer (NPC Assistant – Angola)**

Natasha Malani is one of the dedicated volunteers who not only came from interstate (South Australia), but because she chose the role of NOC Assistant, her commitment of time and money for months of training exceeded most. However, her five weeks in Sydney as NOC Assistant for Nigeria were worth it all, and as Natasha says, 'The challenges, adventures and new friendships give such great memories to take home to Adelaide.'

'As an NPC Assistant I worked with both Macau (China) and East Timor. One of the highlights of the games was when the athlete for the East Timor team was entered into the 5000m race. As the race evolved the bulk of the runners kept up the pace but the runner from East Timor lagged and with each lap he was lagging even more and was lapped repeatedly. As the pack finished the East Timor runner still had a number of laps to finish. As he continued with ever-increasing cheers from the

NPC ASSISTANTS WITH SINGAPORE TEAM AT WELCOME CEREMONY

crowd, he went across to where Portuguese fans were waving the flag and started to shake their hands, then came back onto the track and continued until an official started to lead him off the track and this resulted in the crowd jeering the official. The tempo changed to cheering as another official came running up with a bouquet of flowers, normally given to medal winners. The cheering was deafening and emotions running high as he ran over the finish line with this bouquet of flowers high in the air and also with the biggest smile across his face, to a standing, cheering crowd calling his name, some with tears in their eyes including me. That event to me was what it is all about and why I am grateful to have been there as a volunteer.' ... **Milena Goard**

'When the Deputy Chef de Mission said that he would like a genuine Aboriginal artefact, not a tourist item, I set about getting an item used in initiation rituals. When I presented it to him, it was difficult through language differences to explain the full meaning, so he chose to believe it would bring "strength and good luck".

'The very next day, Kazakhstan won two medals, one Gold one Silver, and continued to win others, some quite unexpected. There were widespread celebrations, and I was thanked for the good luck! Well, I don't know if I brought them luck, but it was nice to share their success.' ... **Kerrie Dougherty (NOC Assistant – Kazakhstan)**

NOC Assistants Ludmila Fedorovitch (Kazakhstan), Tatiana Smolonogov (Uzbekhistan) and Anatoly Kirievsky (Lyrghistan) all found that their delegations were surprised at the number of Russian-speaking NOC Assistants. Obviously they did not understand the multicultural content of Australian society.

All agreed that despite the hectic and demanding schedules they maintained, there were so many memorable moments that will remain in their hearts forever.

When the first group of National Paralympic Committee (NPC) Assistants got together with NPC Services Co-ordinators to celebrate their acceptance into the fledgling program, the evening took on even more special significance.

They were joined by the captain of Australia's Women's Wheelchair Basketball Team, Donna Ritchie. Donna, who is always so appreciative of the volunteer contribution, was accompanied by Dutch Wheelchair Basketballer, Koen Jansens, and was sporting an even larger smile than normal.

Donna and Koen had that day announced their engagement, and the NPC volunteers were thrilled that Donna and Koen had taken time out from their busy schedules to share the moment.

Jeremy Steele (NOC Assistant) and his wife **Margaret** (Spectator Services Host) were stunned when Sydney won the right to host the Olympic and Paralympic Games. Then they went into a state of euphoria like everybody else!

Their volunteering roles were exciting and fulfilling, and being associated with the Gold Medal winning Cameroon Football Team added a different dimension to celebrating. Jeremy says, 'As a conclusion to our volunteering experience this could hardly have been better.'

Alison Radford was one of the cheery ORTA Load Zone Officers between the Transport Mall and Main Dining Hall in the Athletes Village. They saw EVERY athlete COUNTLESS times, as they all ate and all went to events!

Besides becoming acquainted with so many athletes and Village's Workforce, one of Alison's favourite pastimes was watching wheelchair athletes during the Paralympics wheel themselves off buses without the ramps – 'Wheelchair long-jump' she called it!

George Vass was a volunteer at the Guest Pass Centre at the Main Entry to the Athletes Village. These were the friendly people who greeted approved visitors to the Village and issued them with a Guest Pass in exchange for their passport. If the passport wasn't collected that evening, a 'search party' was sent out to the 'hosting delegation'! George couldn't believe the 'thank you' received at the Volunteers Parade, for something he so thoroughly enjoyed.

Julie Georges enjoyed her role even more than expected because she was assisting her fellow volunteers. She was located at one of the staff entry locations to the Athletes Village, and saw a variety of work situations from queues of staff needing assistance, to lonely nights where she would chat with 'Mag & Bag' staff, read a book or write poems. Julie confided, 'I was just glad to be involved.'

'We were given tickets to a morning session of athletics, we were ecstatic. We sat in the stand near the Flame, and down came the rain. Try as it might, the rain was not going to dampen our enthusiasm. We donned our ponchos, and then over the public address system, to our merriment we

NPC Assistants with Donna Ritchie and Koen Jansens

NPC services – regional support East Asia team – (L to R) Katherine Sie, Debbie Simms, Michael Fox and Narelle Best

(RIGHT) DOUG WOOD (NOC ASSISTANT – PAPUA NEW GUINEA), PROUDLY DISPLAYS THE PNG UNIFORM PRESENTED TO HIM FOR THE TEAM WELCOME CEREMONY, ACCOMPANIED BY PARTNER LAUREL RICHARDS AND CHEF DE MISSION, IVAN RAVU

JEANIE LLOYD (NOC ASSISTANT – CAYMAN ISLANDS), REMEMBERS THE THRILL OF WORKING FOR CHIEF-OF-STAFF FOR *THE SUN* NEWSPAPER IN SYDNEY DURING THE MELBOURNE OLYMPICS. JEANIE SAYS, 'THERE ARE NOW SO MANY CONTRASTING STORIES TO TELL.'

heard first, "Singing in the Rain", followed by "Ain't No Sunshine When She Calls", "Bright Sun Shiny Day", "Somewhere Over the Rainbow" and finally "Raindrops Keep Falling on My Head". Glad some inventive Aussie has such a good sense of humour.' ... **Carole Barford (Village Food Assistant) and Paul Apter (Village Venue Staffing)**

'At the Paralympic Volunteers Picnic at Centennial Park in late 1999, I encountered a fellow volunteer, one **Alwyn Murray**, a retired school teacher whom I myself had taught at Kyogle High School in 1949-50. The unexpected reunion was delightful.

Then, at the briefings some months later, where we were allocated our countries, who should be allocated Uganda with me – Alwyn Murray! There had been no personal agency, just pure co-incidence!' ... **Colin Soles**

Sydney's multicultural community played a very positive role in making visitors welcome to this country, but one community that long before Games-time made the volunteers feel appreciated were the Bahamians. NOC Assistants for the Bahamas – **Ellen Coker, Elizabeth Carr and Daniel Hoenig** – were invited to the homes of **Margaret Kerr** and **Lesley Callaghan** on separate occasions for Bahamian feasts (if you go hungry at a Bahamian get together, it is your own fault!). This was an added bonus in giving the NOC Assistants a better insight and understanding of the culture. The hospitality was much appreciated.

'I moved to Australia in early 1998 to marry my Australian husband, coming from coolish Switzerland to the tropical climate of Darwin; it couldn't have been more extreme! It was in Darwin I initially applied to be an NOC Assistant, but by the time I got an interview, we had moved to Alice Springs, a bit closer to Sydney!

'Prior to the Olympics I flew from my residence in Alice Springs to Sydney 12 times to attend training sessions. Some people might call it crazy; I call it enthusiasm and devotion. I feel privileged and special to have been part of the Olympic Volunteers.' ... **Linda Sesta (NOC Assistant – Switzerland)**

John Johnson (NOC Assistant – Vanuatu) had the longest trip of any volunteers to attend one of the NOC Assistant training sessions. He left Shannon Airport in Ireland on Thursday at 5 pm – flew to London – then to Hong Kong and on to Sydney, arriving just in time to get from the airport to the city for a 9 am training session! On arrival John said, 'I'm here in body, but maybe a little tired.' UNDERSTATEMENT!

Thanks for the commitment and contribution to – **John Bartolo** (Resident Relations), **Anna Chulio** (Food Service Assistant and Torch Bearer), **Norita Davidson** (Translator), **Jennifer Smith** (Venue Staffing), **Val Melville** (Olympian 1956 from Bunbury WA), **Peter Goddard** (NOC Assistant – Samoa) and **George Roca** (NOC Assistant and Athlete Escort – Romania).

(L TO R) NOC ASSISTANTS MARK LEWIS, JUDY LAWLER AND JOE SIGURDSSON

LEFT: NEAM NASSIR (NOC ASSISTANT – OMAN) ENJOYING THE CLOSING CEREMONY

RIGHT: MARGARET BOYD (NOC ASSISTANT – ETHIOPIA)

GREEK CONTINGENT

Most Australians, and indeed most volunteers, were not aware that we shared our experience with a group of Greek citizens (Volunteers) who contributed nearly 18 months of their lives to volunteering at SOCOG Headquarters, test events and Games-time venues.

In 1999 the International Olympic Committee placed under its auspices a Master's Programme in Sport Management specially designed by the School of Leisure and Tourism Management (UTS), for sport administrators from Greece.

The idea of the programme originated from the Physical Education Department of the Democritos University of Thrace, Greece, and was proposed to the University of Technology in Sydney (UTS) and to the Sydney Organising Committee for the Olympic Games (SOCOG). Both organisations swiftly understood its potential and benefits, adopted it and made the necessary adjustments to their policies to accommodate it. It was then proposed to the Hellenic Ministry of Sport, which offered a number of scholarships for students. Finally 68 candidates were selected to participate.

Benefits of the Programme

The participants receive an internationally recognised degree in sport management, hands-on experience in the organisation of the Games and lifelong memories and friendships.

The IOC will promote Olympic education and training in an unprecedented way, and ensure that know-how from the Sydney Games is transferred to Athens, the next Olympic City.

SOCOG will make considerable savings in budget, gain access to a large number of people with skills and multiple languages, advance the level of Olympic training and assist the next Organising Committee in organising their Games.

Those who came in mid-1999 were:

Maria Angelopoulou, Kostantinos Anestos, Christina Anthi, Christos Athanasiadis, Theodoros Babaroutsis, Kostantina Bornivelli, Ioannis Chatzibeis, Anna-Maria Chaviara, Margarita Christodoulatou, Stylianos Daskalakis, Amalia Drakou, Maria Eleftheriou, Dimitris Gargaliano, Anastasia Gkoufa, Athanasios Gkounagias, Marianna Grigoraki, Sophia Gritsis, Evangelos Grivakis, Nikolaos Grivas, Sotiria Kafetzi-Apostolopoulou, Aikaterini Kaloudi, Eirini Kama, Athanasios Karagrounas, Panagiota Karaiskou, Marilena Katsadoraki, Apostolos Katsaros, Emmanuil Kavarnos, Anastasios Kostaris, Athanasios Kostopoulos, Spiridoula Kouveli, Ioanna Krokodeilou, Xanthipi Kyriazi, Georgios Leventakis, Nikoletta Loli, Aikaterini Lygkoni, Evanthia Mataranga, Aikaterini Madourou, Smaroula Maniati, Nikolaos Mastrogianopoulos, George Mitrousis, Dimitrios Orfanopoulos, Panagiota Panagiotakopoulou, Georgios Panoutsopoulos, Christos Papagianopoulos, Vasiliki Papakostopoulou, Pavlina Polymeropoulou, Fani Psatha, Apostolos Rigas, Vasiliki Roumelioti, Eleftheria Skarlatou, Eleni Skarpathioti, Nikolaos Sofianos, Haralambos Stamatakis, Ioannis Thamnopoulos, Dionysios Tritaris, Petros Tsiallas, Achileas Tsogas, Maria Tzelepi, Spiridon Vangelis, Georgios Vasilatos, Christina Vasilikou, Marios Vourtsis, Symeon Vrachnos, Anastasia Xaplanteri, Tryfon Zacharopoulos, Theodora Zachou, Kostantinos Zafeiropoulos, Tatiana Zarkada.

While this programme had a lot of benefits as listed previously, and the basic aims were achieved, the participants personally had to endure some challenges. Besides the obvious homesickness and missing their loved ones, initially some of the accommodation was not totally suitable, they had next to no personal time and the workload of attending university, working at SOCOG and studying was overwhelming. In addition to this, their place within the SOCOG structure was not completely clear, and some miscommunication made many of them uneasy until they began to make friends and form a working relationship with other staff.

We thank these people for the contribution they made, and for SHARING AND ENHANCING OUR VOLUNTEER EXPERIENCE.

We wish you well in your personal futures and AN ENJOYABLE AND SUCCESSFUL JOURNEY TO ATHENS 2004.

GREEK CONTINGENT AT ONE YEAR ANNIVERSARY

Marcus Barron (statistics at olympic football – Brisbane)

Ian Podger from oakleigh, victoria with australian basketball team captain Andrew Gaze

members of the barcelona pioneer volunteer team at the one-year-to-go party organised by the heidelberg team

(L to R) volunteers Sandra Logan, John Simpson and Karen Simpson from orange – central western NSW

Emily Ibrahim (protocol supervisor – olympic football – melbourne) shares a silver medal moment with double trap shooter – Russell Mark

TERRIGAL HIGH SCHOOL STUDENTS AS ATHLETE STAND-INS DURING DRESS REHEARSALS

ROLF HENDRIKS (NOC ASSISTANT – NETHERLANDS) CELEBRATES WITH THE GOLD MEDAL WINNING HOCKEY TEAM

TWO-YEARS-TO-GO PARTY – HEIDELBERG PIONEER VOLUNTEER TEAM PROJECT

(L TO R) BERNADETTE AQUILINA, WADE BENNETT AND CHRISTINE MARSH PHOTO BY LESLEY FENTIMAN

(L TO R) SANDRA SCHIPANO, JENNY MORGAN, KEVAN GOSPER (OLYMPIAN), JUDY POLLOCK (OLYMMPIAN) AND ALLISON MUNRO AT THE MELBOURNE CRICKET GROUND

Skye Manion – attaché for Yemen

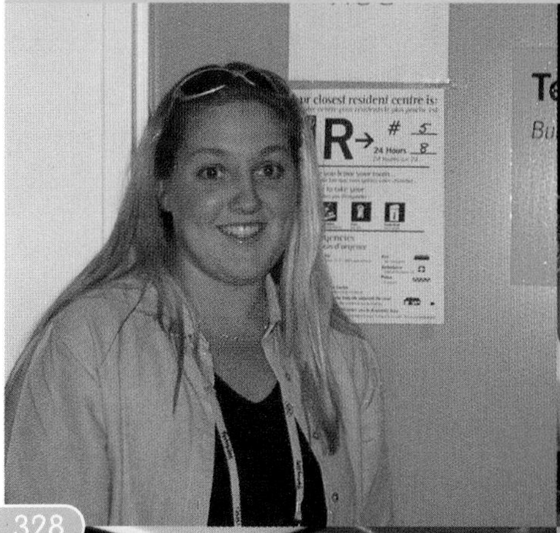

Ray Smee and Judy McMahon (spectator services hosts)

Barbara Bryan photo marshal at the Olympic Stadium

the side of the 'big sheet' the spectators didn't see!

Yvonne Stride Spectator Services Host from Adelaide

Gillian Alm presents a jar of Dubbo Honey to Austrian Paralympic Cyclist Wolfgang Eibeck – as she did for all Austrian medallists

Sylvia Ng (left) and Melissa Wilson – team sports assistants – football – Brisbane

Resident centre 21 staff (l to r) back row – Peggy Crayge, Fiona Woods, Luis Prieto and Donald Whyte. Front Row – Kate Whitelock, Tanya Mavritsky, Kevin McKinlay, Shani Fitzgerald and Usha Ravi

(l to r) Paul Gaffney, Cheryl Dale and Denny Rolleston (NOC assistants for Saint Vincent and the Grenadines)

Relaxation time for door 3 – main dining volunteers after the closing ceremony

(l to r) Geoffrey Hallman, Barbara Smith, Penelope Fox and Robyn Winn (NOC assistants – Kenya)

Volunteer Joyce Roberts meets her cousin Judith Green from Darwin for the first time. Judith won Paralympic gold in swimming SB6 class 100m breaststroke.

PART OF THE GREAT TEAM OF MAIN

DINING VOLUNTEERS

PIONEER VOLUNTEERS AT THEIR

FINAL CHRISTMAS PARTY

INTERNATIONAL AIRPORT IOC RELATIONS

AND PROTOCOL ATTENDANTS

ACCREDITATION OFFICE TEAM – BRISBANE

VENUE STAFFING VOLUNTEER KATHRYN HUGGARD (LEFT), HANDING STAR PRIZE TO SPECTATOR SERVICES VOLUNTEER BETTY SMITH, AT BRISBANE FOOTBALL VENUE

STUDENTS FROM NORTH SYDNEY GIRLS HIGH SCHOOL AS ATHLETE STAND-INS FOR THE OPENING CEREMONY DRESS REHEARSALS

THE ROCCA FAMILY – JOE, CHRISTINE, ANTHONY AND JOSEPH TAKE A BREAK WHILE DISTRIBUTING 'ESKIES' IN PREPARATION FOR THE OLYMPIC CLOSING CEREMONY

REBECCA ARNETT-MANSFIELD (LEFT) MET HER FORMER TEACHER 'MISS CURRY' WHILE BOTH WERE HORSE HANDLERS AND FIELD OF PLAY MARSHALS

PARALYMPIC OPENING CEREMONY PERFORMERS – TRINETTA AND JESSICA FROM HOLY SPIRIT COLLEGE, LAKEMBA

A WONDERFUL TEAM EFFORT

WHILE WE HAVE ACKNOWLEDGED AND SUNG THE PRAISES OF THE VOLUNTEERS, LET US NOT FORGET THAT THE ULTIMATE SUCCESS OF SYDNEY 2000 WAS A TEAM EFFORT

BEGINNING WITH OUR SUCCESSFUL BID TEAM, OUR GREAT SOCOG STAFF (WHO DID NOT DESERVE THE NEGATIVE MEDIA – AND THE RESULTS PROVE IT), THE OLYMPIC CO-ORDINATION AUTHORITY AND THE PEOPLE WHO BUILT OUR VENUES, AND FINALLY THE CONTRACT STAFF WHO JOINED US VOLUNTEERS AT GAMES-TIME

WE WERE PART OF HISTORY

LET US NOW WISH FUTURE HOST CITIES THE SAME SUCCESS IN BRINGING THE PEOPLE OF THE WORLD TOGETHER IN PEACE AND LOVE AND FRIENDSHIP UNDER THE BANNER OF OLYMPISM

ACRONYMS

IOC	— International Olympic Committee
IPC	— International Paralympic Committee
SOCOG	— Sydney Organising Committee for the Olympic Games
SPOC	— Sydney Paralympic Organising Committee
AOC	— Australian Olympic Committee
ORTA	— Olympic Roads and Transport Authority
MPC	— Main Press Centre
IBC	— International Broadcast Centre
MMC	— Main Media Centre
HAAC	— Homebush Arrivals and Accreditation Centre
UDAC	— Uniform Distribution and Accreditation Centre
SIAC	— Sydney International Athletic Centre
NOC	— National Olympic Committee
NPC	— National Paralympic Committee
MOST	— Mobile Operations Support Team

AUTOGRAPHS & MEMORABILIA

AUTOGRAPHS & MEMORABILIA